MEXICO

GULF OF

CAMPECHE

HIDALGO

Huautla
Molango
8856
Zacualtipán
El Cardonal
napán
Huehuetla
S. Bartolo
Tenango de Doria
Actopan
El Arenal Metepec Apulco Xico
Pahuatlán
Pachuca Honey Huauchinango
Tlaxcoapan
Tulancingo
Tihualán
Tuxpam
Coatzintla Tecolutla
Papantla
Nautla
Tenampulco
Tecolutla
Chignahuapan
Teziutlán
Tlaxco
Libres
Teocelo
Tlacolula
Atlixco
P. Delgada
13410 Jalapa
San Carlos
Antigua Veracruz
Veracruz
Otumba
Teotihuacan
Texcoco
TLAXCALA
Tlaxcala 13448
Apizaco
Texmelucan
Huejotzingo
Cholula
Amozoc
Tepeaca
Puebla
Atlixco
Boca del Monte
Maltrata
Tlacotepec
CITLALTEPETL 18077
Orizaba
Córdoba
Medellín
Huatusco
Coscomatepec
Alvarado
P. Roca Partida
Tlacotalpan
Cosamaloapan
Amapa
Tuxtla
Ayochio
Acatlán
IZTACCIHUATL 17670
17880
POPOCATEPETL 17540
Tepoztlán
Cuernavaca
Yautepec
Cuautla
MORELOS
Jojutla
Mixquic
Alta
Chiautla
Acatlán
Tepexi
Tehuacan
Coxcatlán
Tulcingo
Huamuxtitlán
Cieneguilla
Huajuapan
Tamasulapa
Teposcolula
Jayacatlán
Teotitlán
Ojitlan
Tuxtepec
El Burro
Analco
Valle
Cuicatlán
Playa Vicente
Sta. Maria
Choapan
Jaltepec
Suchilapan
Mazatlán
OAXACA
Atlixtac
Tlapa
Patlicha
Metlatonoc
Tlaxiaco
Clacalongo
Lagunas
Etla
Monte Alban
Oaxaca
Zaachila
S. FELIPE 10,250
Teotitlan del Valle
S. Domingo
Mitla Albarradas
ZEMPOALTEPETL 11,139
Barrio
Yalalag
S. Jerónimo
Juchitan
Ayutla
Quetzalapa
Atoyaquillo
Ocotlán
Taviche
Tlacolula
Tehuantepec
Yautepec
Yoloxochitl
Ometepec
Amoltepec
Ejutla
Miahuatlán
Salina Cruz
Pinotepa Nacional
P. Maldonado
Jamiltepec
Juchatengo
Juquila
6183
Mixtepec
Punta Galera
Cozoaltepec
Pochutla
Puerto Angel
Astata

PACIFIC OCEAN

Statute Miles

0   10   20   30   40   50   100

------ Railways

West from Greenwich   98°   96°

STANFORD, LONDON

20°

18°

16°

MEXICAN MOSAIC

also by Rodney Gallop

A Book of the Basques
Portugal: A Book of Folk Ways
Contares do Povo Português (in Portuguese)

by Violet Alford and Rodney Gallop
The Traditional Dance

MEXICAN MOSAIC

Folklore and Tradition

by

RODNEY GALLOP

illustrated
with photographs by the author
and with drawings by his wife

QUILLER PRESS

London

First published in March 1939
by Faber and Faber Limited
This new edition published 1990 *by*
Quiller Press Ltd,
46 *Lillie Road,*
*London SW*6 1*TN*

Copyright © 1939: Rodney Gallop

ISBN 1 870948 44 0

Front and back jacket pictures by Carlos Merida
Jacket design: Linda Wade

PRINTED IN ENGLAND BY BOOKCRAFT LTD

To the memory of
HELGA LARSEN

*and her great knowledge
and love of
Indian Mexico*

'An ancient land, sun-scorched, wind-sculptured . . . .
an ancient, sun-bronzed people, reacting to deep, buried
impulses, following the old trails.'
> ERNEST GRUENING: *Mexico and its Heritage.*

*

'Of all that extensive empire which once acknowledged
the authority of Spain in the New World, no portion, for
interest and importance, can be compared with Mexico.'
WILLIAM PRESCOTT: *History of the Conquest of Mexico.*

*

'It is doubtful if the country of New Spain does not
border on Tartary and Greenland; by the way of California on the former and by New Mexico on the latter.'
> ARCHBISHOP LORENZANA: *Historia de Nueva España.*

*

'¡Oh Mexico, que tales montes te cercan y te coronan!'
> FRAY TORIBIO MOTOLINIA: *Historia de los Indios.*

5

6

Contents

7

Illustrations

9

Illustrations

Drawings in the Text

Drawings in the Text

Foreword

*M*exican Mosaic was first published just 50 years ago, shortly before the outbreak of the Second World War. With Hitler already on the march and the war clouds gathering, it proved to be an unpropitious time to bring out a book on a distant, little known country like Mexico and it has been out of print and virtually unobtainable ever since. Nonetheless, among those familiar with the country and its literature, the passage of time has tended to enhance the book's reputation as one of the most perceptive studies of Indian Mexico and it has come to be regarded as essential reading on the country together with Fanny Calderon de la Barca's *Life in Mexico*, D. H. Lawrence's *Mornings in Mexico* and Patrick O'Hea's *Reminiscences of the Mexican Revolution*. Those who already know the book will welcome this reprinting and now that travellers to Mexico are far more numerous than they were fifty years ago, perhaps a wider public will be able to appreciate the descriptions of Indian life and customs which, firmly rooted as they are in tradition, still form the basis of all that is quintessentially 'Mexican'.

When the first edition appeared, one reviewer surmised that 'Mr. Gallop was apparently connected during his three years' stay in Mexico with some archeological folklore expedition'. Whilst it is understandable that he drew this conclusion, my father was in fact serving in Mexico City as a dedicated career diplomat, and it was only when off duty that he was able to pursue his real passion as a folklorist and musicologist, a passion that had already given birth to books on the Basques and on Portugal, both still looked on as seminal works in their field.

Mexican Mosaic appeared at the same time as Graham Greene's celebrated travel book, *The Lawless Roads*, and inevitably the two works were compared by reviewers, who noted Greene's misanthropic attitude to the country and its inhabitants, resulting in a book which told the reader more about the author than about Mexico. This was compared with my father's empathy with the Indians and ability to communicate with them in the broadest sense of the word, earning their trust and permitting him to witness sacred rituals and relics normally hidden from outsiders. Greene himself reviewed Mexican Mosaic for the *Spectator* and found my father to be 'a rare personality – a man who was happy in Mexico', going on to note that 'he ignores those aspects of Mexico which depress most visitors – the irresponsibility, the hopeless poverty and the political corruption'. It is certainly true that my father was happy in Mexico and was very distressed when a purely fortuitous event, the expropriation of the foreign oil companies by President Lazaro Cardenas' government, resulted in his being withdrawn from the country. He would certainly have been fully aware of the negative aspects and was far from insensitive to poverty, but he preferred to leave these subjects to be written about by transient visitors or those whose specific objective was to deal with such themes. Nor would he have found a three

14

year sojourn in such an outstandingly interesting country as Mexico in the least depressing. As a folklorist and musicologist with a keenly observant eye, he preferred to concentrate on gaining a deep knowledge of the nature and customs of the Mexican Indian and indulging in adventurous travelling off the beaten track, which in the Mexico of half a century ago often involved riding into areas where the motor car had not yet penetrated.

Although my father was in the foreign service and would never have considered 'going native' in the manner of a modern day hippie, he was certainly an unconventional diplomat for his time. Largely avoiding the customary social circuit, he would quickly learn the language, make a host of local friends and turn his attention to the traditions and customs of the country he found himself accredited to. In Mexico in particular his aim was to get behind the mask that the Indian presented to the outside world, the mask that visiting writers so often mistook for the true face, and in getting close to villagers, lift a corner of the curtain behind which they concealed their traditional beliefs and practices. It seems only natural that during his stay my father should have acquired four Aztec godchildren.

There have been many changes in Mexico in the last 50 years, although these are particularly noticeable in the towns and cities, to which so many peasants have migrated. Nevertheless, travelling is easier and buses and lorries now penetrate areas formerly accessible only by horse or mule. There will not be another 'Flying Game' to be discovered, but the Indian lifestyle, traditions and psyche remain largely unaltered and as an introduction to them, I believe this book has never been bettered. This second edition is long overdue and I hope it will bring much pleasure to many travellers in Mexico and may perhaps persuade others that they too should make their way 'Beyond The Mexique Bay' with an open mind and an observant eye.

Nigel Gallop
February 1990

Preface

Unlike most people who write books about Mexico it was not with that object that I went there, and circumstances conspired to prevent me from travelling as extensively as I had hoped, and as true travel-writers are able to do. Except for the journeys to Oaxaca, Michoacan and Huehuetla the experiences described in this book were obtained by taking the fullest advantage of days and week-ends from Mexico City, and they may give some idea of the variety offered by means of transport ranging from mule to aeroplane. These opportunities are open to all, for the beaten track in Mexico is less a geographical fact than an attitude of mind, and experience is not to be measured by distance travelled. To make the most of such brief excursions entails careful preparation and the garnering of much information, unobtainable from tourist agencies or government departments, in regard to ways and means, routes and occasions. In this connexion I owe a great debt of gratitude to friends who have given me the benefit of their help and experience, in particular the late Mrs. Helga Larsen and her sister Miss Bodil Christensen, Madame Stadtler, Herr Robert Weitlaner, Mr. Bernard Bevan, Don Pablo Martínez del Rio, Mr. Cecil James, Mr. Constantine Rickards, Mr. George Conway, Monsieur Paul Van de Velde and Sr. Clemente Velez. I hope that, in its turn, my book will help and encourage others to take up the task which I have had to abandon, and to explore the little known side of Mexico which may be summed up in the one word, tradition.

I. Hot Lands, Cold Lands

Two days of rumbas and daiquiri cocktails at Havana robbed us of the sea-legs which we had so painfully acquired between Vigo and the Azores. Fortunately, the Mexique Bay took pity on us and did not unloose one of those sudden 'northers' which kept travellers of the past rolling about for weeks before they could put into the Gulf ports. Flying fish played round the bows of the ship, and to the south an occasional lighthouse betokened shoal water off unseen Yucatan. Thus passed our last day at sea.

Next morning we came on deck at six o'clock to see the towers and churches of Vera Cruz silhouetted above a low coast a few miles ahead. Over the city, pale and insubstantial, hovered the steep cone of Citlaltepetl, like some Fujiyama of the New World, its snowy summit touched with pink by the newly-risen sun.

From *la villa rica de la Vera Cruz,* the rich city of the True Cross, it took Hernan Cortes nearly three months to reach Montezuma's city of Tenochtitlan in 1519. In 1850 Lady Emmeline Stuart Wortley saw 'the beginning of a railroad which, say the Americans, may perhaps be finished in five hundred years'. To-day, thanks to British enterprise, the traveller passes from the jungle-fringed shores of the Gulf to the high plateau eight thousand feet above sea-level on which Mexico City stands.

19

Hot Lands, Cold Lands

At Vera Cruz it was baking hot even in November, but the railway climbed in turn through the three climatic zones of Mexico, *tierra caliente* or 'hot country' between sea-level and 3,000 feet, *tierra templada* or 'temperate country' from 3,000 to 6,000 feet and *tierra fria* or 'cold country' where, as the saying goes, it is spring in the morning, summer at midday, autumn in the afternoon and winter at night.

Taking the day express (called Anahuac, after the Aztec name of the Valley of Mexico) we passed at first through a rolling tropical landscape. Palms were everywhere, and strange trees to which we could give no name with strange flowers growing among them and bright birds and butterflies fluttering among their branches. In the clearings were groups of palm-thatched cottages and Mexicans riding little donkeys, more faithful to one's preconceptions, in their broad, high-crowned sombreros, than could have seemed possible. Ahead, the trees opened from time to time to reveal a high and apparently unbroken wall of mountains. Soon we were at their very feet, and then, as though in response to some unspoken 'Sesame', the mountains opened and the train was engulfed in a narrow gorge, up which it wound past tumbling waterfalls, through tunnels and over dizzy viaducts. Dense tropical vegetation clothed the slopes, so steep that the vertical trees seemed almost to be growing parallel to them.

So we climbed up into the temperate zone. Dark clouds gathered, for here it rains nearly all the year. The vegetation grew richer and more rank. Banana groves with ripe, clustering fruit, coffee plantations, fields of sugar-cane, flashed past in ever-changing variety. Each wayside station was thronged by Indian women in blue *rebozo* shawls with wares to sell. Some offered fruit and flowers, oranges, bananas, fleshy paw-paw, and posies of sweet-smelling gardenia. Others cried strange foods: *tamales* and *tacos* of highly-spiced meat wrapped round in maize leaves or in *tortillas*, the maize pancakes which are the staple diet of the country. A man in a bright *poncho* dangled in front of us fascinating toys, little men and animals ingeniously made out of straw or maize leaf, hours of patient labour sold for a song. Another specialized in walking sticks, knob-kerries and riding crops, carved and painted in colours which would startle northern eyes.

At Orizaba, four hours from Vera Cruz, we were four thousand feet up. Yet it was from here, or rather from Maltrata, a few stations farther on, that the steepest ascent began. Pine and scrub-oak had replaced the fruit groves of the lower regions, and as the line wound backwards and forwards the peak of Orizaba over 18,000 feet high appeared with bewildering rapidity, now on the right, now on the left, now in front, now behind. The air grew keener and ears began to throb. We looked across on level terms at scrub-covered hills which a few moments before had towered above us. From a couple of thousand feet higher we could, it seemed, have cast a pebble on to the station where we had bargained for oranges and bananas. Then with startling suddenness a crest was crossed, the panorama below was whisked from sight and we were at Boca del Monte, eight thousand feet above the sea, having climbed more than five thousand feet in a fraction under forty-two miles.

After this, the remainder of the journey was something

21

of an anti-climax. There is little rise and fall across the arid wastes of the cold country, the landscape of 'Thunder Over Mexico'. Miles upon miles of *maguey* aloes stretch away to distant smoke-hued sierras. In the villages dun-coloured adobe brick replaces the timber and thatch of the hot country. Far away to the west the great twin volcanoes appeared on the horizon: Popocatepetl, the 'Smoking Mountain' with a light panache of cloud hovering over it in a clear sky: Ixtaccihuatl, the 'White Woman'. As their snowfields were lit by the glow of the setting sun we saw them in our imagination with the eyes of Cortes. For how many days, as he and his gallant little band toiled, fought and intrigued their way up from the Gulf, their ships burnt behind them, must the serene and lofty presence of the two great mountains have kept ever-present in his mind the thought of the great, unknown city, never before seen by European eyes, with its untold wealth and its white palaces. During the years which followed, when their outline became as familiar to me as any horizon, whether of hills or housetops, which limits one's daily round, this fancy never left me and they retained the glamour of a gateway to the unknown.

With the feelings which the threshold of a new life cannot fail to awaken we passed the pre-Aztec pyramids of Teotihuacan, as great an engineering feat as those of ancient Egypt, and a greater mystery. The deepening afterglow was caught and held in the scattered pools which alone are left of the great Lake of Texcoco. Then, as the colour died from the sky, the train came to final rest in the heart of a great, modern city of over a million inhabitants, the capital of Mexico.

II. Tenochtitlan

Few things are more difficult to describe than a place, especially a city, in which one has lived and made one's home. For all his comparative ignorance the casual visitor is at an immense advantage. He can cast his description in narrative form, caring little whether his experience has been of the general or of the particular. The resident on the other hand is less fortunately placed. The daily round, the common task, may furnish all we need to ask, but they will scarcely enlist the reader's interest. All that he shares with the visitor is the ability to fall back upon an array of guide-book information, full of dates, names and historical allusions.

The topography of Mexico City has been catalogued *ad nauseam:* the Zócalo square, the cathedral built on the site of the great *Teocalli* of Tenochtitlan, the Palace, once Viceregal, now presidential, busy Madero Street, the fine National Theatre of Bellas Artes, even the Edificio La Nacional, Mexico's one modest skyscraper. Yet, after all, it is the capital, and as such cannot be ignored. Moreover, it commands attention as the spectrum through which Mexico's kaleidoscopic history may most conveniently be viewed.

Early in the thirteenth century, after a thousand years spent in moving southwards from the Seven Caves of their legendary emergence from underground, a small, unimportant tribe belonging to the great Nahua-speaking family reached the fertile valley of Anahuac and the shores of the great lake which covered the greater part of its floor. Thus came the Aztecs to Mexico. The pictorial account of their wanderings, punctuated with hierogly-phic footsteps, is preserved on maguey parchment in the National Museum. While they hesitated, uncertain where to settle, an omen was vouchsafed to them which may conveniently be described in Prescott's words: 'They there beheld, perched on the stem of a prickly pear, which shot out from the crevice of a rock that was washed by the waves, a royal eagle of extraordinary size and beauty, with a serpent in his talons, and his broad wings opened to the rising sun. They hailed the auspicious omen an-nounced by oracle as indicating the site of their future city, and laid its foundations by sinking piles into the shallows; for the low marshes were half buried under water.' This rock was in all probability Chapultepec, the Hill of Grasshoppers. Accordingly the eagle and serpent remain the emblem of Mexico, although the tribulations of the Aztecs were not quite at an end. In their weakness they were for a while at the mercy of the more settled tribes who had preceded them, Chichimecs and Tepanecs, and it was only a few years later, in A.D. 1324, that they found a more permanent refuge on two little islands in the lake, on one of which they bestowed the name of Ten-ochtitlan, the Place of the Hill of the Prickly Pear.

How by a masterly combination of diplomacy and force they gradually came to dominate their neighbours in the valley and extended their sway far beyond its limits, be-longs to a phase of history which need not be retold here and which culminated in the great empire of Montezuma, built up by the Aztec kings only to be overthrown by Cortes.

Of Tenochtitlan and its sister-city Tlaltelolco vivid descriptions have been left in the letters of Cortes, in the manuscript of the 'Unknown Conquistador' and above all in the wonderful account of the Conquest written by the soldier Bernal Diaz who, in the evening of his days, committed to paper his recollections of the stirring times which he had seen in the prime of life.

'When we saw so many cities and villages built in the water', he writes of his first view of Tenochtitlan from Iztapalapa, 'and that straight and level causeway going towards Mexico, we were amazed and said that it was like the enchantment they tell of in the legend of Amadis, on account of the great towers and *cues* and buildings rising from the water, and all built of masonry. And some of our soldiers even asked whether the things we saw were not a dream.'[1]

A little farther on he speaks with equal enthusiasm of 'the appearance of the palaces in which they lodged us. How spacious and well built they were, of beautiful stone work and cedar wood and the wood of other sweet scented trees, with great rooms and courts, wonderful to behold, covered with awnings of cotton cloth. . . . I was never tired of looking at the diversity of the trees, and noting the scent which each one had, and the paths full of roses and flowers, and the many fruit trees and native roses, and the pond of fresh water.'

Once in the centre of the capital 'Montezuma took Cortes by the hand and told him to look at his great city and all the other cities that were standing in the water. . . .

[1]Bernal Diaz del Castillo: *The Discovery and Conquest of Mexico.* Translated by A. P. Maudslay. London. 1928.

So we took to looking about us. . . . and we beheld on the lake a great multitude of canoes, some coming with supplies of food, others returning loaded with cargoes of merchandise, and we saw that from every house of that great city and of all the other cities that were built in the water it was impossible to pass from house to house except by drawbridges which were made of wood, or in canoes; and we saw in those cities *cues* and oratories like towers and fortresses and all gleaming white, and it was a wonderful thing to behold.'

Except to those blessed with the eye of faith, it is easier to repeople the Acropolis with the shades of Pericles, Aspasia and their contemporaries than to visualize Montezuma's capital as it appeared to the dazzled eyes of the Spaniards. For those same Spaniards destroyed it, stone by stone and brick by brick, when, after the disastrous *Noche Triste* or 'Sad Night' of June 30th, 1520, they painfully reconquered the city from Tacuba by way of the causeway which the Calzada de Tacuba still follows to-day.

More than the destruction of the houses it is the disappearance of the lake which has wrought this change. The seventeenth century historian Fr. Juán de Torquemada naïvely supposes that 'as God permitted the waters which once covered the whole earth, to subside after mankind had been nearly exterminated for their iniquities, so he allowed the waters of the Mexican lake to subside, in token of goodwill and reconciliation after the idolatrous races of the land had been destroyed by the Spaniards.'[1] Neither God nor the Spaniards, however, were the first to interfere with the course of nature in this respect. A century before the Conquest, Nezahualcoyotl, 'Hungry Coy-

[1]Fray Juán de Torquemada: *De la Monarquía Indiana*. Madrid. 1723.

ote' the poet-king of Texcoco,[1] built a great dyke from Iztapalapa to Atzacoalco just beyond Tepeyac which divided the lake into two sections, the eastern of which was salt from the rivers which flowed into it while the western remained full of fresh water. This dyke was known to the Spaniards as the *Albarradón* of Nezahualcoyotl. The works which dried up the bed of the valley and left Lake Texcoco proper an uninhabitable, uncultivable waste, covered with a thin sheet of water in the rainy season and dessicated in winter to a white expanse of dust and salt from which the terrible *tolvaneras* or dust storms overwhelmed the city, were begun in 1607 when the appropriately named Marquis of Salinas was Viceroy. Two or three hundred years elapsed before the work was completed. 'Thus', as Madame Calderón de la Barca wrote a century ago, 'the danger of inundation has diminished, but water and vegetation have diminished also, and the suburbs of the city, which were formerly covered with beautiful gardens, now present to the eye an arid expanse of efflorescent salt.'[2]

Colonial Mexico—the Mexico of Viceroys, coaches, the Inquisition, and a thousand and one stories which read like fairy tales to-day—has not, of course, vanished like Indian Tenochtitlan, but after a hundred years of independence and a quarter of a century of revolutionary progress, it is difficult for those with the nostalgia of the past to recover its atmosphere. New buildings have sprung up amidst the old, churches have been pulled down, façades modernized, so that there is no quarter of the city which to-day exhales

[1]For an account of this remarkable monarch see my article 'Hungry Coyote' in *The Cornhill Magazine* for July 1938.

[2]Madame Calderón de la Barca: *Life in Mexico during a Residence of Two Years in that Country*. London. 1843.

a colonial spirit in the way that many European cities breathe a mediaeval one.

Nevertheless, the diligent seeker will find many exquisite fragments of colonial architecture, museum pieces incrusted in the living fabric of the city. A whole book, for instance, could be devoted to the niches, many of them still containing statues of the Virgin and Saints, which are scolloped out of the angle walls on many a street corner. Many of the older buildings are of *tezontli*, a beautiful rose-red volcanic stone which lends itself admirably to the fine cutting and squaring and the baroque ornament of, for instance, the Iturbide Palace in Calle Madero or the Palace of the Condes de Santiago in Calle Pino Suárez.

The hub of the colonial city, as of the Aztec, is the Zócalo, the wide square on one side of which stands the Cathedral built on the site of the Great Pyramid. Along the eastern side runs the long, low Palace. To me the Zócalo with its surrounding buildings always seems to suffer from a faulty balance of proportions. Either the square is too vast for the buildings, or the latter, owing partly to subsidence, are too low for the square. It is the Cathedral which seems most of all to suffer from this lack of proportion, although it boasts many exquisite Renaissance and Baroque details.

28

Tenochtitlan

One day in the year above all others I delight to be
there, the day of Corpus Christi, when the children of the
city throng into the Cathedral for a blessing and procession, dressed by tradition as little Indians. Tiny creat-
ures of three or four, their faces white or dark according
as European or Indian blood is uppermost, wear the white
cottons, the straw sombreros or the embroidered home-
spuns of the Indian and carry offerings of flowers or the
emblems of the Mexican pilgrim. Emerging from the
Cathedral, they buy toy mules made of maize-leaf or
reeds, stuck with flowers, which for some unexplained
reason are sacred to the day.

Recent years have wrought havoc with the ancient
names of the city's streets. True, the *Calzada del Niño
Perdido* still recalls the time when the Child Jesus was
lost to his parents and was found holding forth in the
Temple. Others have been irretrievably lost, together
with the local legends which they enshrined. There is, for
instance, the curious story of the *Calle del Indio Triste*.
The 'Sad Indian', runs the tale, was an Aztec noble who
earned the protection of the Conquistadores in return for
his services as a spy. He was thus able to retain his great
wealth in houses, lands, jewels and precious birds. Nom-
inally a convert to Christianity, ho continued in secret the
worship of the old gods. Moreover, he led a dissipated life,
so that the time came when he neglected to warn the
Viceroy of a plot against the Spaniards, of which that
official learnt from another source. As a punishment he
was stripped of all his wealth and turned out into the
street where he sat, a forlorn beggar, crouching at the
doors of what had once been his palace, dependent on the
charity of the passers-by. Tormented by hunger and
thirst and by memories of his splendid past his features

took on so miserable an expression that he earned the name of 'El Indio Triste'. He died, according to tradition, of a broken heart, and as a warning to others the Viceroy caused his effigy to be carved in stone and set up at the corner of the Calle de la Carmen and of that which came to bear his name. In the eighteenth century the carving was removed to the Academy of Fine Arts whence it eventually found its way to the National Museum. The features do indeed bear an expression of profound sadness, but archaeologists—iconoclasts where picturesque legends are concerned—consider the figure to be one of the sculptured standard bearers from the great Teocalli. Perhaps that is why the Calle del Indio Triste has now been named Calle del Correo Mayor after the General Post Office.

A similar fate has overtaken the Calle de la Quemada, the Street of the Burnt Woman, Beatriz de Espinosa, who deliberately disfigured her face with fire in order to test the love of her wooer, the violent and jealous young Italian Martin Scipoli, Marquis of Pinamonte and Frantescello; the Calle de los Parados commemorating the two rival lovers who posted themselves at the corners of a block where dwelt the lovely Maria Isabel de Vallejo y Vezca, and who, failing through momentary absence to see the departure of her funeral during an outbreak of plague, remained at their post till their death and, as disembodied spirits, after it; and the Calle de la Joya, called after the exploit of a Spanish merchant Alonso Fernández de Bobadilla who, having murdered his wife and her lover the Fiscal of the Inquisition José Raul de Lara, nailed to his front door with his bloody dagger the bracelet which was the lover's last gift to the lady.

Most of all is to be regretted the passing of the Calle de la Machincuepa, the Street of the Somersault. In this

30

street, there dwelt during the early eighteenth century, an enriched emigrant called Mendo Quiroga y Suárez who had bought himself the title of Marqués del Valle Salado, Marquis of the Valley of Salt, from which he had derived his wealth. Unmarried and childless, he adopted a poor niece from Spain upon whom he lavished his riches. This niece, Paz de Quiroga, repaid his generosity only with unkindness towards him and with insupportable arrogance towards the rest of the world. When her benefactor died, it was found that he had left his vast fortune to Paz, but on one condition, namely that within six months she should go, clad in her finest ball dress and jewels, to the very centre of the Zócalo and there bow to the ground and publicly turn a somersault. For nearly six months Paz hesitated, torn between pride and avarice. Finally avarice won the day, and at the eleventh hour she fulfilled the condition, earning from the delighted crowd the ironic title of Marquesa de la Machincuepa.

The nineteenth century ushered in Mexican independence and nearly a hundred years of kaleidoscopic political change, in which the same elements constantly arranged themselves in new and varied patterns. The tragic error of French intervention led to a still more tragic interlude, the brief, ill-omened empire of Maximilian and Carlota which was played out to its bitter finish on the Cerro de las Campanas at Querétaro. More than any other place in Mexico that episode is evoked by the Palace of Chapultepec, high on the Hill of the Grasshoppers, where the royal pair knew a few fleeting moments of happiness on which their growing anxiety and anguish soon encroached.

The Palace of Chapultepec dates depressingly, but the park which surrounds it with lakes and woods has the eternal youth of inanimate nature. Here the lake-waters once lapped on the shores of Montezuma's pleasure-gardens, commemorated in ancient *ahuehuete* trees under which the last Aztec monarch may have walked. The presence of these giant cypresses is explained in an old legend.

Long ago, before the last eruption, there dwelt in what is now the Pedregal de San Angel, a virtuous Indian maiden, who was much distressed at the sufferings endured by her people owing to the lack of shade. She prayed to the gods that some alleviation might be granted to them, and in answer to her prayer a serpent, perhaps the great Quetzalcoatl himself, descended from the sky and bade her await the coming of One called Ahuehuetzin. In due course there came to her hut an old, old man with a long beard, to whom she gave hospitality. In his gratitude Ahuehuetzin promised to fulfil any wish she might express. She begged him that shade might be granted to her fellow-men, whereupon the old man told her to cut off his beard, cut it into small pieces and plant them in different places. This she did, and wherever a fragment of the beard was planted there sprang up a magnificent *ahuehuete* cypress with Spanish moss like Ahuehuetzin's beard trailing from its green branches.

On a Sunday morning in Chapultepec Park, you may see gentlemen riders in the showy costume of the *charro* on mettlesome *criollo* horses. The original meaning of the word *charro* is an inhabitant of the Spanish province of Salamanca. This is a great bull-breeding district, and where you have bulls you need horsemen to look after them. So in Mexico the name came to mean a horseman pure and simple. There is strong Spanish influence in the *charro's* costume and gear. He wears a broad felt hat, a short jacket or a simple embroidered shirt and long skin-tight trousers. Hat, jacket and trousers are ornate with gold and silver embroidery and braid, so that a gala *charro* suit is an expensive luxury, although tastes have become simpler (or pockets lighter) in the last century. Pistols and *machete* knives complete the equipment. 'What a horror', exclaimed Lady Emmeline Stuart Wortley in 1850, 'is a swallow-tailed coat in comparison, and the crown of all the hideousness of modern European dress, the tight black hat: how frightful it is by the picturesque *sombrero* with its delicate silver cords and hanging tassels.'

The Mexican saddle is large, heavy, and high at the back and front, with a wooden pommel round which the end of the lasso is wound when it has been thrown. Box stirrups hang from long leathers, so that the rider sits with his legs almost straight and grips with his calves. The sharp bit pinches the horse's underlip when the thin, single bridle is tightened, and enables it to be controlled with the slighest pressure.

Very good displays by amateurs can be seen almost every Sunday in the capital as the result of the *charro* movement which has developed in the larger towns in the present century. This movement counts among its devotees numbers of business-men, lawyers, doctors and so on who look forward throughout the week to the day when they can shake up their livers and show their mettle in feats of cowboy skill and daring.

The father of the movement is the 'Grand Old Man' of Mexican riding, Don Carlos Rincón Gallardo, Marqués de Guadalupe and Grandee of Spain. In spite of his white hairs, Carlitos, as his friends call him, has a seat which is the envy of all, and he can still show the younger generation a thing or two.

There are no fewer than seven different *charro* clubs in

and around the capital, most of which have their own *lienzos* or enclosed rings for displays to which the name of *jaripeos* is given. I saw many *jaripeos*, but the best was perhaps one organised at the Rancho del Charro in honour of Tom Mix, the cinema star, who himself donned *charro* kit for the occasion.

After the processional entry of the horsemen the proceedings opened with steer-tailing, an operation which calls for a high degree of skill and judgment. As each steer was released it was driven along a wooden fence towards the spectators. Keeping a little behind it on the near side, the rider seized its tail at the appropriate moment with his right hand. He then swung his right leg over his arm and with the extra purchase which this gave him threw the steer . . . or tried to, for a high percentage of failures testified to the difficulty of this feat.

After the steer-tailing (*colear* it is called in Spanish) there was a pause while the gap hitherto left in the ring was quickly fenced in. The second part of the programme consisted of lassoing and steer- and bronco-riding.

The *charro's* skill with the lariat is extraordinary, and the instrument itself infinitely more delicate than one might suppose. It is made from the spun fibre of the *maguey* and before it can be used must be toughened and tautened by much pulling and stretching. Even then it is very temperamental and sensitive to every change in the weather, so that it can seldom be manipulated the same way on two consecutive days.

On this occasion the *charro's* mastery over the lariat was demonstrated by a man who entered the ring on horseback, and making a wide noose, spun it in the air so that it gradually rose and fell round his body. Then, widening it still further, he began to describe rings round his horse, first at a standstill, then at a walk and finally at a canter which quickened into a gallop. Next, jumping off his horse, without letting the lasso lose its momentum or cease its snake-like writhings, he proceeded to dance backwards and forwards through it with the circle formed first horizontally and then vertically.

After this came the roping of broncos and steers both on foot and on horseback. In addition to straightforward work with the *reata*, the *charros* practise unusual *tours de force* of skill and dexterity. The Marqués de Guadalupe himself executed the so-called *tirón de la muerte*, lassoing his bronco on foot with the end of the lariat fastened round his two feet, so that when the pull came he was dragged along the ground until the horse was thrown or brought to a standstill. Most spectacular and sensational of all, however, was the *salto de la muerte* or 'leap of death'. With the aid of two of his companions, one of the *charros* drove a bronco round the inside of the ring. Then, gradually overtaking it on the near side and choosing his moment carefully, he crossed at full gallop from one horse to the other, riding the startled bronco to a standstill.

The proceedings were brought to a close by a performmance of the *Jarabe Tapatio*, a dance from Jalisco of which the *charros* have made a national affair. On this occasion it was performed by a couple of children. The boy was dressed as a *charro* with a bright Saltillo sarape over one shoulder; the girl as his feminine counterpart the *china poblana*.

The *china poblana* costume has a curious legendary history. *China* means a Chinese woman. *Poblana* is the adjective of Puebla de los Angeles, the beautiful city eighty miles from Mexico beyond the volcanoes. How came a 'Chinese woman' to Puebla? The answer is to be

35

found in the seventeenth century when Sor Catarina de San Juan crossed the Pacific from west to east. Although tradition proclaims her to have been a Chinese princess, Sor Catarina was in reality an Indian girl of high degree, who was carried off by pirates to Cochin, where she embraced Christianity and was baptized by Portuguese Jesuits. She was taken by her masters to Manila in the Philippines, where it so happened that Gálvez, the Spanish Viceroy of Mexico, had ordered the captain of a Spanish ship to buy him a female slave. The captain's choice fell upon Catarina whom he brought to Acapulco in the annual treasure-galleon. By the time they reached the shores of Mexico, however, Gálvez's term of office had ended and he had returned to Spain. A Spanish officer and his childless wife who lived in Puebla then bought Catarina and adopted her. On their death, Catarina devoted herself to a life of contemplation and good works and thus earned a great reputation for sanctity, which she enhanced by the miraculous visions which she claimed to receive. The Church must have looked somewhat askance on these visions, for the story of her life by her Jesuit confessor was condemned by the Inquisition and all copies were burnt. Nevertheless, her fame survived in legend and in another biography by a priest written in 1695 from which these details are taken. Her costume, which Sor Catarina bequeathed to her adopted city and which has spread so widely, betrays its exotic, oriental origin in the silk or bead embroidery with which the low-cut white blouse is adorned and in the brightly spangled green and red skirt. To-day a popular and innocent form of fancy dress (for it is nowhere a true peasant costume) its wearing was looked upon askance in Madame Calderón de la Barca's time. Soon after she had arrived in the country, the wife

of the first Spanish Envoy to independent Mexico was
sent a 'very handsome' Poblana dress 'with the compli-
ments of a lady whom I do not know, the wife of General ——' with the request that she wear it at a forthcoming Fancy Dress Ball. Fortunately, she was warned in
time. The Secretary of State, the Ministers of War and of
the Interior and others, paid her a special visit 'to adjure
me by all that was most alarming, to discard the idea of
making my appearance in a Poblana dress. They assured
that Poblanas generally were *femmes de rien*, that they
wore no stockings, and that the wife of the Spanish Minister should by no means assume, even for one evening,
such a costume.' The warning was rubbed in by a note
from an old busybody called José Arnaiz, who wrote: 'The
dress of a Poblana is that of a woman of no character. The
lady of the Spanish Minister is a *lady* in every sense of the
word. *However much she may have compromised herself*'
(my italics) 'she ought to go neither as a Poblana nor in
any other character but her own.' Madame de la Barca
accordingly went to the ball in the dress of 'a virtuous
Roman Contadina, simple enough to be run up in one
day.'

Sor Catarina and Madame de la Barca have taken us far
from the bright little girl at the Rancho del Charro who
so admirably simulated the alternating coyness and petulance of the Jarabe Tapatio. Like many European pair
dances this represents a courtship in which the lady at one
moment leads her lover on, at the next spurns him.
There is no contact between them until the inevitable
happy ending after the man has pleaded with the maiden,
gone off in a huff, returned drunk and finally overcome
her resistance. The music consists of a number of short
pieces, always repeated in the same order and correspond-

ing to the different episodes of the dance. Their pleasantly
obvious 'tonic-dominant' character unmistakably betrays
their European origin, as do also their steps and figures.
The man dances debonairly with body slightly bent and
hands folded behind his back. The lady holds the front of
her skirt in both hands, pointing a demure toe. Facing one
another the couple advance, cross and circle round each
other. At one moment with a deft gesture, he winds his
sarape round her spinning figure and a moment later she
returns the compliment. Then he arrogantly throws his
hat down on the ground, and with tiny steps she dances
round the brim. Finally, in token of submission she bends
down while he swings his leg over her head. Completely
vanquished, for this is no dance for feminists, she picks up
the hat and puts it on, and, both facing the same way, they
dance the final figure which culminates in his falling before her on one knee on which she rests her foot while he
kisses her hand.

No one dances the Jarabe Tapatio with a greater air
than the Marqués de Guadalupe, and he is as great an
authority on the correct costume for a *China* as for a
Charro. He himself relates with gusto how once he was
invited down into the arena to display the dance with a
fair unknown. After the dance the lady begged him to
tell her whether her costume was correct in every detail.
'Candour compels me to tell you, Señorita,' he replied,
'that there is one thing wrong. Every true *China Poblana*
wears lace-edged drawers. *You are wearing bloomers.*'

III. Indian Background, 1

The Indian tradition, shattered beyond recall in the capital and larger towns, lives on in the country. Continuity is uninterrupted on the very outskirts of Mexico City, where one has only to scratch the surface of the ground to find concrete traces of the pre-Spanish inhabitants.

Once or twice I had an opportunity of doing a little private digging with some friends in a maize field near Atzcapotzalco only twenty minutes from my own front-door. The Aztec-speaking farmers of the land dug a trench some three or four yards long and a yard or so wide. For a while we watched them. Then, as the earth began to yield the evidences of a bygone age, we could contain ourselves no longer. Jumping into the ditch we joined in the work with trowels and bare hands and for the rest of the day were as happy as a party of children at the seaside. We made no sensational discoveries. The most interesting perhaps was a set of ten shark's teeth, each pierced in two places, which had clearly once been threaded together as a necklace. Remains of one sort or another began only about eighteen inches down. There were quantities of sherds, some with a dull red glaze, others with graceful Aztec patterns, human bones, fragments of charred wood, lumps of natural pigment, bone needles and prehistoric razor blades of volcanic obsidian glass, skilfully flaked from the original core, veined and translucent as one held them up to the light. Once we came upon a little jug unbroken, once upon an incense burner with a moulded human face, once upon a clay whistle, and to spur us on there was always the possibility, however remote, that we should discover a skull of rock-crystal or a mask of gold or jade or turquoise inlay.

For another eighteen inches stretched the Aztec layer. Below this began the artefacts of the Toltecs, a people of whom far less is known but who may have attained a higher degree of culture than their conquerors. For nine or ten feet down does the Toltec strata extend before giving place to relics of a yet earlier civilisation, that of peoples of whom little or nothing is known, and to which for the sake of convenience the name of Archaic is given.

If the old rule of thumb were reliable and one could count upon the earth's surface being covered at the rate of three feet per thousand years, one could be sure not only that the Nahua-speaking peoples, to whom for convenience we can extend the name of Aztec, had been in possession of the valley of Mexico for four or five hundred years before 1520 (which is not far from the mark), but that the Toltec civilisation lasted from about 2000 B.C. to A.D. 1000, and that the six feet of Archaic strata correspond with the period from 4000 to 2000 B.C.

Unfortunately, erosion and other factors render any such calculations utterly unreliable, and contemporary archaeologists are inclined to compress into a very much shorter span the period represented by these remains. It is certain that the Archaic culture goes back to before the last great volcanic eruption in the Valley, for at Copilco near San Angel skeletons and the artefacts which they used in life have been found under the petrified lava-flow known as the Pedregal at the foot of the now extinct volcano of Ajusco. Unfortunately, geologists are at a loss to date this eruption even approximately. The one thing certain is that from the earliest days of its inhabitation there must have been continuity of civilization in the Valley, for the Mexican Indians of to-day grind their maize on three legged *metate* mortars and use spindle whorls for spinning exactly similar in design to those found beneath the lava-flow, and at the coming of the Spaniards the Aztecs were still worshipping and sacrificing their victims at pyramids similar in type to the Archaic pyramid of Cuicuilco, on the further side of the Pedregal, round which the lava still whirls in petrified current and cross-current.[1]

Who were these first Indian inhabitants of Mexico, and whence did they come?

Many fantastic answers have been propounded to this question, involving lost continents and passages of the Pacific quite beyond the powers of primitive man. Two things seem certain: America was populated from Asia, and this occurred at, anthropologically speaking, a relatively recent date, say ten to fifteen thousand years ago. Scarcely less certain is it that those first 'Pilgrim Fathers', the primitive Siberian tribes, entered America in successive waves by way of the Bering Strait and gradually filtered down through the whole length of the two continents. It is difficult to understand how within so short a time all the varying languages and physical types of America can have been evolved, but it must be remembered that these tribes came over at a very embryonic stage of civilisation, at which some of them, in their original habitat, have ever since remained. They knew neither

[1]For a fuller account of Mexican archaeological sites see my article 'Ancient Monuments of Mexico' in *The Geographical Magazine* for September 1938.

agriculture, pottery nor weaving. Hence the very different lines on which American and Asiatic civilisation developed, and hence incidentally the clearest indication that from neolithic times till the Conquest there was no intercommunication between the two continents[1].

We may now leave the past for the present and turn to the Indian inhabitants of Mexico in whom the traditions 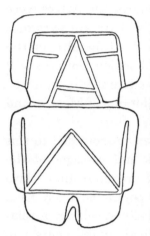 of their indigenous ancestors are perpetuated. When I first came to Mexico my ideas about them were very hazy. I knew, for instance, that Mexico boasted almost the highest proportion of Indian blood in any Latin American republic. I had heard of Aztecs and Mayas and imagined that all Mexican Indians fell under one or other of these two categories. I had a vague idea that if one adventured into the wildest parts of the country, among still semi-savage peoples one might find traces of the ancient languages. I had to learn that over one-third of Mexico's eighteen millions are of pure Indian stock, and over half of mixed, but predominantly Indian blood; that upwards of sixty different Indian languages are still spoken (sixteen of them in the state of Oaxaca alone), of which no less than fourteen are said not to share a single root in common; and that well over a million people do not speak any Spanish, apart from the far larger number who are bilingual. Nearly a million people, for instance, speak the Nahua

[1]For an admirably clear and comprehensive account of American origins see Pablo Martínez del Río: *Los Orígenes Americanos*. Mexico. 1936, and its forthcoming English translation.

dialects, to which in Mexico the name of *mexicano* is generally given, although we may for convenience call them Aztec. Over a quarter million speak Maya, nearly as many Otomi and its allied dialects, about 200,000 each Zapotec and Mixtec, and so on down to minor tribes who to-day number only a few hundred souls.

At this stage it is important to draw a clear distinction between the northern and the southern parts of the country, the boundary between which may very roughly be set at the Tropic of Cancer. The fever-ridden hot lands of a great part of the south have been described by Mr. William Spratling as 'Mexico's subconscious', and a journey through the vast empty spaces of the north suggests that the simile might be extended to call these 'Mexico's *un*-conscious'. From Torreón to Zacatecas, for instance, is nearly ten hours by rail, during which no large town is passed, no village church even, only agglomerations of adobe houses which have sprung up round junctions or wayside stations. Hour in, hour out, the train puffs across desolate, sandy wastes, where little or no rain falls even in the wet season, and the soil, white with saltpetre, nourishes only prickly pear, candelabra cactus and feathery mesquite scrub.

On either side the desert stretches away to long, straddling mountains five, ten, twenty miles distant. When the earth's surface is concave the eye distinguishes every cross-hatching of the plain away to the far slopes. At times it appears convex. Then the mountains are seen hull-down, like ships in the trough of a wave, barely topping the near horizon. In winter the sky is unbroken blue: in summer a few white clouds, as in an Italian primitive, splash cobalt shadows on the ranges of burnt sienna. Rare is any sign of cultivation or habitation. The traveller is

43

assailed with a desolate sense of emptiness, of a landscape that has never sprung to life or that has been drained by the merciless sun of any spirituality which it may once have possessed.

Always there is the compensation of the light, the diaphanous early-morning light of the days when the world was young. Its attains its greatest brilliance in the Laguna, a vast bowl among the hills of Durango and Coahuila, where British initiative, among others, has harnessed the waters of the River Nazas and made the desert flower with the white and gold of cotton and wheat. Here, the light can only be compared with that of Aegean Delos, birthplace of Apollo. As in Greece, the mountains have the whiteness of wood-ash against the deep blue of the sky. At noon they are insubstantial and two-dimensional as a theatrical backcloth. In the late afternoon they take on solidity as the light falls athwart their angular ridges and come to look as though moulded out of tinfoil. The last rays of the sun tinge them with that vivid petunia which earned Athens the name of violet-crowned, and in a liquid purple-brown they are finally lost in the dulling crimson afterglow.

Although pre-Conquest America is supposed to have had a population of forty millions it is improbable that Northern Mexico ever supported a larger Indian population than it does to-day. It was left to the Spaniards through the great impulse which they gave to mining and cattle-breeding to open it up. They colonized it with Indians from other parts of the country, with whom they interbred to form the predominantly *mestizo* population who live there to-day.

There are, of course, indigenous Indian tribes in the North, whose descendants still cling tenaciously to the rocky escarpments of the two Sierra Madres, the eastern and the western. Such tribes are the Yaquis, Coras, Tara-

Viva Mexico!

Popocatepetl

Mexican landscape (State of Hidalgo)

Lassoing a bronco

Huichole Indians

Tortilla sellers, Amecameca

Baskets   Sombreros

The basket-maker, Ixmiquilpan

Otomi potter

humaras, Apaches, and others. In physical appearance and mode of life they are more closely related to the nomadic, hunting tribes of the American south-west than to the settled agricultural population of southern Mexico. They are *bronco*, untamed, their spirit still unbroken. There are Yaquis, for instance, in Arizona as well as in Sonora. Within living memory the Governments of Mexico and the United States of America combined to round-up the savage Apache Indians who invariably took refuge on one side of the border after committing outrages on the other. A small group of thirty or forty eluded the net, and are still at large. A friend of mine who lives in Chihuahua was once out shooting on the edge of the Sierra Madre in uninhabited country when he saw a wisp of smoke curling into the sky a mile or two away. Unfortunately, one of his beaters fired a shot before he could stop him, and within a minute or two the smoke had disappeared, the fire from which it rose abruptly extinguished. A deep canyon lay between him and the spot. When he reached it he found the warm ashes of an encampment of thirty or forty persons, the outlawed Apaches. Somewhat imprudently he set out to follow them, but after two days of vain pursuit he found the trail leading into such terrible country, almost impassable and yielding nourishment for neither man nor beast, that he was obliged to abandon it.

It was not people such as these who left to posterity the legacy of the pyramids and palaces, the jewels of gold and jade, of Anahuac and Yucatan. Pushing up into the north in their untiring search for treasure the Spaniards of the sixteenth century found savages at the lowest ebb of human culture. In the long, narrow peninsula of Lower California, for instance, the Jesuit missionaries found three tribes, the Cochimis, Guaycuras and Percues, living in conditions of utter savagery. They had no dwellings but slept in caves, leaf shelters or hollows in the ground, roughly roofed with stones. Their only food consisted of roots and berries eked out with the produce of arrow and harpoon. The men went naked, the women in skin loin-cloths. They had no social organization, no religious be-liefs or practices, no tradition of their origin except a vague idea that they had come from the north. They had not even reached the stage of making pottery, but contented themselves with utensils of stone, wood, bone or shell. They were in fact a relic of the Stone Age, and failed to survive their contact with civilization, most of them per-ishing miserably in two great smallpox epidemics in 1709 and 1856. To-day a small handful of them survive in the north of the peninsula under the name of Cahuilas.

To find such primitive conditions in the present day it is necessary to go to the Seris or the Lacandones. The for-mer live on the Isla de los Tiburones in the Gulf of Cali-fornia, and the latter in the sodden rain-forests of the largely unexplored border between Chiapas and the Gua-temalan Peten.

Tribes like these, however, form an insignificant minor-ity in Indian Mexico. In his book *Peace by Revolution* Mr. Frank Tannenbaum quotes one of his friends as remarking that there are three classes of Mexican Indians, 'those on the plantations who feel themselves the white man's in-ferior and look on the ground while talking to a stranger; those in the villages who feel themselves a white man's equal and look straight at him while addressing him; and those in the mountain tops who consider themselves a white man's superior and look down upon him while ad-dressing him'. Good examples of this last class are the Yaquis of Sonora and the Huicholes of Nayarit, both of whom are still spiritually untamed. The plantation Indians are rapidly disappearing as a class as a result of the agrarian policy, pursued since the revolution of 1910, of breaking up the big estates, restoring to the Indians the ancient *ejidos* or communal smallholdings of which they were despoiled after the Conquest and endowing with land those who hitherto had had none. They have gone thus to swell the ranks of the largest of Mr. Tannenbaum's three categories, that of the village Indians who have retained all the qualities of a peasant deeply rooted in his traditions. These are the true bearers of the ancestral tradition, the unbroken chain which links the Archaic period with the twentieth century.

In spite of the very considerable disparity between tribe and tribe in language, physical appearance, customs and mode of life there is a fundamental uniformity among the Indians of Mexico which makes it possible to generalize about them at least to some extent.

The physical type generally lacks the thin, aquiline features of the Redskin, and corresponds more with one's preconception of the South than of the North American Indian. The colour of the skin varies from a light coffee through ruddy gold to a deep tawny bronze. The hair, of an even blackness, is thick and close even in old age. A bald Indian is the rarest thing in the world. On the other hand, the facial hair is thin and scanty, and its straggling wisps account for the deep impression made on Montezuma's warriors by the thick beards of the Conquistadores.

The shape of the head varies considerably, one of the commonest and most characteristic forms in the men being a long sugar-loaf point rising steeply from the brows. In the women the back of the head is often gracefully rounded, its curve enhanced by their long black tresses,

flowing loose or knotted in two long plaits on either side of
a neat parting.

Their Asiatic origin is only too clearly evidenced in
their features; the broad face, the high mongoloid cheek-
bones, the full, fleshy lips, brilliant white teeth and broad
nose, often squat, with wide-set nostrils. There is nothing
resilient, no hint of bone and muscle in their forms which
are full, solid and rounded. The muscle is there as their
strength and endurance show, but its play lies hidden beneath the thick skin, like the deep currents of the sea beneath a surface calm. I have seen many Indians, especially
among the Totonacs, who from the back might have been
Japanese. Others bear a close resemblance to the people of
the East Indies and Polynesia. The distinguishing feature
is the eyes. Much has been written about Indian eyes, and
much remains to be written. D. H. Lawrence, if I remember right (for I cannot bring myself to reread *The Plumed
Serpent*), called them cold and serpent-like, felt in them a
sense of creeping evil, saw in them a look of implacable
hatred for the white man. Once or twice only I have seen
that look of racial hatred, and then more often in a *mestizo*
than in a true Indian. In any case Lawrence took a very
personal view of Mexico as of most other things.

To describe it more exactly, the Indian eye is large and
well-shaped with clear whites, an intensely dark pupil and
in its centre a pin-point of glinting light. The disconcerting thing is that, although one can read nothing in its
depths, it is not veiled or turned inward, but bright with
the hard, unchanging brilliance of polished obsidian. It is
utterly impossible to read through these eyes the thoughts
or feelings of their owner, and one is left with an impression of void opacity, of challenging inscrutability, which
is completed by the deft sweep of a *sarape* rug or *rebozo*

shawl like the closing of a door or the extinction of a light.

As baffling to read as the expression in Indian eyes is the Indian temperament. It is, at the best of times, an invidious task to weigh the character of a race whose hospitality one has enjoyed, and in this case it is also one of real difficulty. Yet there are certain aspects of the Indian outlook which it may be neither presumptuous nor invidious to outline here. In the first place the Indian seems to have preserved from pre-Cortesian times the ceremonial attitude towards life. 'Living in subservience to their divinities,' writes Dr. George Vaillant, 'the Central Americans seemed little interested in their own emotional weaknesses or sentimentality, and this impersonality, often austere, defines their art.'[1] Their present day descendants seem to be curiously (and it may be added agreeably) lacking in personal ambition and acquisitiveness. It counts far more with them to be able to adhere to their self-ordained pattern of life. If one wants to induce an Indian to take a course of action for which he is disinclined, it is perfectly useless to appeal to his self-interest. A good instance of this attitude is quoted in the sixteenth century by Padre Durán. One wintry day he passed an Indian, undernourished and underclad, on his way to market with a load of firewood which he hoped to sell for two *reales*. In the kindness of his heart Father Durán gave him the money and bade him return home and use the firewood to warm himself. Looking back a few minutes later he saw the Indian still following him, and turned back to remonstrate with him. 'Take back your money if it means so much to you,' was the characteristic reply. 'As for me, I am going to market to

[1]George C. Vaillant: *Artists and Craftsmen in Ancient Central America*, p. 21. New York. 1935.

sell my wood'. To have turned back would have meant breaking his own self-imposed pattern of life, and against this no question of material advantage weighed with him.

This trait, coupled with their paganism, no doubt accounts for the low opinion of the Indians held by the early Spaniards. On several occasions the Pope had to intervene to point out that the Indian was to be regarded as a human being above the level of animals. Nevertheless, in the colonial period those who shared this view were only a small minority. In spite of the fact that for twenty-five years the redemption of the Indian and the restoration of his rights have formed the chief plank in Government policy, something of this attitude still remains in the phrase *gente de razón* (reasoning beings) smugly applied to themselves by all those with a few drops of white blood in their veins as even by pure Indians who have forgotten their native idiom. One of the few to defend the Indian in the eighteenth century was the historian Clavijero. 'The Spaniards', he wrote, 'say in the manner of a proverb that the Indians neither feel injuries nor are grateful for benefits. Yet never did Europeans make such poor use of their own reason as when they doubted that of the American native.'[1]

The Indian's detachment does not mean that he is not a very warm-hearted person, ready to put himself to endless trouble to oblige a friend or even a stranger. His courtesy is proverbial and is all the more engaging for being instinctive and corresponding to no external, purely formal, code of behaviour. In making you free of his hut of palm-thatch or sun-baked adobe brick its owner will allude to it as '*your* poor house' and in contradistinction to the Spaniard he really means this.

[1]Francisco Xavier Clavijero: *Historia Antigua de México*. Madrid. 1780.

Indian Background

An American girl told me of the unconsciously humorous remark which this attitude once prompted. She was talking at Amecameca to an Indian with a little girl by his side. 'Is that your little daughter?' she asked him. 'Yes' came the reply, and then with grave courtesy, '*y la de Usted* . . . and yours!'

The Indians have a fundamental vein of gentleness which is none the less real for the contrast which it presents to their sporadic outbreaks of uncontained violence. This quality has communicated itself even to the Spanish language which they speak with a sing-song cadence falling strangely on the ears of those accustomed to the robust intonation of Castile. Into this intonation one instinctively falls when talking to them, and it is as well that one should do so, for they are quick to detect and resent the slightest nuance of tone which is abrupt or peremptory.

In their outlook there is a quality at the same time aristocratic and democratic. Provided that you have no illusions of your own superiority, the Indian does not in the least feel called upon to assert his, and is prepared to meet you on a footing of complete, unquestioning equality. So sure is he of his own position, so secure in the standing which he has occupied for hundreds of years, that he does not deem it necessary to remind you of his legend of the creation. When the creator, so runs his version, made man from a lump of dough his first attempt was underdone and produced the pallid white man. Determined not to repeat his mistake he went to the other extreme, and the burnt and blackened negro was the result. Only at the third attempt did he judge things correctly and produce the happy mean, baked to the warm brown of the Indian.

In Indian children, as in the grown-ups, gentleness and instinctive good manners are combined with spontaneous

51

good humour. Seraphic, Flandrau calls them in his *Viva Mexico*. If you smile at them they find it almost impossible not to smile back. Little Mexican boys are most em-

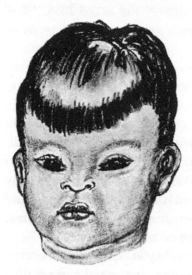

phatically not made of 'slugs and snails and puppy-dogs' tails'. 'So docile and gentle are they,' wrote Father Motolinia in the sixteenth century, 'that ten Spanish children make more noise than a thousand Indians.' It is almost as though the old Adam had been left out of their make-up, and the traveller has no cause to fear their mockery or volleys of stones as in some European countries. If asked their name they will lengthen it with the formulae of courtesy, thus Margarito Romero González *con su permiso para servirle a Usted* (with your permission and at your service). The little girls are compact miniatures of their elders, blessed with an admirable composure. Most of their games are founded on the 'works and days' of grown-ups and played with miniature household utensils, pots, pans and gourd bowls, and other toys home-made out of clay, wood, straw or maize stalk. It has sometimes occurred to me to wonder whether the detached, contemplative attitude of mind of the Indian is not due at least in part to the Olympian outlook which the baby commands during the first two or three years of his life when he views the world from the shawl which binds him tightly to the back of his mother or elder sister.

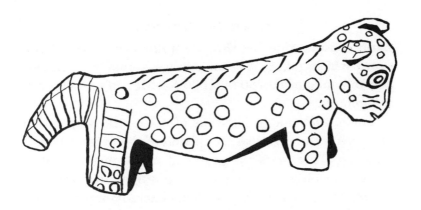

IV. Indian Background, 2

Just as in spite of tribal differences there is a recognizable highest common factor in the physique and character of the Mexican Indians, so their culture, both material and spiritual, has a well-marked unity, in spite of differences of climate and altitude. The unifying element is the cultivation of maize. It was only when they began the cultivation of the thin wild Indian corn called by the Aztecs *teocentli* or food of the gods that the rude, hunting tribes settled down in one place and moved forward from the hunting to the agricultural stage of civilization. It has been suggested that the first home of Indian corn was in the Huasteca, inland from Tampico. As the cultivated plant gradually developed the big cob which we know to-day, so did an assured supply of food permit the people to develop the culture which culminated in the Old Empire of the Mayas, the civilization of Teotihuacan and the splendour of Montezuma's capital. To-day maize is grown from sea-level to 10,000 feet and forms, as it has done since pre-history, the staple diet of the whole country. Monsieur Van de Velde calculates that the Zapotec village of San Pablo Cuatro Venados with its 676 inhabitants consumes no less than $2\frac{1}{4}$ million maize *tortillas* a year,[1] which, taking it as an average, would give the respectable total of 60,750,000,000 for Mexico's 18,000,000 inhabitants.

The *tortilla* is a griddle-cake of maize, the preparation of which is the principal occupation of the peasant housewife. First she soaks the grains of maize in lime-water. Next, crouching to her work, she rubs them to a dough on the *metate*, a slightly curved slab, generally of porous volcanic stone, set on three legs, of which one is longer than the others so that the slab is slightly tilted away from her. For this operation she uses a rolling-pin, likewise of volcanic stone, called *metlalpilli* (lit. 'the child of the *metate*'). Lumps of this dough are then slapped from hand to hand and turned the while until they assume the circular shape of the thin, flat *tortilla* which is finally grilled over a charcoal fire in a very shallow earthenware bowl called a *comal*. Like a sudden burst of applause the rhythmic clapping of tortilla-women recalls the unseen snapping of castanets just before the curtain goes up on the ballet of the 'Three Cornered Hat'. With the gobbling of turkeys it forms the *leit-motiv* of rural Mexico.

Even now, four hundred years after the Conquest, the Indians tend to keep to the diet of their ancestors, to prefer pork or venison to beef, and to eschew eggs and milk.

In most parts chile peppers are used for seasoning in innumerable varieties each hotter than the last, attaining their crowning glory in *mole poblana* and black *mole*, turkey or chicken stewed in a hot, dark sauce in comparison with which Bengal curry is as cooling as sherbet. Curiously enough, in British India a similar dish is known under

[1]G. Russell Steininger and Paul Van de Velde: *Three Dollars a Year*. New York. 1935.

the selfsame name of *mole*, having travelled thither perhaps by way of Acapulco and the Pacific.

Needless to say, a good number of native delicacies do
not commend themselves to white men's palates, or at the
least are acquired tastes. Many of them are drawn from
the insect world. Of these one of the best-known is the
gusano de maguey, a small white caterpillar which grows
inside the maguey aloe. It is supposed to contain phos-
phorus and to have excellent nutritive and digestive prop-
erties. Personally I rather like it. Fried in butter or oil and

eaten with *huacamole* (a salad of avocado pear, chile and
onions) maguey worms are not unlike crisply fried pota-
toes. Other dishes are grasshopper *tacos*, the insects being
fried and wrapped in *tortillas*; *santiaguillos* found in tree-
trunks in the Huasteca country; the *jolín* of Chiapas; and
xumiles, hotter than any chile, a large greenish bug found
among pine-trees in Guerrero. *Ahuautli*, the eggs of the
March fly, *axayacatl*, skimmed off Lake Texcoco, mixed
into a paste with white of egg and fried, are said to be
both nourishing and a preventative for rheumatism. They
are mentioned by Bernal Diaz as 'a sort of scum tasting
not unlike cheese' and alluded to by Thomas Gage (1626)
in the following appetizing passage: 'The several kinds of

meats to be sold was without number, as Snakes without
head and tail, little dogs gelt, Moles, Rats, Long-worms,
Lice, yea, and a kind of earth; for at one season in the
year they had nets of Mail, with the which they raked up a
certain dust that is bred upon the water of the lake of
Mexico, and that is kneaded together like unto Oaze of the
sea. They gathered much of this and kept it in heaps, and
made thereof Cakes like unto Brick-bats . . . and they did
eat this Meal with as good a stomach as we eat Cheese. . . .'[1]
To me the nearest thing which it suggests is the hard and
rather gritty roe of a herring, and I cannot say that I ate
it with particularly 'good stomach'.

Both coffee and chocolate are grown in the hot country,
especially in the state of Chiapas, and curiously enough it
is not of the two the indigenous product which is the more
widely consumed by the Indians to-day. Few English-
speaking people when pronouncing the word 'chocolate'
realize that they are merely using a corruption of the
Aztec word *xocolatl*, meaning the drink prepared with the
cacahuatl bean, the fruit of the *cacahuaquahuitl* tree. In
Aztec times chocolate was essentially an aristocratic drink,
so much so that only the Emperor and his chief Lords and
Priests partook of the beverage with the object of restoring
the energies lost in religious vigils. So precious were the
beans that they were used as coinage, 'blessed money' as
Peter Martyr exclaimed, 'which exempts its possessors from
avarice since it cannot be long hoarded nor hidden underground.' Their use spread with the sending of cocoa beans
to Europe by Cortes and his successors, and the manner of
preparing it changed. In Montezuma's time the beans
were crushed in a jar with a little water and well beaten

[1]Thomas Gage: *The English American, his Travail by Sea and
Land, or A New Survey of the West Indies*. London. 1648.

up and stirred. The oily scum which rose to the surface was taken off, and only added in again after the remainder had been mixed with *nixtamal* (maize dough) and heated on the fire. It was then allowed to cool, seasoned with aromatic herbs, chile peppers and honey, whipped up once more and served cold in a gourd bowl into which it was poured from a height. The Spaniards preferred to flavour it with vanilla, cinnamon and Spanish aniseed.

When prepared in the old fashion it was not only nourishing, but a powerful stimulant and aphrodisiac, a property which no doubt accounts for the controversy which it provoked in Spain. Books and pamphlets were written for and against it, and the Pope forbade monks and nuns to partake of it on account of its diabolical power to awaken the flesh. Even to-day my Oaxacan servants tell me that the best cure for a scorpion sting is to rub garlic on the place and to drink chocolate.

The excessive addiction to chocolate of the Spanish aristocracy of Chiapa la Real once cost a worthy Bishop his life, as related by Thomas Gage, the renegade English Dominican who came to Mexico early in the seventeenth century. 'The women of that city', he writes, 'pretend much weakness and squeamishness of stomach, which they say is so great that they are not able to continue in the church while a Mass is briefly huddled over, much less while a solemn high Mass is sung and sermon preached, unless they drink a cup of hot chocolate and eat a bit of sweatmeats to strengthen their stomachs. For this purpose it was much used by them to make their maids bring to them to church in the middle of the mass or sermon a cup of chocolate, which could not be done at all, or most of them, without a great confusion and interrupting both Mass and sermon.' Persuasion and threats having alike proved of no avail to put an end to this abuse, the Bishop, Bernardino de Salazar, laid a ban of excommunication on 'all such as should presume at the time of service to eat or drink within the church.' The ladies, however, 'began to stomach him the more and to slight him with scornful and reproachful words; others slighted his excommunication, drinking in iniquity in the church, as the fish doth water, which caused one day such an uproar in the Cathedral that many swords were drawn against the priests and prebends, who attempted to take away from the maids the cups of chocolate which they brought unto their mistresses.' Things did not even stop there. The ladies next transferred their devotions to the Franciscan and Dominican monastery churches whose monks, like Friar Thomas himself, viewed the weaknesses of the flesh with a more indulgent eye. To this trick the Bishop replied with a better, for he 'began to stomach the friars, and to set up another excommunication, binding all the city to resort unto their own cathedral church, which the women would not obey, but kept their houses for a whole month.'

All this 'stomaching' was bound to lead to trouble. The Bishop fell ill. Unable to find a physician willing to attend him he moved to the Dominican monastery whose Prior he trusted, and there a few days later he died, of poison administered to him in the very beverage of which he had so zealously condemned the use. 'And it became afterwards', continues Gage, 'a proverb in that country, Beware of the chocolate of Chiapa; which made me so cautious that I would not drink afterwards of it in any house where I had not very great satisfaction of the whole family.' Even to-day, where Chicago would say 'they took him for a ride' conservative Chiapas is content with the phrase *le dieron su chocolate* 'they gave him his chocolate'.

Pulque, the ancient *ochtli*, is a drink derived from the maguey aloe. Every nine years this plant shoots forth the long flowering stalk familiar to many as the 'century plant'. Immediately before this a great quantity of sap gathers in the heart of the plant. This sap, known as *agua miel* (honey-water) from its sweetness, is sucked out through a long gourd called an *acocote*, and is fermented into pulque, a sort of mead of moderate alcoholic strength tasting something like a cross between flat beer and sour buttermilk. In wineskins made from the whole skin of a pig, pulque is taken to town where it is sold in special taverns called *pulquerías*, the names of which are often consciously or unconsciously humorous. Near Tlalnepant-la there is one called *Vamos a Ver a Cruz*, a pun on the two meanings of 'Let's go to Vera Cruz' and 'Let's go and see Cruz' (a girl's name). The festive spirit is implicit in such names as *Sal que Puedes* (Leave if you can), *Dos al Fandango* (Two in the Fandango), *Me siento Aviador* (I feel like an Airman) and *El Gato Vasilante* (The Staggering Cat). Wiser warnings are conveyed by the names of *El Gran Mareo* (The Big Hangover) and *B.B.Y.V.T.* (*Bebe y Vete*: Drink and Depart). Others reflect an incongruous elegance on which the interior is apt to be an ironic commentary, such as *El Tenplo del Amor* (The Temple of Love), *Entre Violetas* (Among Violets), *La Cascada de Rosas* (The Shower of Roses), *El Palacio Encantado* (The Enchanted Palace) and *El Gorgeo de las Aves* (The Twittering of the Birds).

Best of all names of *pulquerías* in its delicious paradox is the classic *El Recuerdo del Porvenir* (The Memory of the Future).

Indian Background

One of the names most frequently met is *La Reina Xochitl*, an allusion to the legend of the origin of *pulque*. Towards the end of the Toltec Empire of Tula, according to the chronicler Ixtlilxochitl, King Tecpancaltzin was visited by one of his subjects called Papantzin who with his daughter Xochitl (Flower) offered the King the *miel de maguey* (maguey honey) which they had discovered. Perhaps the 'honey' had fermented by the time it reached him for the King's ardour was aroused by the girl whom he imprisoned in a fortress and seduced. In due course a child was born to them, Meconetzin, Son of the Maguey, who bore on his body the signs predicted by the astrologer Hueman, as being those which would distinguish the King in whose reign Tula's ruin was to be encompassed. In due course the prophecy was fulfilled, Tula falling a victim to wars, plagues and pestilence and Queen Xochitl meeting a valiant death at the hands of her enemies.

The maguey is known in Mexico as *la vaca verde* (the green cow), so many of the people's wants does it supply. Apart from *pulque* and *mescal* (a spirit distilled from the heart of the plant), soap is made from the roots, and fences or even huts from the tough leaves. If these are carefully skinned a clear parchment is obtained on which many of the pre-Spanish codices were painted. The most important of its by-products perhaps is the fibre known as *ixtle* from which ropes, nets and bags are made, and clothes sewn and embroidered with needles furnished by the hard spikes of the points which can be made to come away with the fibre attached.

Those who have come into contact with the Indian in Canada and United States are generally struck by the great difference between the Indian culture of North and of Central America. Miss Erna Fergusson who has described in *Dancing Gods* the tribal dances and ceremonies of the American south-west, was keenly disappointed when she came south to write *Fiesta in Mexico* to find how rare were the pure, uncorrupted survivals of Indian myth and ritual. Comparison between the two Indian worlds is misleading, however. The European invaders of North America came to colonize; those of Central and South America to enrich themselves and if possible to return whence they came. It has been estimated that during the three centuries of the colonial period, not more than 300,000 Spaniards settled in Mexico. The Pilgrim Fathers and their successors found the New World sparsely populated by fierce, nomadic tribes, at a low stage of civilization, with whom there was little or no possibility of compromise, a fact which to some extent explains, if it cannot excuse, the famous adage that 'the only good Indian is a dead Indian.' The Spanish Conquistadores found Mexico thickly populated by a settled people whose civilization awoke their astonished admiration. Quite apart from any questions of colour bar, circumstances precluded the evolution of a mixed race in North America, and the Indians have been exterminated except for a few survivors, many of them penned in reservations, who either preserve their blood and traditions uncontaminated or have practically lost their racial character. This accounts for the fact that North American Indian culture, such as it is, appears nowhere to have blended with the European.

In spite of the ravages of warfare and the white man's scourges of drink and disease there was never any question of the Mexican Indians being wiped out. The history of Mexico is one of assimilation rather than of annihilation, and although they ruled the country for 300 years it was in the long run the Spaniards and their culture which were assimilated.

Mexico has therefore been the scene of a long process of cultural and biological evolution quite unparalleled north of the Rio Grande.

This fusion of the two cultures, the native and the European, is particularly noticeable in the domain of costume. Some pre-Conquest garments have remained; others have disappeared; others again have been modified as the result of European influence. Male costume almost throughout the Republic consists of white cotton pyjama suits and the *sarape*, the decorative woollen blanket flung round the shoulders or worn poncho-fashion with a hole cut in the middle, which evolved out of the Aztec *tilma* or mantle. Indian men are shod with *huaraches*, the ancient sandals, consisting of a leather sole with no upper other than the leather thongs with which they are secured. The women go barefoot. Their dress shows more variation than the men's. In some parts it consists of a blouse and skirt of European cut with the ubiquitous *rebozo*, a shawl of Spanish origin. The indigenous dress, however, survives in whole or in part in many districts. It is based exclusively on rectangular pieces of material. Thus the *chincuete* skirt generally consists of two horizontal strips of wool woven on a pre-Cortesian hand-loom, sewn together and carried round the waist, either folded in pleats or barely meeting according to the prosperity of the wearer. The *quexquemitl* is a sort of little cape made of two rectangular strips of material, the end of one being stitched to the side of the other and vice versa. In many parts of the hot country, notably in the states of Vera Cruz and Oaxaca, the garment generally worn is a *huipil* of white cotton, cut like an inverted sack with holes for the head and arms.

62

Indian Background

In the districts less invaded by the civilization of the machine age, these garments are woven in a variety of patterns owing much to both native and European influence, worked with the loving care of a people blessed with a tradition of handicraft.

In cases of illness the Indians rely less on medical science than on a traditional lore which goes back into the mists of antiquity. Their notions of the nature of disease are as variable as they are vague. The Popolacas dwelling on the borders of Puebla and Oaxaca believe at the instance of their witch-doctors that illness of whatever nature is due to the loss of some part of the patient's soul which has been carried off by an animal. An essential part of the treatment is the witch-doctor's hunt in the hills for the animal which he deems responsible. When he catches it he hands it over to the patient, and then drums on some hollow object, shouting and bellowing his adjurations to the soul to return, in the chorus of which all those present join.

Not all conceptions of illness are as vague and erroneous as this, and in the greater part of the country the seat, if not the exact nature, of the complaint is generally recognized. In the rarified air of the tableland, the heart is naturally a susceptible organ which calls for frequent attention. The prevalence of intestinal infections due to bad water makes stomach complaints frequent, as does the effect on the digestion of the nervous disorders caused by the altitude. Most Mexicans will take to bed from time to time with a complaint which they call a *derrame de bilis* or 'flow of bile' and which they will freely admit has been brought on by an attack of rage. They go so far as to say that if you lose your temper after eating a custard apple or two cold eggs, you will die and there is no doubt that the congestion which so imprudent an action may cause, sometimes has serious if not fatal results.

The remedies which they apply in these and other complaints are a curious mixture of superstition and empirical herb-lore in which the latter predominates.[1] When King George V lay on his death-bed an English resident in Mexico City was approached separately by two Indians of his acquaintance. The first begged him to telegraph home that if the King were to drink two pints of the blood of a freshly killed stag his life would be saved. The other offered to give him, for transmission by air mail, a secret Aztec remedy distilled from seven herbs gathered at the new moon.

At almost any market you may find a *curandera* or herb-woman in charge of her stall. She is generally a gnarled old hag crouching over a *petate* mat on which are spread in neat little heaps an astonishing variety of dessicated leaves, stalks, flowers, nuts, bulbs and roots and animal fragments from mountain and seashore. At Oaxaca I saw a green woodpecker and at San Bartolo Otzolotepec the head of a red *pico real* for that indeterminate complaint known as *el aire* 'the air.' At the latter place delicate pink mussel shells were also on sale. You must pour lemon juice on them, said the *curandera,* and apply it to

[1] For a fuller account of Indian medicinal lore, based largely on my wife's researches, see my article 'Magic and Medicine in Mexico' in *The Cornhill Magazine* for February, 1939.

wounds or boils. For heart trouble her specific was the little flower of the *manita* (digitalis) and a leaf from the *huevillo* or 'little egg' as she called the closed magnolia bud, taken together in a glass of wine. Alternatively, she was prepared to recommend *corazón de piedra*, heart of stone, that is to say fragments from the centre of a broken stone.

In many of these remedies there is sound sense. Seashells almost certainly contain minute quantities of iodine; digitalis is a well-known heart specific; the bean widely given for snake-bite contains strychnine; and in applying the kidneys of cattle or toad-skins to staunch bleeding wounds, the Indians have only been anticipating by a few centuries the discovery of adrenalin. These cures are but the dispersed fragments of the elaborate medicinal lore practised by the ancient Aztecs and chronicled in minute detail by Fray Bernardino de Sahagún and other early writers.

One day, in Mexico City, we bought some guinea-pigs for the children. Our washerwoman was interested and approving. We had, of course, bought them for our health, she intimated. This new use for guinea-pigs puzzled us, and we told her that they were only intended as pets. Nevertheless, she maintained stoutly that where guinea-pigs were kept people did not fall ill, and although it may have been mere coincidence we were in fact remarkably free from illness during our stay in Mexico. This belief puzzled me considerably until I learned that in Peru, if not in Mexico, guinea-pigs play a considerable part in folk medicine. Thus, in the High Andes, if an Indian feels pain the spot is rubbed with a live guinea-pig, with the idea that the evil shall pass into the animal. This is then skinned and examined and the patient's complaint diagnosed from the condition of its muscles and heart.

Amulets of a more usual type are common in Mexico, one of the most popular being the *ojo de venado* or deer's eye, a large pill-shaped brown bean which grows on the *tepalcingo* tree. An Otomi woman in El Cardonal had one hung round her baby's neck against the evil eye and admitted that she had paid the large sum of ten centavos for it. In Contreras, we found animals protected against the same menace by a chile hung round the neck on a string. When cats and dogs are ill you tie three (or a multiple of three) lemons round their neck in the same way.

Such ravages has the industrial age worked in the traditional heritage of the world, reducing us all to a drab uniformity, that one is apt to seek vestiges of the past in the inner recesses of men's minds rather than in their outward lives. For this reason it comes as a surprise to find that as a general rule the Indians of Mexico have preserved their spiritual beliefs less faithfully than their material civilization. This can be explained in part by the fact that the civil and ecclesiastical hierarchy of the Indians were more effectively wiped out than the common people and in part by the proselytizing activities of the Catholic Church which made its influence felt even in districts which had not submitted to the military and civil rule of the Spaniards.

In 1936, Mrs. Helga Larsen paid a visit to Maya tribes in Quintana Roo who still to-day have no contact with the Mexican administration and preserve their ancient social system based on a military hierarchy. After six days journey through uninhabited jungle she reached their village and was fortunate enough to be present at a big religious feast which lasted for several days, the details of which, thanks to her knowledge of the Maya tongue, she was able to follow. To her astonishment she found that the ceremonies of these people, who of course knew no Spanish, were predominantly Catholic in character. Their church was a large hut divided into what may well be called a nave, a chancel and an apse-shaped sanctuary. The congregation filled the nave, and their participation in the ceremonies could all be related to pure Maya myth and ritual. The 'priests' who officiated in the chancel performed rites of a purely Catholic character including the use of a dog-latin which they themselves did not understand. The object of their cult is neither the Trinity nor the Saints but the Cross, an actual cross which is believed to be preserved immured in the apse. During the War of the Castes a century ago, the defeated Mayas complained that the dice had been loaded against them as 'the Christians had all the gods'. To satisfy them, a Cross was miraculously discovered and given to them, and it is in all probability this which to-day is the object of their idolatry.

If the Church was able to make its influence felt in places as remote as this, it is little wonder that undiluted paganism is extremely difficult to discover to-day and that within a relatively short time of the Conquest most vestiges of the old faiths were extirpated or transformed and endowed with a new Christian purpose and meaning.

In this task, the Church was aided by the curiously empirical mental processes of the Indians who seem to construct by addition rather than by development, or, to use a mathematical simile, by arithmetical rather than by geometrical progression. An apt illustration of this trait is to be found in the complex symbolical ideographs which adorn pre-Cortesian sculpture and codices, and which are clearly the result, not of the development of a simple germ, but of the accretion to it of new and different motives. Similarly, when as so frequently happened in

the fertile valley of Mexico, a new wave of primitive hunting tribes descended on the more cultivated, settled agricultural population, they rarely fused the identities and attributes of their respective divinities but installed the new beside the old, thus contributing to the appalling complexity and overcrowding of the Aztec Olympus, in which the Toltec Quetzalcoatl rubbed shoulders with the Aztec Huitzilopochtli and Xiuhtecutli or Huehueteotl, the 'Old Old God' of fire with Mixcoatl, the Chichimec god of war.

In this Olympus, the Indian made no difficulty in finding a place for the Christian Trinity, the Virgin and the Saints. Only when it was suggested to him that he should renounce and expel the old gods did he oppose a resistance which was generally passive rather than active.

Another factor worked in favour of a fusion of the faiths. This was the number of points in common between Christianity and the pre-Cortesian cults, such as the Cross (symbolizing, in ancient Mexico, the four cardinal points), the Virgin birth (of Quetzalcoatl), the use of incense, and of holy water, bread and oil, flagellation, penitence and fasting, amulets, charms and scapularies. There are few Indians to-day who are not professed Catholics, but there are also few who do not make some more or less unconscious concessions to the beliefs and practices of their ancestors. In the remoter parts offerings are made to idols in some hidden cave, stone deities are dressed up in surplices and baptized with the names of Christian Saints, ancient effigies are hidden beneath the altars of Catholic churches or built into the jar-shaped mud-granaries of Tlaxcala or Morelos to bring blessing upon the corn.

Conscious attempts to revive the old worship on the lines of D. H. Lawrence's *The Plumed Serpent* are unknown either in history or in the present day. Virtually the only exception was the tragic rising of the Chamula Indians in 1869, led by an inspired priestess called Agustina Gomez Checheb who preached a return to the old gods. On this occasion, in order that the rebels might fight Christianity with its own magic, an Indian boy allowed himself to be crucified as a mediator.

A few years ago, an ardent patriot attempted to introduce the substitution of Quetzalcoatl for the imported Father Christmas. The idea was not widely adopted, but before it was abandoned it caused at least one minor tragedy. A child in Mexico City was told by his free-thinking father to direct his appeals to Quetzalcoatl, and by his *bien pensant* mother to remain faithful to Santa Claus. Being a practical minded child, he wrote to both asking for presents. It so happened that his father was rich and his mother was poor. The result was that Father Christmas came out of the contest with much less kudos than Quetzalcoatl.

V. Anahuac

Si a morar en Indias fueres
Que sea donde los volcanes vieres

'If to the Indies you go to dwell, let it be where you may see the volcanoes,' runs a Spanish proverb of the colonial period. It may be doubted, however, whether it was the natural beauty of the country within sight of the great snowclad peaks which inspired this old saw so much as its healthiness after the fever-ridden swamps and jungles of the coasts, and its fertility compared with the arid deserts of the north.

Tierra fria in and around the wide valley of Anahuac is indeed a privileged land. It may be true that a height of 7,500 feet above the sea is half as high again as is healthy for those bred and nurtured at lower levels, but against this may be set the perfection of the climate 'never colder than an English April, never hotter than an English June'. The year falls into two well-defined halves, the wet season and the dry, the first roughly from May to October and the second from October to May.

When you arrive in Mexico people will tell you that throughout the winter not a single drop of rain falls while in summer every day dawns bright and clear, clouds up at noon and deluges with rain from two to four in the afternoon so punctually that you can set your watch by it. When this does not happen, they will say that it always used to be so but that the weather is not what it was in their young days. All over the world newcomers seem to be assured that the weather is not what it used to be.

All the same, the accounts one hears of the Mexican weather are the relative, if not the absolute, truth. The dry and wet seasons are clearly distinguished. The rains begin in about May and then, after a sort of St. Martin's winter, a fine spell called the *días caniculares* or dog days, they set in in good earnest. In the valley of Mexico it seldom, if ever, rains before lunch and at Cuernavaca and Taxco most of the rain falls at night. In the valley the days generally dawn misty, clear at about eleven, cloud up in the middle of the day and discharge thunder, lightning and torrential showers for most of the afternoon. Early in October strong winds from the north bring the last storm and then blow the clouds away for good. They are called *el cordonazo de San Francisco*, St. Francis's flagellation, and in my first year in Mexico the rains were actually turned off like a tap on St. Francis's Day, October 4th. The next three months are the most delicious time in the whole Mexican year. The air is clear and rain-washed. The earth has blossomed forth with the transient beauty of dry places. Green grass clothes the hills, splashed with the blue, the purple, the gold, the crimson of wild flowers. The world seems for a brief while to have regained, Faustlike, its lost youth. By Christmas, an unseasonable Yuletide to the Anglo-Saxon, all this beauty has withered. The flowers have been scorched alike by the vertical sun of the tropics and by the first hard frosts. The grass is dry and sere. There will be showers in February and March, when northers strike upon the coast of Vera Cruz, but they will do little or nothing to quench the thirsty soil. *Febrero loco, Marzo otro poco*. February mad, and March

71

a little also, runs the proverb. But March is far from coming in like a lion though it may go out like a lamb. Mexico knows nothing of Atlantic gales and east winds from the Baltic. This is indeed the beginning of the driest and hottest part of the year. A diaphanous curtain of dust hangs in the air draining all colour from the landscape and veiling the volcanoes for weeks at a time. Down near Cuautla in April, I have seen the sun set as a red ball through Turneresque mists, just as it does in a London December. Vicious little winds whip the dust into whirlwinds, called by the Spaniards *tolvaneras* and by the Aztecs *ecamalacatl* 'spindles of the air', in the belief that they are spindles set whirling by the souls of the dead. Like waterspouts these thin, brown, curling columns travel across the face of the land until they break upon a hillside or fizzle out like the end of a Roman candle. From Texcoco great dust storms bear down upon the city of Mexico blotting out the eastern sky, the penalty of the drainage of the ancient lake. Eyes smart, throats are sore, nerves grow taut and tempers frayed, so that it comes as a relief when the annual cycle is completed and the refreshing rain falls once more upon the land.

In the changing weather one thing alone remains con-stant, the beauty of the land in its infinite variety. The two great volcanoes, Popocatepetl and Ixtaccihuatl, seldom look the same on two consecutive days. There are mornings when their eternal snows have the cool, glassy translucence of ice. Sometimes they are pale clouds, motionless and insubstantial, painted on a backcloth of airy blue. Another day the rains will bring them startlingly near to the

city, every jagged edge visible to the naked eye, flaring up
in the sunset in a crimson blaze.

To the north and south and west the valley is ringed
round with lesser mountains, chief among them Ajusco,
the only volcano which has ever poured burning lava
down into the inhabited valley. The prospect down many
a city street is closed, like a cul de sac, by Ajusco's solid
mass. He, too, has his moods. Seldom touched with snow,
he is unimposing in a clear, quiet sky. But a dark ceiling
of clouds will bring his steeply curving skyline looming up
into the heavens, menacing once more the people of Anahuac.

Across the floor of the valley, from Iztapalapa to Tlalma-
nalco, runs a line of lesser hills, as though the big mountains had spawned in the waters of the lake, each repeat-
ing the pattern of the skyline, with the unmistakable outline, and in most cases the hollowed-out crater, of a volcano.

One of the strangest tracts of country in the whole valley is the Pedregal, already mentioned in the previous
chapter, the petrified lava flow which once swept down
from Ajusco and remains as a memorial to that great pre-
historic eruption which buried the first traces of man.
Several miles in breadth, it lies between San Angel, Coyoacan, Tlalpam and the outlying spurs of the *sierra*, a tossing
sea of rocks with the low, lumpy horizon of an ocean swell
broken by an occasional pepper-tree. To walk across it is
the strangest sensation. The little huts of the Indians cease
at its edge and there is no hint of human life except an
occasional goatherd, often ignorant of Spanish. The
stranger is never in danger of being lost, for the shores
of habitation are never out of sight, yet to the inexperi-
enced eye there is not a single identifiable landmark in the

73

whole of the Pedregal, and to retrace one's steps exactly would be just as difficult as to steer a boat to a submerged rock a mile or two out to sea.

Twice I have walked out in the Pedregal, piloted by boys from Coyoacan, to the two objects of interest which it has to show, a serpent and a human figure carved upon flat rocks turned upwards to the sky. The human figure, or *diablito* (little devil) as they call it, is of no great interest either artistic or archaeological. More striking is the serpent, twelve or fifteen feet in length, recalling both in its style and in the conch-shells drawn between its undulations the serpents running along the base of the Quetzalcoatl pyramid at Teotihuacan. It is difficult to believe that it is not the work of one familiar with the symbolism, and trained in the art, of the ancient cults. How came it to be carved in this lonely place which can never have been inhabited since the last eruption of Ajusco? That is the problem which can never be solved with any certainty. A tentative explanation, however, has been suggested to me by rumours of pagan rites still practised in secret in the Pedregal. It is possible that when the old faiths were driven underground by the proselytizing Conquistadores, they may have been kept up in this lonely and inaccessible spot from which the approach of an intruder could be observed half an hour before his arrival. May not the serpent of the Pedregal have marked the site of a survival of the Quetzalcoatl cult into colonial times?

Be that as it may, a walk through the Pedregal in the rainy season is its own reward if only for the introduction it provides to Mexico's rich variety of wild flowers.

I would like the flowers of Anahuac to have some place in this book as they do in the enjoyment of rambles in the valley and in the surrounding hills. Here a grave difficulty

presents itself, that of names. Mexican flowers, like trees
and birds, naturally possess learned Latin names intelli-
gible only to specialists. I am, alas, no botanist, but then
neither in all probability are most of my readers. To the
latter such names will mean little, and Indian names,
varying with locality and dialect, will mean even less.
Spanish names, where such exist, are either useless or
actually misleading. Faced with the richness and un-
familiarity of the flora of the New World, the invaders
bestowed on it either names of an engaging simplicity
such as the equivalent of 'blue bird' or 'white flower' or
the names of those most similar to them in Spain. Thus
the Mexican *gorrión* and *encina* bear about as much resemblance to the European sparrow and holm-oak as does
the Canadian robin to the English variety. No such difficulty presents itself in the case of the blue lupins and
great pink thistles which in winter light up the dark pine
woods at about 10,000 feet, of the scarlet dahlias or of the
cosmos which at the end of the rainy season stand in pools
of rosy mauve on the slopes between Chapultepec and Los
Remedios. Sometimes a knowledge of garden flowers will
help, as with the scarlet trumpets of penstimmon and
salvia and the rust-red zinnias which spring up between
the rocks of the Pedregal. Yet how can I hope to catalogue
the countless different yellow blossoms ranging from small
sun-flowers to the tiny *cinco llagas* in whose five purple
stains the pious see a representation of the five wounds of
Christ?

Following from the capital the course of Cortes's retreat after the Noche Triste along what were then the
shores of the lake, a road runs out through Tacuba, Atzca-
pozalco and Tlalnepantla to Cuautitlan, a rustic *pueblo* of

low houses, the provincialism of which has passed into the proverb that *todo fuera de Mexico es Cuautitlan* (everything outside Mexico City is Cuautitlan). The road ends a little further on at Tepozotlan, a shrine which must be visited by every pilgrim in search of Mexican colonial art.

Paradoxically enough, the arts in Mexico are the product not of Spanish influence on an Indian foundation but of Indian influence on a Spanish foundation. In other words, the Spaniards substituted their own for the pre-existing Indian arts, and the Indians stamped them in turn with their unmistakable cachet. Nowhere is this more obvious than in the field of architecture. The Conquest put an abrupt end to the building of Indian temple-pyramids, replacing them, not unnaturally, with churches built on European models. Nevertheless, Mexican architecture developed on divergent lines from Spanish, and in ornament especially the Indian masons influenced its evolution as much or more than the Spanish or Italian architects who worked in the New World. This influence naturally did not make itself felt immediately. The first monastery churches built in the sixteenth century at such places as Actopan, Santiago Acolman, Atlatlahuacan, Yecapixtla, Huejotzingo and many others are austere buildings of the basilica type, consisting of a single lofty nave often without a tower and with a low-pitched crenellated roof which emphasizes their dual aspect of church and fortress. At the most their severity is softened by a few faint memories of Gothic decoration and by some discreet excursions into the Plateresque, but the exuberant phantasy of the Romanesque and Gothic styles is conspicuously absent from the classical severity of their cloisters.

Not until Renaissance architecture evolved into the Baroque did Mexican architecture achieve individuality.

Donde los Volcanes Vieres

Popocatepetl from the saddle

Tepozotlan

Puebla

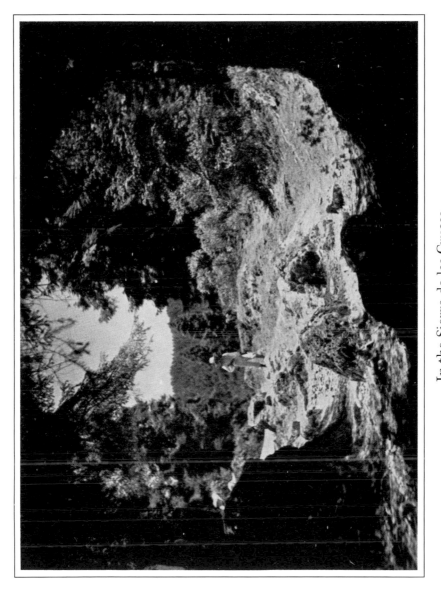

In the Sierra de las Cruces

Lucas, Loreto and Ventura

The Christmas pig at Mixquic

The chapel on the hill

The Day of the Dead

Anahuac

In the eternal sunlight of Mexico and amidst its tropical vegetation the Baroque style seems to spring more naturally from the soil than those architectural styles which may seem more satisfying in northern lands. Its wealth of ornament afforded Mexican tastes full scope, and it was carried in Mexico to a higher pitch of Churrigueresque exuberance than anywhere else in the world.

All this may be seen in the church of the monastery of Tepozotlan, founded by the Franciscans in 1546 and taken over by the Jesuits in 1584. One glance at the exterior of the church shows it to date from at least a hundred and fifty years later when the Churrigueresque style had fastened on Mexican imaginations. Built in stone of a pale ochre colour the west front springs into the air with the leaping gesture of a flame. The single tower is some 140 feet high. The west door is framed and crowned by elaborate carving in a relief which attains at times a depth of a foot or more.

Inside, the Baroque style achieves an expression even more unmistakably Mexican. Carved in no less deep relief, the altars are covered from top to bottom with gold leaf. Yet the effect is not tawdry, for the gold is of a subdued, ruddy hue and smoulders and burns in the darkness of the nave. It is the woodcarver rather than the gilder who has let his imagination run riot. Among the ornate volutes and foliations peer the pink and white faces of cherubs, fixed in inane, chubby smiles. Saints in their niches are bright with the exquisite enamel work on gesso which goes by the name of *estofado*. Over a side-altar two false lattice windows mask only the bare wall as though to spite all functional principles. In the chapel of the Holy Ghost the native craftsmen have drawn inspiration from four different styles, Plateresque, Baroque, Churrigueresque and

Mudejar. Black female torsos bearing on their heads gold-en baskets piled high with vari-coloured fruit are repeated in a recurrent pattern, and the eye is carried upwards to an octagonal dome where the Holy Dove floats in an ethereal light.

Four other churches rival Tepozotlan as the ultimate expression of Mexican Baroque. Except for Santo Domingo in Oaxaca, which will be mentioned again, all are in or near Puebla de los Angeles, about 75 miles from Mexico City. Puebla is indeed a perfect museum of colonial art, and, although outside the limits of Anahuac, may conveniently be described here, for like the valley it lies *donde los volcanes vieres*. For the site of a new city to supplant the neighbouring Aztec pilgrimage centre of Cholula, the Conquistadores chose a place where no Indian town had previously stood, and Puebla is laid out in squares on a rational system. It has something of the character, crisply austere, of a Castilian city, such as Salamanca or Segovia. The two-storied houses are faced with red-brown tiles in panels framed by structural walls of light-hued stone.

The only discordant note is struck by the fantastic Casa del Alfeñique, once a lordly mansion, which to-day houses the State Museum. More than any other aberration of the Baroque style which I have ever seen, it suggests white of egg and icing-sugar. The very name means sugar-icing and is connected with the legend of its foundation. A young Puebla girl was once visited on her birthday by an unwelcome suitor bringing as a present a magnificent iced cake. 'When will you marry me?' he asked her, not for the first time, as he laid it at her feet. 'When you build me a house just like that cake', she replied in a fit of petulance. The result was the Casa del Alfeñique, and the girl was held to her bargain.

Anahuac

Of the three Baroque churches mentioned above, the Chapel of the Rosary in Santo Domingo, is the least remarkable because the least specifically Indian. The other two lie some miles outside Puebla in the direction of Cholula and Atlixco. San Francisco Ecatepec (Hill of the Air) on its windswept knoll is graced with an eighteenth century façade of *azulejo* tiles, brown, blue and yellow, which leaves the bewildered beholder undecided whether to admire or deplore. The interior is a smaller but a more perfect and homogeneous Tepozotlan. The pulpit, hewn from a single block of stone, is a miracle of carving and colouring. Beneath the organ loft a scene in polichrome stucco represents the traditional meeting in Rome, the *topetón* or 'bump' as the folk colloquially call it, between St. Francis and St. Dominic.

Most remarkable of all is the church of Santa Maria Tonazintla, a mile away, in whose name the Aztec and Christian Mother Goddesses meet and mingle. As we approached the church we met a tiny funeral procession coming away. An old woman walked ahead, strewing rose-petals. Then came an Indian, unusually tall, bearing on his head a child's coffin smothered in flowers. These were not laid upon it in lifeless horizontality but sprang up in tall sprays of gladiola, their outlines softened by a misty veil of gypsophila. Behind, walked the bereaved family and with them the musicians, a flute, a fiddle and a guitar, playing a melody from some comic opera. The music was gay and lively as befits the demise of an *angelito*, a little angel, who to the Indian as to the Spanish idea will go straight to Heaven.

The trail of petals led us to the church. If any doubts remained of the ability of the Indian to take the elements of European decoration, assimilate them and transmute

79

them into something unmistakably, triumphantly Indian, Santa Maria Tonazintla would dispel them. The visitor finds himself in a fantastic world of plasterwork, a kaleidoscope of gold, red and blue on a white ground, covering walls, arches and dome with an inextricable maze of scrolls and volutes from which only after a time the eye disentangles the pink and white limbs of angels and cherubs in every conceivable posture. Still closer inspection reveals a wealth of detail which can have originated only in the Indian mind: great masks like those worn in the Indian dances; angels with feather headdresses which recall Aztec codices rather than European missals; a tiny figure in cotton drawers bearing on its back the *huacal* or wooden crate in which the Indian carries his goods. However bewildering, the whole thing is light and airy, neither sombre nor garish but quite other-worldly, far removed from any art which one has hitherto connected with Christianity.

*   *   *

In sober and ascetic contrast to this baroque exuberance is the Desierto de San Miguel de los Carmelitos Descalzos, better known as the Desierto de los Leones (Desert of the Lions). It stands high on the forest clad slopes of the Montes de Santa Fé, nearly 10,000 feet above the sea. The monastery church and buildings were begun in 1605 and finished in 1611 as a retreat for the Carmelite Order which had established itself in New Spain in 1585 at the suggestion of Santa Teresa de Jesus. This lonely and forbidding spot, often wrapped in rain-clouds when the sun shines clear in the valley below, was called Culiuca in Aztec times. An obscure legend explains the choice of the site by a miraculous appearance of St. John the Baptist in the semblance of a young Indian from the neighbouring

village of San Mateo. How he was recognised as the Prodrome is far from clear. A similar obscurity surrounds the
lions of the name. Some say that they relate to two brothers called León who disputed the ownership of the site
with the *cacique* of Coyoacan. Others more boldly main-
tain that the forest was truly the haunt of these beasts.
'The Sons of Carmel', according to an old chronicler of the
Order, 'conjured the lions who abandoned the place which
was then populated by birds and deer'.

The spot was prolific in miracles. While the church was
being built there was a shortage of food among the labourers. One of the monks who had gone to look for wild fruits
on the mountain side found a large basket full of white
bread. Later there mysteriously appeared two horses laden
with bread with a paper saying 'Aquesto para el Desierto'
(This for the Desert).

The object of the Desert was retreat accompanied by
prayer, fasting, meditation, penance and mortification of
the flesh. Gage, who visited it in 1626, is very sceptical as
to the manner in which this purpose was fulfilled.

'Were all wildernesses like it', he writes, 'to live in a
wilderness would be better than to live in a city. About the
Cloister they have fashioned out many holes and caves in,
under and among the rocks, like Eremites lodgings, with
a room to lie in, and an Oratory to pray in, with pictures
and Images, and rare devices for mortification, as disci-
plines of wire, rods of Iron, hair-cloths, girdles with sharp
wire points to girdle about their bare flesh, and many such
like toys which hang about their Oratories, to make people
admire their mortified and holy lives . . . They are weekly
changed from the Cloister, and when their week is ended,
others are sent, and they return unto their Cloister; they
carry with them their bottles of wine, sweet-meats and

other provisions; as for fruits the trees about do drop them into their mouths. It is wonderful to see the strange devices of fountains of water which are about the gardens; but much more strange and wonderful to see the resort of Coaches, and gallants, and Ladies and Citizens from Mexico thither, to walk and make merry in those desert pleasures and to see those hypocrites, whom they look upon as living Saints, and so think nothing too good for them, to cherish them in their desert conflicts with Satan. None goes to them but carries some sweet-meats or some other dainty dish to nourish and feed them withal . . .'

No doubt the renegade Dominican exaggerated in his virulent prejudice against all things Catholic, but it seems to have been the Desert's proximity to the capital and the resultant relaxation of the Order's severities which made the monks move in 1814 to a remoter spot two hours ride from Tenancingo in the south-western corner of the State of Mexico. For every thousand people who visit the Desert of the Lions to wander through its ruined corridors and subterranean chambers or to climb up through the pines past little hermitages to the Cruz Blanca, one or two at the most attain the incomparably more beautiful Desierto de Niscango.

Though abandoned to the melancholy solitude of things which no longer serve their purpose the monastery is neither ruined nor uncared for. The hill on which it stands rises a thousand or fifteen hundred feet above the green valley of Tenancingo which serves as a step between the cold plain of Toluca and the temperate bowl of Morelos. In colour the trail rings the changes with the changing soil between ochre, orange and rose-red. The hillside is clothed with trees and vegetation, and on the eastern slopes near the summit the monastery stands embowered in a forest of magnificent cedars and *encinos*, rising to a height of a hundred feet or more. In three places, named respectively the Balconies of the Devil, of St. Michael and of St. Elijah (sic) clearings in the trees open up the vast panorama which the hill commands in every direction. To the west the furthest *sierras* must be in Michoacan. Southwards one looks down into Morelos and the tangled hills which carry the eye into Guerrero. To the north-east a sea of pines sweeps up to the Pico de Zempoala and the Montes de Ocuila, with Popocatepetl and Ixtaccihuatl climbing above their craggy mass. I know no place which better conveys the vast surge of the Mexican landscape, the slow rhythmic lines of its majestic contours. Nature here is prodigal in space as in growth. She allows herself room to stretch, and her gesture is that of a giant lazily extending his limbs to their full extent.

*   *   *

In the hope of seeing the Indian life of Lake Texcoco more or less as it used to be, the tourist is taken out to Xochimilco, however short a time he may spend in the city, to see the famous Aztec floating gardens. Xochimilco, the 'place of the flowering cornfield', once formed part of the freshwater lake. It can still be reached by water from the capital along the Viga canal through Santa Anita, scene in the early hours a week before Good Friday of a *fiesta* which the last few years have robbed  of its native beauty and spontaneity. By water Xochimilco is five hours away, by car only half an hour, and this has been its undoing. The exquisite natural loveliness of the place is unchanged, the native life flows on surprisingly unaltered, the Indians supplying the capital with flowers and vegetables as they did before the Conquest. But the magic has fled since Xochimilco has been invaded by the paraphernalia of the pleasure resort. Canoes shoot out from the banks to press beer or coca-cola upon you. Shady backwaters are loud with the stridency of radio and lined with cheap restaurants catering for noisy Sunday crowds who bring with them an atmosphere of Coney Island or Hampstead Heath.

The real Xochimilco has not vanished, however. It has only receded before the advancing tide of modernity to Tlahuac and Mixquic.

From Xochimilco, Mixquic is a further five hours by water or half an hour by car. You take the road which winds out towards Milpa Alta following the foot of the hills through Santa Cruz Acalpixla, San Gregorio Atlapulco and Tulyehualco. To the right the hills are sharp and jagged with volcanic rock thrown out by the great pre-historic eruption of Ajusco. In the wet season they are one unending rock-garden. To the left the volcanoes stand serenely above the dry floor of the lake, through which the uninterupted water-way is marked by a green line of *ahuejote* trees.

At San Antonio Tecomitl you turn to the left through Tetelco and in five minutes you are at Mixquic. If you are wise you will follow through the village past the church as though you were heading for Chalco. At the far end of the *pueblo* there is a bridge with an enchanting view of Popocatepetl framed in trees and mirrored in the water, a landscape all green and blue and white. Stop here, walk into the orchard on the left and ask for Lucas Garcia.

84

Lucas and his wife Leonora are pure Aztecs and have five
enchanting little girls called Benita, Maria Luisa, Loreto,
Ventura and Hypolita. Singularly little foreign blood
appears to have come to Mixquic,
which is mentioned by Bernal Diaz
as one of the lake-towns subject to
Tenochtitlan. In the churchyard
an ancient idol still stands, together with carved stone rings
from the *tlachtli* ball-game. Inside
the church I once saw a Danza de
Pastorcitas, a garland dance by the little girls of the village
dressed in white with blue ribbons, the eldest perhaps
twelve, the youngest certainly not more than two, yet following the steps and figures with grave concentration.
Even hundreds of miles from the capital it would have been
difficult to find better and purer Aztec types.

For a consideration Lucas Garcia consented on the first
of many occasions to take us out on the water in his flat-
bottomed punt. He stood at one end with an oar and a
pointed pole and his wife crouched at the other with a
round-bladed paddle. Loreto, Ventura and Hypolita came
too. Hypolita who could not yet talk wanted to step out
on to the deceptive looking beds of water-weeds. Loreto,
with the motherly instinct of Indian six-year-olds, held
her back and comforted her when, in a momentary fit of
petulance, she cried.

It would be difficult to imagine a more idyllic landscape
in the bright afternoon sun. The tall, evergreen *ahuejote*
trees stand up out of the water, with willow-leaves and
the slim forms of the Lombardy poplar. Down the water-
avenues one glimpses the eternal snows of the Smoking
Mountain and the White Woman. On their summits, says

Lucas, *hay encanto*, there is enchantment. It would be very dangerous to go there. Open spaces of water are few, for the greater part of what was once a lake has been reclaimed as *chinampas*, floating gardens, artificially woven of reeds and mud, anchored in place and eventually grown to the bottom by their plunging roots. These little plots of maize, vegetables or flowers are made fertile with slime from the bottom and with water splashed up by paddle-blades. On one of them stood a bamboo cross in a diamond frame, with two little candles before it, set up on the day the year's work was begun. It served as a perch for a perky *lagartijero* butcher-bird with pearl-grey feathers.

Ever narrower have grown the channels, clogged with water-plants between banks of solid-looking turf which give beneath your feet and sink a foot below the surface when you place your weight upon them. There are flowers on the land and flowers in the water. For the markets of Mexico the people of Mixquic grow stocks, carnations, arum lilies, violets, pansies, delphiniums and hollyhocks. In the narrow channels their mirrored reflection blooms beside water-lilies white and yellow and the mauve hyacinth flower of the *lirio huachinango*. Among them swim slim, viperish water-snakes, with upturned heads and forked tongues.

Lucas picks a water-lily bud with a long trailing stalk. He splits the stalk up to within an inch or two of the end. Then with dexterous fingers he pulls away the pith in alternate inches leaving in between only the outer skin of the stalk. When it is done he hangs it round Marjorie's neck, a chain of jade beads with an ivory pendant.

None of the water-weeds are used in folk-medicine, but from the grassy margins he plucks medicinal herbs and tells us of their uses. *Ahuehueche* and *hierba del perrito* with its little yellow snapdragon flower for the stomach; *gordolobo* for the lungs; *perrito del agua* for skin troubles.

In a backwater three men are fishing in white cottons rolled above the knee which, with their broad hats, give the scene the quality of a Japanese woodcut. Two of them have short poles with which they stab the beds of weeds while the third plunges into them a gigantic triangular fishing-net. They show us their catch. To our astonishment goldfish gleam among the black *ajolote*.

Where the huts of the village back on to the water, punts like our own are clustered. They have long names, some of them quaintly facetious. *El Enamorador de las Muchachas* (The Maidens' Wooer), *Adios mis Dos Amores* (Farewell, my two loves), *La Diosa Benus* (sic), *No más para mi dueño soy* (I am my master's alone), *En el Monte Naci en la agua me batice* (In the hills I was born, in the water I was baptized), *Cuando me viste te fastidió cuando me retiré me suspiras* (When you saw me you were bored, now that I have gone you sigh for me). The hills and the water join at the far end of the *chinampas* where a spring bubbles up in a deep and limpid pool, which was our favourite goal. Looking back through the trees at the countless white figures pursuing their various occupations in diminishing perspective it was difficult to tell where was land and where was water.

One day, when we had not been to see the Garcias for some time, we found that a son had been added to the family. In two days, Leonora told us, he would be twenty-five days old, and I wondered what atavistic tradition made her reckon the days in multiples of five instead of in weeks or months. The baby was called Adán, but he had not yet been christened because this would cost three pesos and

87

they would have to scrape and save to put so much money together.

An idea sprang to my mind. It would in any case be interesting to attend an Indian christening. More, an Aztec godchild would be a sentimental link between me and the side of Mexico which most appealed to me. So I told them that we would pay for the christening if we might attend it, adding diffidently that if they would like it I should be only too glad to be the baby's godfather. This offer was accepted with alacrity, more indeed than I had bargained for. When we came to fix a date it transpired that not only Adán but Loreto, Ventura and Hypolita had not yet been christened. However, in for a penny, in for a pound, so I took on the responsibilities of godfathership to all four.

It was a great day when we all drove in the car to the church, Adán in his christening robes and the three little girls in the conventional white silk dresses which we had bought for them, with socks and shoes on their feet which had never before been shod. In turn I held them up as the priest went through the rites of water, oil and salt, and the sacristan repeated in their name the brief 'Volim' which made them members of the Holy Roman Catholic and Apostolic Church. They all behaved beautifully, my godson crying just enough to reassure us that the old Adam had in fact been driven out of him. As we came out of the vestry into the sunlight I was assailed by scores of children with the traditional cry of 'Bolo, padrinito!' (An obol, little godfather). Fortunately I had been warned beforehand, and a shower of *centavitos* sent them all grovelling on the ground to return a moment later unashamedly for more. Henceforward I am linked to Lucas and Leonora by the sacred ties of godfathership. We call each other *Com-*

padrito and *Comadrita*, while my godchildren, who in true Aztec fashion turn their 'r' into 'l', address me as *Padelinito*.

I have grown very attached to them all: to my *compadre* Lucas with his high-pitched sing-song voice and the unending stories of which I never can follow more than half; to my *comadre* Leonora who like so many Indian wives has twice his responsibility and sense; to Benita, solemn as befits the eldest, and to dimpled, almond-eyed Maria Luisa; to Loreto the mischievous, to coy Ventura and to grubby little Hypolita; and of course to Adán, the origin of our relationship[1].

One day on the way back from Mixquic we stopped at Xochimilco to see the blessing of the animals. It was January 17th, the day of San Antonio Abad, St. Anthony the Abbot, patron saint of livestock and not to be confused with his matchmaking namesake of Lisbon and Padua. While Mass was being said in the great colonial church, the people were congregating in the cloister. There were men with ponies, cattle and pigs, but for the most part it was the children who had brought their domestic pets to be blessed. They hugged puppies and kittens, turkeys, cocks, hens and rabbits all done up with ribbons and bows like Easter eggs. There were even song-birds in cages and bees in little boxes. Our own children had brought their guinea-pigs, and their fair colouring contrasted with the brown faces and dusky locks of the little Aztecs. One black pig had a yellow bow so big that it looked like a pair of preposterous great ears. In the old days it used to be the custom to dye the animals in brilliant colours for the cere-

[1]Since this was written my *compadre* Lucas has died from intestinal fever but Leonora and the children are carrying on, and I hope that some of those who read this book may visit them and hire their boat.

mony, but a pink dove, a purple cock and a pair of canary-yellow dogs seemed to be all that was left of this tradition.

When Mass was over the priest appeared in the gallery of the cloister and after pronouncing a brief benediction proceeded to asperge the crowd below. There was an immediate rush to that corner of the cloister, and hundreds

of arms were uplifted grasping the animals so that they should not miss being sprinkled with the 'outward and visible' sign of benediction. Many were left disappointed when he withdrew. But a few minutes later he came out into the cloister itself. This time he was nearly rushed off his feet. '*Padrecito, Padrecito*', cried the children as they drove him back and pinned him against the white-washed wall. A panicky hen, held under his very nose, nearly swept his glasses off in its terrified flutterings. At last he was able to stand up on a ledge and from this vantage-point continued his aspersions until not a drop of holy water was left, and many of the animals, I suspect, had been blessed at least half a dozen times.

VI. Fiesta

There was a time when I almost thought seriously of calling this book '*Days in Mexican Churchyards*' so great a part did the pursuit of *fiestas* play in our excursions. Some of these *fiestas* are nation-wide, such as the *Quema del Judas*; the burning in effigy of Judas on Easter Eve, a purely European tradition; and the Day of the Dead which is a fusion between the ancient cult of Mictlantecutli, Lord of the Underworld, and the Christian observances of Halloween and All Souls.

The Festival of the Dead is celebrated on two days, November 1st and 2nd. The first is devoted to *los muertos chicos*, the little dead, who died in childhood. On the second everyone spends the day in the cemetery. The graves are swept clean and decorated with *cempoalxochitl* (Aztec 'twenty blossoms') the golden marigold which figured in many ancient ceremonies. Candles are lit, and throughout the day the people sit huddled over the tombs in silent communion with their dead, nibbling from time to time at the food which they have brought partly as an offering, partly as a picnic.

On this same day the dustman leaves at my house a discreet little card. It bears the astonishing heading *El Cami-*

91

Fiesta

onero de la Limpia Pide su Calavera (The Driver of the Rubbish Cart asks for his Skull). Underneath is a woodcut of a well-spread table with a grinning skull painted on the table cloth and a little verse:

> *Respetable Patroncito:*
> *No olvide LA CALAVERA*
> *Que le pide el Camionero,*
> *Yo espero de su bondad*
> *Que con pedir no se ofenda,*
> *Pero en este día los patrones*
> *Deben darnos nuestra ofrenda.*
> *(Worthy Master:*
> *Do not forget the skull*
> *Which the Dustman begs of you,*
> *I trust that in your goodness*
> *You will not be offended at my asking,*
> *For on this day our clients*
> *Must give us our offering)*

The poem clarifies the heading. The 'skull' in this case is a tip, and the dustman duly gets it. He will, no doubt, spend part of it at the pastrycook's on little sugar skulls with eyes of shiny purple paper, which he will take home for his children to scrunch.

Such universal celebrations are rare, however. The majority are founded on purely local cults, linked to a place and occasion which, as often as not, can be explained as easily by paganism as by Christianity. It was the deliberate policy of the Catholic missionaries to take over as much as possible of the paraphernalia of the old faiths and to harness them to the purposes of Christianity. For this reason the Cathedral of Mexico was built on the site of the great Teocalli; a Christian church sits awkwardly among

the ruins of Mitla; and the great mound of Cholula like
many a lesser known pyramid is crowned with a Catholic
place of worship. Sometimes a subtler method was used,
and miraculous appearances of the Virgin were vouchsafed to the humble at places of Aztec pilgrimage. Of such
coincidences the two great pilgrimage shrines of Guadalupe and Remedios on the outskirts of the capital are good
examples.

The hill of Tepeyac, a low spur of the Sierra de Guadalupe, was the site in ancient times of an important cult of
Tonantzin. Soon after the Conquest, the Aztec goddess
of fertility was displaced by Our Lady of Guadalupe,
named after the famous shrine in Spain. So often has the
story been told that I may be excused for giving the
legend in the sober, well-turned phrases of the oft-quoted
Madame Calderón de la Barca:

'In 1531, ten years and four months after the conquest
of Mexico, the fortunate Indian whose name was Juan
Diego, and who was a native of Cuatitlan, went to the
suburb of Tlaltelolco to learn the Christian doctrine which
the Franciscan monks taught there. As he was passing by
the mountain of Tepeyac, the Holy Virgin suddenly appeared before him and ordered him to go, in her name, to
the bishop, the Ylustrisimo D. Fr. Juan de Zumárraga,
and to make known to him that she desired to have a
place of worship erected in her honour, on that spot. The
next day the Indian passed by the same place, when again
the Holy Virgin appeared before him, and demanded the
result of his commission. Juan Diego replied that in
spite of his endeavours, he had not been able to obtain an
audience of the bishop. 'Return', said the Virgin, 'and say
that it is I, the Virgin Mary, the Mother of God, who send
thee'. Juan Diego obeyed the divine orders, yet still the

bishop would not give him credence, merely desiring him to bring some sign or token of the Virgin's will. He returned with this message on the twelfth of December, when, for the third time, he beheld the apparition of the Virgin. She now commanded him to climb to the top of the barren rock of Tepeyac, to gather the roses which he should find there, and to bring them to her. The humble messenger obeyed, though well knowing that on that spot were neither flowers nor any trace of vegetation. Nevertheless, he found the roses, which he gathered and brought to the Virgin Mary, who, throwing them into his *tilma* (cloak), said, 'Return, show these to thy bishop, and tell him that these are the credentials of thy mission.' Juan Diego set out for the episcopal house, which stood on the ground occupied by the hospital, now called San Juan de Dios, and when he found himself in the presence of the prelate, he unfolded his *tilma* to show him the roses, when there appeared imprinted on it the miraculous image which has existed for more than three centuries.'

Nuestra Señora de Guadalupe, whose *fiesta* is observed by tens and hundreds of thousands on December 12th, has always been the principal invocation under which the Indians have worshipped the Virgin. Across the corner of the valley, within easy sight of Tepeyac on a foothill of the Sierra de las Cruces stands the church of her rival, Nuestra Señora de los Remedios, whose *fiesta* is celebrated on September 8th. She is *la Virgen Gachupina*, the Virgin of the Spaniards. Bernal Diaz makes reference to the *cue* or pagan temple which stood on the spot at the time of the Conquest, and the Indians who are no more inclined towards monotheism to-day than they were then, pay her a devotion little less fervorous than that which they accord to Our Lady of Guadalupe. The image which forms the object of this cult is said to have been brought from Spain by Cortes, or rather by one of his soldiers called Villafuerte who, after the 'Sad Night', hid it in the heart of a maguey aloe where it was subsequently found by an Indian and housed in a magnificent church specially built to receive it. Hence the apparent national penchant displayed by Our Lady of Remedios. The rivalry between the two Virgins reached its apogee during the struggle for independence when they were regarded as the champions of the opposing forces. On the defeat of Hidalgo, the priestly champion of an independent Mexico, the image of the Virgen de los Remedios was conducted in triumph to Mexico City dressed in a general's uniform, but when the tide of battle turned her trappings were torn from her by a real, live General who signed her passport with an order (incidentally never executed) for her expulsion from the newborn Republic.

All over the country lesser images of Christ, the Virgin and the Saints are preserved in village churches, and the old pagan celebrations of the agricultural year needed only to be altered by a day or two to fall within the Catholic Calendar of Saints.

A good example is the Festival of the Assumption of the Virgin on August 15th, which coincides with the beginning of the harvest and has taken over the relics of ancient harvest ceremonies. The maize fields are blessed, the first sheathes cut and bright nosegays fastened to the standing corn. In 1937, we came upon a *fiesta* at Tecaxic, a mile or two from the ancient site of Calixtlahuaca. In the churchyard of the Virgen de los Angeles a harvest dance, the Danza de los Montoneros, was in progress. They had taken ripe maize stalks from the fields and planted them in little humps of earth in imitation of a *milpa*. Young men and boys in white *cotones* with bandana handkerchiefs represented the harvesters and first executed a dance with hoes. Others dressed in ragged clothes with masks of animal skin and carrying long whips and stuffed badgers, weasels and hares were supposed to be the *milperos*, the guardians of the crop. Every now and then they would collect and crack their whips with an ear-splitting sound, presumably to scare away the vermin. At one stage each in turn was seized by the labourers, thrown on his face with a stuffed animal laid across his back and beaten. It occurred to me that they must in some way be identified with the very pests against which it was their function to protect the crop. Towards evening, to the music of rustic fiddles, the dancers harvested the corn and in joyful procession carried the sheathes into the church.

Many of the biggest *fiestas* are held on the different Fridays (of all days!) in Lent. The great Indian pilgrimage to the shrine of Chalma, for instance, is held on the *primer viernes*, the first Friday, and the *fiesta* of Nuestro Señor de la Santa Vera Cruz at Taxco on the fourth. So little prejudice seems to exist against Lenten feasts that Yautepec in Morelos celebrates its Carnival on the first Sunday in Lent so as not to conflict with Tepoztlan which brings out its *Huehuenche* dancers on the Sunday before. All the same, accurate and certain information about the dates of *fiestas* is not easy to obtain. For one reason or another they may be held one year and dropped the next, changed to the Sunday before or after the Saint's day or postponed for a week or two. *Fiesta*-hunting therefore, is as liable to disappointments and blank days as any other form of the chase.

Mexican legislation confines the purely religious part of

the *fiesta* to the church precincts, and for many years the holy images have ceased to be carried in procession through the streets. Only once have I seen, in a remote village on Palm Sunday, a statue of Christ on the Ass smothered in flowers, maize stalks and paper rosettes, carried surreptitiously out of a side-door of the church and hurried through the back streets to a chapel on the outskirts where it was to remain till Good Friday.

At Santiago Temoaya, at the western foot of the Sierra de las Cruces, a vast statue of St. James mounted on a more-than-life-size horse looked down the aisle on St. James's Day, the back of its platform resting on the altar steps, to which men only were admitted. Candles and copal incense burned before the Saint, and a steady stream of Indians climbed on to the back of the platform and reverently kissed the spurred heel and the off hind leg of the horse. Many carried little children and stroking the Saint's calf with a curiously caressing gesture rubbed into their offspring the virtue derived from it. In the afternoon, to the braying of a brass band in the organ-loft, the platform was hoisted on to the shoulders of a score of men and like the Car of Juggernaut, the Saint was painfully carried twice round the inside of the churchyard.

Mexicans, incidentally, seem to cherish a special fondness for what they call *los santos charros*, the mounted Saints, chiefly St. James and St. Martin. Santiago Tlaxala claimed to us that Temoaya's St. James was really theirs but had been stolen during the Revolution and transported across the *sierra*. One day, they hinted, a couple of hundred armed men would go to reclaim their own, and there would be wigs on the green, for those of Temoaya were *muy broncos* (very fierce). Further along the *sierra* at Santiago Tepatlaxco St. James once lost a wooden arm,

97

and the villagers, so they told us, called in not a carpenter but a *curandero*, a herb doctor, to put him right.

Music, dance and fireworks are the three indispensable ingredients in a Mexican *fiesta*, and most important of them are the fireworks. It is surprising how much money quite small villages can raise for gunpowder which they expend in one grand and glorious outburst of petards and rockets, deafening to the ears and shattering to the nerves. This traditional fondness for fireworks is the subject of a story which goes back to the time when Mexico had just achieved her independence. 'What do you suppose the Mexicans will be doing now?' wistfully remarked King Ferdinand VII to a Mexican at his court one morning. 'Letting off rockets Your Majesty', was the answer. 'Well what are they doing now', asked the King again that afternoon. 'Letting off more rockets', answered the Mexican. That night, if the story is to be believed, the King again reverted to the subject. 'Now what will they be doing in Mexico?' he asked. 'Still letting off rockets, Your Majesty.'

There is something almost theatrical in the setting of a Mexican *fiesta*. In the background, the church lifts its tall belfry-towers high over the adobe or palm huts of the faithful, in a contrast of which the implications are inescapable. Round the churchyard there generally runs a stone wall, scolloped out between the pilasters which are moulded with graceful baroque ornamentation and crowned, often enough, with classical urns. On a *fiesta* day, the wall becomes an exquisite frieze of Indian figures, clustered and festooned round the pillars, their white forms falling into the graceful postures and groupings which are the natural heritage of the Indian.

Against the wall, round the trees, over the tombs, are sprawled little family groups, cooking their meals, putting

98

on their dancers' trappings, or sitting in motionless huddled attitudes, wandering out now and again to do the round of the booths outside. These booths are shaded by cotton awnings or petate mats. In them are to be found all the strange foods and drinks of the Indian festive board, peasant pottery in soft browns and greens, and clay whistles in the form of animals which have their counterpart in Europe and yet, as archaeological evidence shows, were used for rain-magic before even America was discovered.

The most disappointing feature of Mexican *fiestas* is their music. When a European civilization is grafted upon a native culture the result is generally a hybrid music combining European melody with native rhythms. Negro spirituals, Cuban rumbas, the native songs of the West African coast are all cases in point. In Mexico, however, little that is truly native has survived, and Europe has

not given of its best, so that the result is on the whole disconcertingly characterless.

It is indeed uncertain whether music ever played a preponderant part in ancient Mexican life. Undoubtedly both vocal and instrumental music existed. Several

of the drawings in the Florentine Codex, which illustrates Sahagún's immortal work,[1] show musicians playing drums

[1]Bernardino de Sahagún: *Historia General de las Cosas de Nueva España*. Mexico. 1829-30. This sixteenth-century work is also available in French and German translations.

and gourd rattles. In one such drawing, scrolls issuing from their mouths are clearly intended to represent song. Nevertheless, to-day the Indians are not natural, spontaneous singers. It is the rarest thing, for instance, to hear servant-girls sing about the house as they do in Europe, or to listen across a valley to those snatches of song from the lips of shepherds or ploughmen which are such a joy in Spain or the Balkans. The probability is that music, like so much else, was reserved in the Indian scheme of things to ritual and religious purposes, and with the death of the old gods indigenous melody has disappeared from most of Mexico.

Pre-Cortesian native instruments have not vanished so completely. Apart from the conch-shell, ancient wind instruments have been modified by European influence into flutes, pipes and clarinets of simple construction and familiar type. Percussion instruments, on the other hand, have preserved their original character, and it is possible that the rudimentary rhythms played on them to-day have not changed greatly in the last four centuries. There are two kinds of drum, the vertical *huehuetl* and the horizontal *teponaztli*.

Of the first of these there were three types. When the people of Tenochititlan heard the sound of the simple *huehuetl*, a hollowed tree-trunk, standing on three feet and covered with deerskin, they responded cheerfully to this summons to the dance. The sound of the *tlapan-huehuetl* covered with panther-skin was less welcome as a call to war, while the sinister throb of the great snakeskin *teohuehuetl*, drum of the gods, was a signal that human victims were being sacrificed. Bernal Diaz had good cause to know that dread sound, and there is more than one reference to it in his narrative. 'As we were retreating', he writes after one of the unsuccessful attacks which marked the last stage of the siege, 'We heard the sound of trumpets from the great Cue . . . and also a drum, a most dismal sound indeed it was, like an instrument of demons, as it resounded so that one could hear it two leagues off. . . . At that moment . . . they were offering the hearts of ten of our comrades and much blood to the idols.'

The *teponaztli* is more unusual in type. It consists of a section of a log laid horizontally on the ground or on a stand and hollowed out from underneath. The upper circumference is cut through with an incision in the shape of an H, thus leaving two tongues of wood which vibrate when struck. As the two tongues are of different thickness they give out different notes when struck, the effect being approximately that of a kettle-drum with an interval usually of a fourth.

A number of pre-Cortesian drums of these types finely carved with Aztec symbols are preserved in museums and private collections both in Mexico and abroad. A few are jealously guarded in Indian villages. Apart from the fine *teponaztli* of Tepoztlan, there is one in the Matlalzinca village of San Juan Acingo (state of Mexico) of which M. Jacques Soustelle discovered the existence, as described in his book '*Mexique: Terre Indienne*', although he was unable to prevail on the Indians to let him see it. Two months before my departure from Mexico a combination of tact and patience was rewarded, and for the first time, this remarkable instrument was shown to an outsider and photographed. Carved in the shape of a wolf, with the head and legs in the round, it had a blue ribbon and a green tied round its neck and was kept on a lead the whole time it was on view (See Plate 48).

Modern *huehuetls* and, much more rarely, *teponaztlis*

are still made in one or two places. The first time I saw
these instruments played was at the sanctuary of Sacro
Monte on a steep hill above Amecameca commanding the
finest of all views of the volcanoes. It was on the Sunday
before Lent, the first day of a *fiesta* lasting a week, of
which the climax is reached on Ash Wednesday. As I
reached the top of the steep Via Crucis between ancient
ahuehuete trees, a sound of music reached my ears, and I
saw, outside the chapel of Nuestro Señor del Sacro Monte,
a small band consisting of a *huehuetl*, two *teponaztlis*, a
side-drum and a strident clarinet. They were playing
people to church. Eager to photograph them I approached
and asked the players' permission. They raised no object-
ion, and I was just about to take my photograph when a
fat little man in blue overalls and a battered 'gent.'s
boater' came up and told them on no account to let themselves be photographed. I was doing it to make Mexico
look ridiculous, he said. He had been *allá* (over there) and
he knew. There was this to be said in his favour that un-
scrupulous press-photographers from Mexico's northern
neighbour have on more than one occasion gone out of
their way to photograph the most sordid subjects which
they could find and to print them with cruel and malici-
ous captions. The result has been a certain susceptibility
among the ill-informed and half-educated from which the
innocent rather than the guilty are the first to suffer. I
explained to my friend, however, that I had never been
allá and that I was English. At this his attitude changed
completely and indeed disconcertingly. He struck a solemn
pose with one arm uplifted as though in blessing. 'What
were the last words of the great Queen Victoria on her
death-bed?' he asked rhetorically. I thought I had better
disguise my ignorance of this important fact. 'That's

right', I said, 'tell the musicians what they were.' He did. Queen Victoria's last message, it seemed, had been that no drop of Mexican blood should ever be shed for British interests. We clasped hands in a gesture of international fraternity, and I had no further difficulty with my photographs.

For the most part the music of *fiesta* is furnished by brass bands, for which the Indians have more inclination than executive skill, and by simpler combinations of instruments accompanying the dances, such as pipe and tabor, drum and clarinet, fiddle and drums, and so on. The tunes played on these instruments show very pronounced European influence, many of them resembling Country dances of the early eighteenth century. It is not, however, the regional dialects of European music but its *Hauptsprache*, as spoken in the eighteenth century above all in Italy and Austria, which has left its mark on Mexican music.

In the dance the contending forces, the native and the European are more evenly matched. It is known that dancing played a far greater part than music in the life of the Aztec court, and if there are few dances of which it can be said with certainty that they are still performed unchanged, contemporary accounts have left a fairly clear idea of those done by Montezuma's subjects.

'They were taught by dancing masters', writes the historian Clavijero, 'to execute the most complicated steps in strict time and to sing in tune the hymns with which they accompanied the dance.' Some of these dances were for men alone, others for men and women, and others again were reserved for priests or warriors. Another historian leaves a valuable description of the so-called Great Dance, as it might have been seen at, say, the feast of

103

Macuilxochitl or Five Flower. This Great Dance was performed by several hundred persons gathered round the musicians in a series of concentric rings. The innermost rings were formed by priests and other persons of importance, the younger and less distinguished being relegated to the outer circles. Each kept his place in relation to the others in such a way as to form lines radiating from the centre. While those near the middle moved with slow dignity, the outermost had to exercise all their agility to keep in line. There were different costumes for the different hymns and dances, the basis of all being cloaks and headdresses of brightly coloured feathers. The nobles wore their finest array with gold ornaments and jewels, carrying in one hand a shield and in the other a gourd rattle. 'In the spaces between the lines of dancers', wrote Clavijero, 'there also danced certain buffoons, imitating the dress of other regions, or disguised as wild and other beasts, and making the people laugh with their antics.'

To the ceremonial Great Dance corresponded a Little Dance which was principally performed in the palaces for the amusement of the nobles, in the temples as an act of private devotion or in lesser houses at weddings or other family feasts. A smaller number of dancers took part, in two parallel lines facing each other or both turned in the same direction, with occasional *pas seuls* between the two lines.

'Such were the ordinary forms of the dance', concludes Clavijero, 'but there were other very different ones in which they represented some religious myth, historical incident or some description of war, hunting or agriculture. Not only did the lords, priests and pupils of the religious seminaries dance, but even the King, in the temple on some religious occasion or in his palace for recreation,

104

being accorded on either occasion a special place appropriate to his rank.'

To-day, as more than four hundred years ago, most Indian dances are ceremonial in character. The pair dances such as the Jarabe, Sandunga, Jarana and Huapango are of foreign origin and of colonial *mestizo* character. This is not to say that ceremonial dances have remained unchanged. Of only a very few and those in the remotest places, could this with truth be said. In the rare places where conscious paganism survives it is accompanied by pagan dances. Everywhere else these have been transformed and adapted to Catholic requirements or even replaced by dances imported from Europe, which in turn have been assimilated by the Indians and stamped with their indelible mark.

None of these Indian dances are done for pleasure, recreation or conscious artistic self-expression. One and all are offered to some Virgin or Saint in fulfilment of a vow, by groups organized for this special purpose under a leader called a *Mayordomo*. Carrying their accoutrements they may come for days over the mountains to a *fiesta*.

On arrival they enter the church devoutly, often on their knees, burning candles and seeking a benediction not only on themselves but on their dancing gear. After Mass they dance either in the interior of the church or in the sunlit brilliance of the churchyard, each group with its own musicians. To many *fiestas* only one or two such groups will come. Others attract larger numbers.

Fiestas and dances are sprinkled through this book as and when occasion arises, but there are one or two within easy reach of Mexico City for which room may conveniently be found in this chapter.

Apart from the national patriotic festivals, Carnival,

the child of the Roman Saturnalia, is perhaps the only secular occasion for traditional festivities. There is certainly little that is religious in character about the great *fiesta* celebrated on this occasion at Huejotzingo. The little *pueblo* which played an important part in the Conquest as Cortes's principal ally after Tlaxcala is in the state of Puebla about fifteen miles away from the city of that name. It consists of one-storied adobe houses clustering round a great sixteenth century convent and a wide market square, one side of which is formed by the main road.

When we arrived at about eleven in the morning on Shrove Tuesday, this square was alive with brightly dressed figures in pink and white masks, bearded and moustachioed, all busily engaged in dancing, if the word can properly be applied to their grotesque hopping step, and in filling and firing off ancient muzzle-loading muskets as fast as they could.

The noise made it difficult to collect one's thoughts and sort out the armed forces into their different categories. Fortunately, at about noon, they withdrew to the outskirts of the town and then, several hundred in number, marched in once more in ordered array. In front came the dozen or two players of the leading rôles, mounted on lively *criollo* ponies. There were Agustín Lorenzo the Bandit, with a black handkerchief across his face; a very masculine 'Lady' in a pink dress, a plumed hat and a thick white veil which discouraged any comments on 'her' personal appearance; an Indian messenger got up as a Redskin; and the Captains of the various *comparsas* or detachments. Of these the first were the Apache Indians, resplendent in plumed skirts and feather headdresses all the colours of the rainbow. Their masks and occasionally their faces were adorned with ferocious warpaint, and

106

their music of clarinet and *huehuetl* drum was punctuated with wild war whoops. Next came the *Zapadores* or Sappers in bearded, white-faced masks crowned by enormous bearskins adorned with the Eagle and Serpent device of Mexico. They were followed by the *Zacapoaxtlas* or Indians of the Sierra de Puebla whose highly inappropriate uniform consisted of skirted tunics in black, white and green, slit up the sides and cut short at the knee to reveal frilly white drawers, and of broad hats with bunches of paper streamers hanging down on either side. The *Zouaves* in blue and red wore masks which were a clever caricature of white French faces and contrasted oddly with their brown arms. On their haversacks were painted crossed French flags with the legend *Viva Francia*! The rear was brought up by the tatterdemalion crew of the Serrano Indians in battered hats and rough hairy masks. Like the Apaches they uttered raucous cries and each carried slung across his back the stuffed *cacomixtli* skunk associated with many Indian Folk-Fools. Once they had marched round the market square, the variegated army again started dancing, skirmishing and letting off their muskets. Gradually some sort of purpose began to emerge out of their activities. People gathered round the two-storied municipal building, on the first-floor balcony of which the 'Lady' had taken refuge. Several times the Redskin rode backwards and forwards with messages between her and the bandit Agustín Lorenzo. Suddenly there was a swirl of dust at the far end of the plaza and the bandit himself galloped on to the scene with a dozen of his men. In the most unladylike manner the 'Lady' shinned over the balcony, dropped to the ground with the aid of a rope, and mounted a spare horse. Then, firing their pistols in the air, the bandits galloped off hell for leather amidst a

107

deafening discharge from the whole army which for a moment ceased its internecine warfare to unite in a vain attempt to prevent the elopement.

A few minutes later the bandits swept down on the plaza once more to raid a mule-train bearing treasure on its way from Mexico City to the coast. There then followed a midday lull during which the troops scattered in little groups all over the square, and the bandits exercised their traditional privilege of 'assaulting' the shops the owners of which, with mock unwillingness, surrendered food and drink to them.

At about three o'clock, the troops begin to muster again in the centre of the plaza. A straw hut has been erected to represent the bandits' lair in the Barranca del Zopilote (Buzzards' Gulch). Inside it Agustín Lorenzo and the 'Lady' are married, and the latter sets about her domestic tasks, making tortillas and so on. But the army has tracked them to their retreat, and presently they are surrounded by the whole motley crew. There is one last glorious and deafening engagement. The air is thick with smoke. Then the army storms the stronghold, we have a momentary glimpse of the 'Lady' making good her escape at the back, and the hut goes up in flames.

Varied fragments of history, legend and ancient ceremony must have gone to the making of this kaleidoscopic pageant. The whole conception of a mock-battle may come from the Dance of the Moors and Christians which is recorded at a very early date as near as Puebla and Tlaxcala. In the most grandiose of all European Battles of the Moors and Christians, that held annually at Alcoy in the province of Valencia, more than a thousand people take part, organized in all sorts of different *comparsas* including one of *indios bravos*. Up till quite lately a group of

Huejotzingo: an Apache

Huejotzingo: the French General and his Zouaves

The Passion Play: Pontius Pilate and Claudia

Preparing Christ for the Scourging

Ótomi musicians, Santiago Temoaya

Weaving hands

The Shrine of Chalma

Pilgrims

Votive Pictures

Moors and Christians, Taxco

'Turks' figured at Huejotzingo, and it is easy to understand how other and more extraneous elements may have been introduced into this framework. The *Morisma* played in Mexico City in 1538 to celebrate the conclusion of peace between François I and Charles V and described in a later chapter, included not only the familiar mimic warfare between Christian and Infidel but a battle between two bands of savage Indians, another between Indians and horsemen, and, as *pièce de résistance*, a representation of the storming of Rhodes by the Turks, the fortress being defended by a hundred Commanders of the Order of Knights under a Grand Master and Captain General whose rôle is supposed to have been played by Cortes himself.

My idea is that some phantasmagorical *Morisma* of this type may well have been played annually at Huejotzingo, possibly in a gradually degenerating form, until, some time in the nineteenth century, it was revised in the light of local history and local legend.

The main coach-road to Vera Cruz from the capital used not to follow the route of the Mexican Railway but that of to-day's motor road through Huejotzingo, Puebla and Jalapa. Before reaching the first of these places it crossed at a height of 10,000 feet the fir-covered slopes of the Sierra Nevada, a long spur of Ixtaccihuatl. On the eastern side of the crest lies Rio Frio, of sinister repute, where brigand bands known as *los plateados* used to lie in wait for the coaches of the wealthy and for the rich mule-trains bearing to the coast the treasure of the Mexican silver mines. Whether Agustín Lorenzo was one of their leaders, whether indeed he ever lived at all, is uncertain. Like Robin Hood, he has become a figure of myth and mime. His fame has spread far beyond the state of Puebla,

and performances in which he figures are found at Jojutla
in Morelos (Candlemas) and in Guerrero at San Juan de
los Naranjos (Holy Cross). Legends about him differ
widely, each state claiming him for their own.

The version most generally accepted at Huejotzingo is
that he used to descend on the highway from his lair on
the rocky slopes of the great volcanoes, leaving the white
captive who was his mistress sealed up in a cave with en-
nough food to last until his return. One day, of course, he
did not return, and the maiden perished of hunger.

The presence of Zouaves under a French General is
more easily explained. One of the great national festivals
of Mexico is May 5th, anniversary of the day in 1862,
when the Mexicans defeated the French invaders at
Puebla. It is typical of the confusion of ideas prevailing
in the Huejotzingo festivities that there is no clear-cut
battle between these Zouaves and the Mexican troops, for
they, together with the Zapadores and the Zacapoaxtlas
are certainly modelled on the *Batallas del 5 de Mayo*
which are still enacted on that day in a number of villages
in the states of Puebla and Mexico and in the Federal
District.

A year later we went to a Carnival battle of a very
different type. The scene was Huixquilucan, a small *pueblo* tucked away in a fold of the Sierra de las Cruces. The
pueblo itself is *mestizo* in character, but it is the market
town for a country district inhabited by pure Otomis.
Paradoxically enough, Carnival is here postponed from
the week-end before Ash Wednesday, to the week-end
after, as many people go on the great pilgrimage to Chalma on the first Friday in Lent and are already on the road
at the beginning of the week.

Huixquilucan is dominated by the parish church, a fine

early baroque building with a moulded porch. At either end of the village stands a little chapel, one rose-pink dedicated to St. Martin, the other a dazzling white dedicated to St. John the Baptist. These twin chapels divide the village into two opposing camps, between which the rivalry used to be so great that it was dangerous for parishioners of the one to venture into the confines of the other. There was no intermarriage between them, the first case occurring only about fifteen years ago. In recent years, however, animosity has died down to the point where it is expressed only in a glorious Carnival battle between the opposing forces. St. Martin, in his chapel at the western end of the village, is depicted by an equestrian statue clothed in a handsome *charro* costume complete with spurs, pistol and cartridge belt. Each year, he is presented with a new *sombrero* so that his collection must be one of the finest in the country. The poor Saint, alas, has no one to whom to display his finery, and many years ago his parishioners chose a sweetheart for him, in the person of the Virgen de la Candelaria (Our Lady of Candlemas), who thrones it beside St. John in the rival chapel. Every night, say his parishioners, their Saint visits his lady, and San Jacinto, who is also housed in St. John's chapel, connives at their philandering, holding St. Martin's horse and acting as sentinel. These innuendos touch the honour of St. John's parishioners in its most tender spot, and never fail to arouse their fury, so that the annual combat has come to be regarded in the light almost of a duel fought over a lady's reputation. Two barriers are set up in the main street, twenty or thirty yards apart, the intervening space being a no man's land the penalty of entry into which is to be hailed off to gaol. From one barrier to the other an incessant fire is kept up not only of insults but

111

of rockets, squibs, petards, rotten eggs and eggshells filled with paint, generally ending with a volley of stones if with nothing worse.

We reached the village too early. It is not difficult to do this in Mexico. For a while we sat in St. Martin's churchyard while the village seemingly slumbered in the afternoon sun. Then curious little yelping cries began to be heard from the hillside farms and mountain paths. Crudely masked and clad in incongruous, ragged clothes, some of them as women, the *huehuenche* masqueraders were gathering to do battle. In the village, however, a bitter disappointment awaited us. The previous year, when we had not yet known of the festival, the combatants had got so out-of-hand and had used their stones and machetes with such a will that there had been a casualty list of two killed and many injured. The authorities had very sensibly decided not to risk a recurrence of these events and had filled the street with rural guards with strict injunctions to keep the two armies apart. It was disappointing, but much as we regretted not having been present the previous year, we had no desire to see men butchered to make a folklorist's holiday. We were able to obtain some idea of what the spectacle must have been, however, for St. John's barricade had been set up and was manned by a howling mob of masqueraders who hurled insults indiscriminately into the West. '. . . . *tu madre, San Martín*' they yelled, throwing the traditional taunt at the Saint's mother. But, alas, St. Martin's adherents were not there to counter with the warning that they were coming for La Candelaria as their Saint felt cold, and with the time-honoured cry of '*San Juan, chiche pelada*' (St. John, bare breasts), an allusion to the very scanty costume of the Prodrome's image. Aspersions on the Saint's virility

112

wasted their sweetness on the desert air. *Los de San Martín* were out of sight round the corner, separated from the enemy by half a dozen loaded muskets, and trying hard to pretend that they couldn't hear the hullabaloo. We went away hoping that by the following year calm might have been restored to the point at which the combat could once more take place safely, and inclined to join in one of the verses of the song of the Huixquilucan *huehuenches*:

> *Yo suplico a las autoridades*
> *Que no quiten esta diversión,*
> *Que tengan gusto los indios*
> *Y también los de razón.*
> *(I beg the authorities*
> *Not to stop this entertainment*
> *So that the Indians may take pleasure*
> *And also the people 'of reason')*

From the secular hilarity of the Carnival, it is a far cry to the religious drama of the Passion Play. Nativity and Passion Plays were among the methods used by the Catholic missionaries to make the story of the Gospel live before Indian eyes and to impress it on Indian minds. Devoutly obedient, the Indians adopted the sacred drama as their own and came themselves to play the chief parts in it.

Early in the afternoon of Maundy Thursday, we reached the village on the shores of Lake Texcoco. The Twelve Apostles with candles and palm branches in their hands were kneeling in vigil before the Altar, clothed in cotton cloaks and robes in brightly contrasting colours, green and blue, red and yellow, purple and green. The effect of simplicity was enhanced by their dark Indian faces and the *huarache* sandals with which they were shod. Presently they came out into the sunlight and,

113

beneath a tree in the churchyard, partook of the Last Supper. At one end of the long heavily-laden table the Priest presided, reading from the Gospel. At the other stood a statue of Christ who, apart from the Virgin Mary, was the only figure not represented by a human actor. The meal was no simple repast of bread and wine, but a six-course dinner beginning with soup and continuing through boiled fish with parsley sauce and fried chicken to dessert. The courses were served by Indian girls in clean dresses and aprons, and to each in turn the Apostles with all due gravity and reverence did the fullest justice.

On Good Friday we were early on the scene. Strange figures in masks and tinsel-decked robes, representing Jews and Romans, were hanging about, and a small trestle stage had been erected outside the church. The betrayal of Judas was vividly enacted with all the bargaining associated with a Mexican business transaction, and presently the traitor went with a crowd of Romans and Pharisees to arrest Christ. The Captain of the Roman soldiers wore a cocked hat, a black uniform tail coat with red and yellow epaulettes and braid, white riding breeches and top boots. His men were in theatrical costumes with visored helmets or veils of butter muslin. The Pharisees in bearded black masks and purple robes clanked chains dismally. The High Priests were also masked, with horned crowns on their heads. The statue of Christ was carried in procession from the church and set up before the stage where Pontius Pilate had already taken his seat with his satellites. Pilate's pink and white beardless mask had an incongruous air of benign innocence. His wife Claudia, the only female rôle, was played by a charming Indian girl in white with blue ribbons, who told the story of her dream with deep conviction. Then in a free Spanish translation

114

followed the familiar interrogatory. Caiphas demanded the death sentence. Barabbas, a small boy naked save for a loincloth, was freed. Finally Pilate washed his hands of the affair with a jug and basin provided for the purpose, and the sentence of crucifixion was proclaimed by a Roman soldier galloping up and down before the court of judgment.

There followed a noontide pause, while the Priest preached from a pulpit at the church door the sermons of the Scourging and of the Three Falls. At about three o'clock, the procession formed up for the journey to Golgotha. First, however, a strange and apocryphal episode had to be played out. To bear the cross, Simon of Cyrene was not picked out of the crowd, as the Gospel relates. He lay concealed on a stony hillside rising above the village and had first to be found. A battue was organised. Jews, mounted Romans and all the children of the village scoured the slope in search of him. So well hidden was he that it took them nearly an hour to find him, the little figures silhouetted against the horizon, beating backwards and forwards in their vain search. At last he was discovered, a small boy of twelve, and lifted on to the platform with the statue of Christ, where he held the end of the cross and worked the ingenious mechanism by which the three falls were simulated.

To the doleful strains of a rustic flute and drum, the procession wound twice round the churchyard and then into the church for the solemn climax of the Crucifixion. The sun had gone in now, and a vast black storm cloud was coming up from the volcanoes. The first raindrops fell as we entered the church on the heels of the pressing crowd. Within all was gloom, lit only by dim candles and occasional flashes of lightning. They had taken the image of Christ to the east end, where a vast drop cloth representing Golgotha concealed the Altar. A sinister sound of hammering reached our ears. Nearer and nearer drew the storm and louder grew the reverberations of the thunder, tossed from mountain to mountain. Now, above the heads of the crowd, the cross was raised aloft, a contorted Christ hanging from its arms. At the same moment, the building was shaken by the mightiest thunder clap of all. Well might one imagine the veil of the temple rent in twain. The crowd swayed this way and that, and an eerie music of flute and drum stole upon the ear. . . .

Thus, in this Aztec village, as in mediaeval Europe, was the story of the Cross played out before the faithful.

VII. Pilgrims to Chalma

Not far to the west of the capital the Federal District marches with the state of Mexico. The boundary stones run across a bare hillside just beyond the Chapultepec Heights, and Los Remedios is within state not federal jurisdiction. The capital of the state of Mexico is Toluca, lying at the foot of hills at the far end of a spacious plain, higher by nearly a thousand feet than Mexico City. The road, a fine tarred highway, winds up below the Desierto de los Leones, between rocky fir-clad escarpments. At a height of over 10,000 feet it crosses the Sierra de las Cruces, then drops again and runs straight into Toluca between reed-beds and lush green meadows watered by the Rio Lerma. Ahead and slightly to the left is the great mass of Xinantecatl or, as the Spaniards call it, the Nevado de Toluca, a volcano 15,000 feet high, wooded on its lower slopes, bare snow-flecked rock above, cut by the thin line of a motor-road which leads to within a thousand feet of the summit.

To the north of the main Toluca road most of the villages are inhabited by Otomis. They are a queer, wild, shy people. If the Aztecs, the Mayas, the Tarascans and the Zapotecs can point with pride to the culture and achieve-

117

ments of their ancestors, the Otomis have always been described as the Boeotians of Indian Mexico. Where they dwell few remains are found of temples or artefacts. Perhaps this is because they were driven up into the hills by more advanced invaders, but it seems almost as though something in their nature had made them recalcitrant to progress. Only in the fifteenth century were they reduced to settled village life by the Lords of Texcoco, and the Spaniards did not fully subjugate them till the middle of the seventeenth. They call themselves the *nya-nyu* which apparently means 'those who speak the *nyu* or Otomi tongue'. The latter is monosyllabic, with five different vowel intonations, and in sound has a marked though purely superficial resemblance to Chinese.

Otomi and its kindred dialects are spoken to-day by about a quarter of a million people who spread like a fan to the north of Mexico City in the states of Mexico, Guanajuato, Queretaro, Hidalgo and Puebla. The Laredo highway takes you through the heart of their country round Actopan, Ixmiquilpan and Zimapan. To the east they extend into the Sierra de Puebla, in which Mexican Macedonia they rub shoulders with Aztecs, Totonacs and Tepehuas.

Many of our Sunday rambles and one ride of three days took us into Otomi country in the Sierra de las Cruces which is strangely inaccessible by either road or rail. Probably the best way of reaching it is to drive to Toluca and then turn back at a sharp angle over rough roads which bring you to the foot of the range you crossed an hour before. In about two hours it is thus possible to reach San Bartolo Otzolotepec or San Francisco Xonacatlan. San Bartolo has a fascinating Sunday market which attracts many wild, uncouth-looking people down from the hills. Besides sarapes and cottons the men wear *ayates* of maguey fibre worked with exquisite floral and animal designs in red, blue, green, yellow, orange and purple. The *ayate* has been described as a carrying-cloth, and it often serves as such, but so often is it wrapped round the shoulders like a cloak that it is difficult not to see in it a survival of the pre-Cortesian *tilma*. The designs are not embroidered but actually woven into the fabric on the hand-loom on which it is made. Generally the design is of one colour across the whole width of the *ayate*, and if the coloured wool runs out it may change half-way down a design. Some of the finest *ayates*, however, have different coloured patterns woven in the same line with unbelievable skill and patience.

The warp is first made by winding the thread in a figure of eight round two posts about a foot high stuck vertically in the ground four or five feet apart. Then it is transferred to the hand-loom one end of which is fastened round the weaver-woman's waist while the other is tied at a steep angle to  a door-post or tree exactly as shown in one of Sahagún's illustrations.

It was in the villages on the slopes of these hills and at their foot that we most often saw in use the ancient *coa* or Aztec planting stick, a wooden spade-like implement with a more or less heart-shaped blade. Three or four men, each armed with a *coa*, walked slowly down the newly ploughed furrows. Every pace or two they bent down and loosened the earth with the blade. Then, straightening themselves, they inverted the *coa*, and stabbed the ground with the handle, making a small round hole. Behind, at a few paces distance, walked the women sowing from gourd bowls full of seed. Into each hole they dropped two or three grains of maize, then with a curious shuffling movement of their bare feet filled it over with the loose earth. Their actions had a rhythmic, stylized quality suggestive of the ballet, and it occurred to me that in the movements of the sowers might be found the origin of many Indian ritual dance-steps.

From all the Otomi villages of the wide Toluca plain, as from many others, the Indians flock in pilgrimage to the shrine of Chalma on the first Friday in Lent. We, too, went in 1937, not penitentially trudging for days beneath heavy loads, but in a series of stages which began by car and, gradually running through the whole gamut of trans-port, ended appropriately on foot. Just before Toluca a dirt road leads off to the left through Metepec and Mexical-cingo to Tenango del Valle in the far south-western corner of the plain. Then it drops in wide curves through pine-woods from *tierra fria* to *tierra templada* and the green valley floor of Tenancingo. Except to the north where it is dominated by the snowy Nevado, grander by far than from the plateau, the valley is surrounded by hills whose flow-ing contours suggest Europe or New England rather than Mexico. The impression is enhanced by fields of emerald wheat and by lanes hedged with rambler rose and bramble. The town, clustered at the foot of a steep conical hill which must have caught the attention of the ancients, has a charm which cannot be defined in terms of *Sehens-würdigkeiten*.

Here, acting on good advice, we left our own car and for the ten miles to Malinalco hired an ancient flivver be-

longing to Don Donaciano, the genial proprietor of the
Hotel La Paz. For a few miles, as the road led across the
valley floor, this precaution seemed unnecessary. Then
the Ford chugged over a pine-clad crest and suddenly it
seemed as though we were looking down into the crater of
a volcano, a crater which instead of vomiting fire and
smoke had blossomed like a garden. In a wide amphitheatre precipitous cliffs dropped sheer to the green sea
which washed their foot. A series of terrifying hairpins
carried the narrow, rocky road down to Malinalco upon
which it seemed to swoop like a falcon upon its prey. The
seedy-looking chauffeur drove with cool skill and composure. A larger car would have had to back round the
corners and would in all probability have shattered its
vitals on the rocks with which the road ends.

After Tenancingo we had begun to overtake the rearguard of the pilgrims, and the spacious, cliff-shadowed
plaza of Malinalco was full of them, resting, cooking or
eating their simple fare. They came in little groups of anything from three or four to a score from each *pueblo*,
ranging in age from grandmothers to infants in arms. On
their backs they carried their food, rugs and cooking utensils in *ayates* or *huacales*, home-made crates, heavy burdens on arduous mountain trails. Tiny babies were slung
in their mothers' *rebozos*. Most of the older children footed
it with the rest, though a few were strapped to mules or
donkeys or to the crates on their fathers' backs. There was
something infinitely moving in the long straggling procession, impelled by faith and devotion. City-folk would
have fallen by the wayside. Village Indians would never
think of doing so. Yet, in spite of their wiry endurance,
the pilgrimage is no country stroll for them. They were
sustained as they went by long sugar-canes which, like

121

pilgrim staffs, they carried in their hands. Half the people in Malinalco were selling them a heart stimulant, *cabellito de angel*, 'angel's hair', the silky strands from a flowering shrub, in appearance like the pink shaving brushes of the *clavileño* tree.

Malinalco is one of those exquisitely lovely places which linger undiscovered in out-of-the-way Mexico. Its houses are hidden, its broad ways shaded by flowering shrubs and fruit trees, the *guayaba*, the *zapote*, the mamey and mango. Each side-path from the broad track is closed by a backcloth of towering rock with maybe a rose-coloured church silhouetted against it. Its climate is the perfection of *tierra templada* at about 5,000 feet, the light of a tropical brilliance, the heat dry, and the air fresh and fragrant. Birds flit in and out among the trees, a flash of red or blue or yellow. From among the leafy recesses comes the liquid thrush-like song of the *clarín* or the brittle glassy note of the *cenzontli*, '*klein nur unsichtbar und grau*' like Mörike's cuckoo. Swallow-tail butterflies flutter across the path, black and yellow, purple-brown, or white as a winding sheet.

Apart from its natural beauty Malinalco is of considerable archaeological interest. Clambering up in the heat of the day to a high pinnacle of rock overhanging the village we found an Aztec pyramid hewn out of the solid rock and only recently excavated. The usual steep stairway leads up to a sanctuary the entrance of which is formed by an arch, unfortunately broken away to-day, engraved with a serpent. The Aztec builders never achieved the construction of the true arch, and this one, made by cutting through the rock beneath it, is unique. The sanctuary is circular. In the centre and on either side are carved three eagles and at the back a tiger. Their bodies are merely indicated in low relief, but their heads are firmly modelled in the round, so that the tiger looks like one of those skins with stuffed heads and glassy eyes which graced our Victorian drawing-rooms.

The pilgrimage had caused a scarcity of horses in Malinalco. All were busy transporting pilgrims or food, and for a while it looked as though we should not be able to go on that afternoon. By good fortune, however, we found a shaggy Indian boy of fifteen who had brought two donkeys in with fire-wood from the Montes de Ocuila. Chalma was not on his way home, but he consented for a small sum to add three hours on to his return jour-ney. He began by being very dour and suspicious of the three foreigners and insisted on having half his payment down in advance, but as time went on he relaxed.

Not even a Tenancingo Ford could have gone beyond Malinalco along the trail to Chalma, which resembled alternately a goat-track and the bed of a mountain torrent. It followed the foot of an enormous bastion of rock with precipitous contreforts. In the late afternoon light the scenery had the glint and fire of a cut and polished gem-stone. To our drover we remarked on its beauty. 'Yes', he said, 'God made it so, for Our Lord himself walked among these mountains.'

It must be hard for the Indians to realise that Christ never came to Mexico and did not Himself visit this place where for four hundred years His miraculous image has been venerated. Here He would have seen, if not all the power and glory, all the natural beauty of the world.

Trudging along in the now continuous stream of pilgrims, exchanging a smile here and a friendly word there, gave us a curious feeling at once mediaeval and communal, admitted us to the brotherhood of 'painful peregrinations' shared. We might have been on the road to Santiago de Compostella or to our own Canterbury. That old lady in her blue *rebozo* and broad hat, might she not be the Wife of Bath and her companions the Miller, the Reeve, the Maunciple and the rest? The mediaeval impression was completed by the few pilgrims we crossed coming away from the shrine (for the festival lasts a whole week) with little prints of the Señor de Chalma rolled up and fastened to the crowns of their hats.

The sanctuary lies at the foot of high cliffs in the mouth of a narrow, rocky valley. Each pinnacle of rock in this wild amphitheatre is crowned with a wooden crucifix. Down the valley a little mountain torrent comes tumbling clear and cold, bordered by scarlet-blossomed *colorín* trees. Startling and almost incongruous in this lonely spot are the severe lines of the massive seventeenth-century church which recalls, in the contrast it offers to its setting, the church built round San Ignacio's cottage at Loyola in Spanish Basque Guipúzcoa.

The history of Chalma is depicted in three enormous oil-paintings, darkened with age, which hang in the sacristy of the church. It is related in greater detail in the *Historia de Chalma* written by the Augustinian Father Fr. Joaquín Sardo and printed in Mexico City *en casa de Arizpe* in 1810. Before the Conquest it seems that this wild and lonely valley was the resort of 'lions, tigers, wolves and a multitude of beasts and poisonous reptiles such as vipers and scorpions, vile companions of the infernal and malign being which dwelt therein'. It was, in fact, rather worse than Ireland before the coming of St.

Patrick. The 'infernal and malign being' was a large stone idol, supposedly that of Oztocteotl, Aztec god of caves, which was worshipped in a natural cavern in the rock with pagan rites and human sacrifices. Not until about twenty years after the Conquest was the Gospel brought to this corner of the State of Mexico, partly owing to the wildness of the country and partly to the difficulty of the Ocuiltec dialect which was spoken there. In 1539, however, two Augustinian fathers, Fr. Sebastian de Tolentino and Fr. Nicolas de Perea reached Ocuila two hours away and with the fervour and eloquence of their oratory made many converts. One of these told them of the rites practised at Chalma, and conducted them to the spot, where Father Perea, who had some knowledge of the Ocuiltec tongue, endeavoured to persuade the Indians of the error of their ways. Loath as Father Sardo is to admit it, he was not immediately successful. 'The quiet forcefulness with which Fr. Nicolas de Perea had preached to these unfortunates had such effect on their minds that they could not resist the knowledge of truth. But, neutralized by the vehemence of the internal conflict which they necessarily suffered in their spirit, attacked on the one hand by the irresistible force of such powerful reasoning, and on the other by the astute fallacy of the common enemy and by the violent impulses of that superstitious religion which they had inherited from their ancestors, they looked at each other in such surprise that they feared to take the final resolution to detest the adoration of that impious image and to embrace wholeheartedly the faith of Jesus Christ . . .' In other words they required further persuasion. As to what exactly happened next accounts vary. Some say that the Indians themselves attacked the image and broke it in pieces; others that the Indians went back to their homes in indignation. The most generally accepted account, however, suggests that while the common people returned home their caciques continued to discuss the matter with the missionaries and asked for time to consider so serious a matter as a change of religion. A miracle was clearly required, and one was duly forthcoming. Both Fathers thought it more prudent to withdraw and to return a few days afterwards with their converts from Ocuila bearing a wooden cross which they intended to set up in place of the idol. What was their astonishment on arriving at the cave to find the idol shivered into fragments and an image of the crucified Christ in its place, while the floor of the cave was 'carpeted with various and exquisite flowers'. This happened either on the day of the Archangel Michael to whom the chapel was subsequently dedicated, or on the eve of Whitsunday which is still the occasion of an important pilgrimage to the spot.

Fr. Joaquín admits some doubt as to the origin of the crucifix. Was it really brought by the angels, he asks, or only by the two missionaries? 'Those who wish to be guided in everything by the standards of human wisdom opine that it is unnecessary to have recourse to angels for what lies within the power of man's accomplishment.'

Whatever its origin, it was not long before the image began to demonstrate its thaumaturgical powers. The wild beasts and vermin which had infested the valley disappeared. An Indian who had climbed a tree to gather flowers for the altar fell into a deep canyon, but his life was miraculously spared, as was that of a woman ill to the point of death with 'gallic humours', whatever they may be.

Miracles, indeed, have never ceased. A woman who

126

trudged beside us on the homeward trail told us that she had been troubled with sore toothache and had spent three pesos at the dentist's in vain. At Chalma she had found earth from the holy cave on sale and had bought some and applied it to the tooth with the result that the pain had immediately stopped. 'Did it never return?' we asked. 'No', she said, 'you see as soon as I applied the earth the tooth fell out'. 'How wonderful a thing', she added, 'is Faith'!

For many years, in spite of the many pilgrims attracted by its fame, the site was virtually deserted. Seventy years passed before a holy man, Fr. Bartolomé de Jesus Maria, established himself there and built a series of galleries across the cliff face and the mouth of the cave, with rooms where the pilgrims might sleep.

The construction of the monastery in 1683 and the translation to its church of the holy image cannot have been accomplished without much hesitation and anxiety. So many thaumaturgical images have signified their displeasure on similar occasions by returning miraculously to the place of their first appearance. Fr. Joaquín, however, compares the cave to the shell in which a pearl is found and the monastery to the jewellers' masterpiece in which it is set, and in effect, on being 'carried to the new shrine with the greatest solemnity, veneration and magnificence and with the popular rejoicings which can be imagined, the sacred image began forthwith to show how much to its liking was this pious act and opening the hands of its liberal clemency diffused itself in abundant misericord, kindness and favours.'

127

Pilgrims to Chalma

I have spoken of the solitary grandeur of the place, but in point of fact nothing could have been less lonely than Chalma on the evening of our arrival. It is said that as many as thirty thousand people come on each of the great pilgrimages of the First Friday in Lent and the *Pascua Chica* or 'Little Easter' of Pentecost. The bare slopes in front of the church, where the amphitheatre of rock opens out into the valley, had been turned into a vast Indian encampment, the brilliant evening light softened by the smoke of a thousand campfires. We stabled in the *mesón*, a vast caravanserai open to the sky, full of mules and donkeys contentedly browsing dry maize stalks. I set out for the monastery alone in search of lodging, and it must have taken me at least twenty minutes to struggle through the dense crowds round the booths which had sprung up mushroom-like for the *fiesta*. By good luck Padre Antonio, the priest in charge, was able to give us the last of the rooms on the upper gallery of the cloister. Its only furniture was a single bed and a child's chair, rather inadequate sleeping accommodation for three people, but the floor was specklessly clean and, when covered with a *sarape*, not too hard to prevent the two of us who occupied it from sleeping soundly for the two nights that we stayed there.

The intervening day was the Friday, the highpoint of the festival. We spent it in wandering round the church and its precincts and the surrounding countryside, never tiring of the varied spectacle which it presented.

All day long, little groups of pilgrims were arriving from different directions, bowed under their burdens, grey with the dust of the trail. Making their way in single file through the crowded churchyard they entered the church and fell upon their knees before the altar, intoning in their high-pitched voices verses of the *Salutación* and *Alabado*, hymns to the Señor de Chalma, sung to the traditional tune of the pilgrimage:

Glorioso Señor de Chalma	*Glorious Lord of Chalma*
Padre de mi corazón	*Father of my heart*
Adoro con toda mi alma	*With all my soul I adore*
Tu dichosa aparición.	*Your auspicious apparition.*
A un idolo sucedió	*An idol was succeeded by*
El simulacro del cielo.	*The image of the Heavens.*
De Oztocteotl la idolatría	*The idolatry of Oztocteotl*
Desterró el Dios verdadero.	*Was driven out by the true God.*
En una cueva se halló	*In a cave there was found*
Tesoro rico e imenso,	*A treasure rich and great,*
El mismo que hoy adoramos	*The same which we adore to-day*
En su magnífico templo.	*In its magnificent temple.*
Arboles de la montaña	*Trees upon the mountains*
Cuyas ramas mueve el viento,	*Whose branches are swayed by the wind,*
Dad voces de bendición	*Pour blessings aloud*
A ese montero divino.	*On this divine mountain-dweller.*
Caudaloso rio que corres	*Deep stream flowing*
De esta Casa al cerro	*From this House of God to the hills*
Canta a Cristo, fuente viva,	*Sing to Christ, living stream,*
Limpios cristales rompiendo.	*Breaking clear and crystal-line.*

Slow, simple, gravely harmonized in thirds, this melody was the *leitmotiv* of the festival. Never stilled, it was taken up by one group after another, in varying pitch and key, at times in free, untrammelled canon. Even in the still hours of the night we would be awoken by its distant echoes and imagine some devout little band arriving or departing. It served, too, for the *Despedimento*, the hymn of farewell, which with tears rolling down their cheeks the pilgrims would sing, facing the altar on their knees, and slowly retreating backwards to the door of the church, their eyes fixed in rapt devotion on the image which was their solace in their trials and tribulations and which they would not see again for another year:

Adiós, Cristo milagroso,	*Farewell, miraculous Christ,*
Adiós, brillante lucero,	*Farewell, brilliant star,*
Adiós, Santuario dichoso	*Farewell, blissful Sanctuary,*
Hasta el año venidero.	*Until the coming year.*

The scene which the hymn conjures up most vividly to my memory is that of a calvary high up on the trail to Ocuila where I sat for an hour or so. Four wooden crosses raised their gaunt outlines against a background of rocky crag, with flowers at their foot and white ribbons fluttering from their arms. While I sat there, a big band of Otomi pilgrims, forty or fifty strong, from somewhere up on the cold plateau near Ixtlahuaca, came by on their homeward way. Turning aside from the stony track they fell on their knees before the calvary in a long line four or five deep and sang through the many verses of the hymn. Then, rising to their feet, they resumed their weary journey, burnt by the sun, wet with the dew, through rocky gorges and over bare uplands three or four days to their distant village home.

De Cuernavaca y de Iguala From Cuernavaca and from Iguala,

Pilgrims to Chalma

De Zacualpan y Angangueo,	From Zacualpan and Angangueo,
Se les cumplió su deseo,	Their desire has been fulfilled,
A los de Taxco y Tetecala,	Those from Taxco and Tetecala,
De Ixmiquilpan y Cuezala,	From Ixmiquilpan and Cuezala,
Todos llorando se ván;	All depart in tears;
De Yautepec y Amatlán	From Yautepec and Amatlán,
Se despiden con esmero,	They take their leave with care.
Adiós Chalma, dulce imán,	Farewell, Chalma, sweet magnet,
Hasta el año venidero.	Farewell till the coming year.

At night Chalma called for the engraving-tool of a Rembrandt. Not only on the bare hills had the Indians bivouacked under improvised shelters of sarape or petate. They filled the smoke-blackened rooms of Fr. Bartolomé's galleries across the cliff-face. Singly or in family groups they sprawled across the galleries and stairways of the monastery and cloister. They had overflowed into the churchyard and even into the dim-lit church. At night they were still and motionless, in the day-time busy with a thousand varied activities, religious or domestic. They bought little sacred souvenirs and had them blessed in the sacristy, or offered tiny silver ex-votos in the shape of a child, a horse, a donkey for whose welfare they prayed, or of some evil, a scorpion for instance, from which they wished to be delivered. At the spring women were washing and scrubbing an exquisitely embroidered cloth in which they had brought a household Virgin to be blessed by the Christ to whom she had given birth. Down in the ice-cold stream they

131

washed themselves, confident no doubt that they would emerge spiritually purified as well as physically cleansed.

The church was always full of worshippers, and of children dancing the eighteenth century measures, so like our own Country dances, of the Danza de los Pastores. High up above the altar was the miraculous image itself, in a glass case to which a spiral stairway gave access from behind. There was always a long line of Indians awaiting their turn to leave the imprint of their lips upon it.

On either side of the great west door the walls are packed to the ceiling with *retablos*, the naïve pictures offered by the faithful, illustrating and describing the miracles wrought by the Señor de Chalma. Such pictures are found in many churches and are the work either of the donors themselves or of rustic artists from whom they are commissioned.

While I was contemplating the horrific representations of railway accidents, motor-car smashes and so on, a new picture was placed beside it, the donor showing no compunction in removing an old and blackened *retablo* to make room for his own. The new picture depicted a man and a dog gazing into the sky at the crucified Christ. No animal-lover can fail to be touched by the legend which it bore:

'Vine a la fiesta que se hace en veneración a la Imagen de N.S. Jesucristo y perdi un perrito que traia: habiendo regresado a mi pueblo que es muy lejos sin esperanzas de volverle a ver invoque al Señor de Chalma y pocos días despues llegó a mi casa por lo cual doy rendidas gracias a Nuestro Señor Manuel Martinez San Lorenzo Cuauhtemoc 1936.'

(I came to the fiesta held in veneration of the Image of Our Lord Jesus Christ and lost a little dog which I had

brought; having returned to my village which is very distant without hope of seeing him again I invoked the Señor
de Chalma and a few days afterwards he arrived at my
house for which I give hearty thanks to Our Lord Manuel
Martinez San Lorenzo Cuauhtemoc 1936.)

Although the centre of worship has long since shifted
from the cave to the church, the former is still revered
and visited. We found it hidden away behind Fr. Bartolomé's galleries, graced with a small altar and with a
statue of St. Michael in place of the miraculous crucifix.
An old Indian woman had placed her hand against the
wall and was busy drawing it in outline with a piece of
charcoal. Looking round I noticed numbers of similar outlines of hands and, at a lower level, of feet. I asked her
why she did it. Looking a little embarrassed, she replied:
'Para un recuerdo' (For a souvenir); and I was left wondering whether unconsciously she was not perpetuating
some ancient superstition.

The outer part of the churchyard, just inside the gate,
was full of booths of vendors of religious emblems. Immediately in front of the open church door, however, a
space was reserved by tacit consent for the groups of religious dancers who had come from afar to dance out the
fulfilment of their vows. The tall, plumed headdresses of
the Apaches, the crescent-topped crowns of the Moors and
Christians, the quaint bull-headpiece of the Torito, waved
and swirled above the heads of the crowd.

One of the dances most frequently seen in Central
Mexico and at the same time one of the most interesting
is that known as the Dance of the Apaches or Concheros.
Its performers are all members of one big religious
brotherhood with wide ramifications, secret rites and

initiation ceremonies from which outsiders are rigorously
excluded. They may not even hand over their banners or
dancers' trappings without a little ceremony in which

they kneel, kiss the
surrendered object
and cross themselves.
Their dress is a slight-
ly self-conscious imi-
tation of ancient
Aztec costume with
brightly coloured, tin-
selled tunics and fea-
thered headdresses
and reminiscences of
Redskin garb which may account for their puzzling use of
the name Apache nearly a thousand miles from any rem-
nant of that unruly border tribe. Their other name of
Concheros (Shell-Men) they owe to the guitars of arma-
dillo shell which they carry and on which they strum the
rhythmic accompaniment to their dance. Both their dancing and singing has a quality of tense, fanatical, ecstatic
fervour which I have seen in no other Indian dance and
which can be almost frightening. At Los Remedios on
September 8th there must have been nearly a dozen
groups of them, some from as far away as Guanajuato,
dancing either in small self-contained rings or in wider
circles in which two or three groups had merged. They
strongly resented these circles being broken, and each
group was accompanied by a masked Devil armed with a
little whip whose duty it was to keep order and who irre-
sistibly recalled Clavijero's masked buffoons. With gro-
tesquely carved features and animal horns some of these
masks are positively terrifying. One at Los Remedios had

seven snakes with feather fangs springing from its forehead which may possibly have enshrined some dim, unconscious memory of Chicomecoatl, Seven Snake, one of the chief Aztec goddesses of fertility (See Plate 32). At the shrine of Sacro Monte above Amecameca I once saw one of these Devils take off his mask, blindfold himself and advance on his knees, wailing and groaning, through the churchyard and into the church, guided on either side by a dancer.

'How poor are they that have not patience!' The Indian, poor in many material things, is rich in this spiritual gift, and his dances continue for hours and hours, sometimes indeed for days on end. They are frankly monotonous, but that of the Apaches with its strong rhythms has an extraordinary cumulative effect on the beholder which must be multiplied a hundredfold in the performers, among whom, exceptionally in Indian dancing, women are included, and even tiny children not more than three years old.

Standing in a wide circle they strike up a persistent rhythm on their guitars. Then at a given signal they begin, each in his place, the vigorous almost vicious stamping and jumping steps which they have studiously rehearsed together. Some of these steps can be related to European dancing, but most of them are of pronouncedly Indian character. Even when the feet are, so to speak, talking a European language one has only to look at the swaying, rounded shoulders, crouched over the guitars, to feel the spell of Indian magic.

Any Indian character which, on the other hand, the Dance of the Moors and Christians may possess has been acquired by adoption, so to speak, for it is completely European in origin and was brought to Mexico by Catholic

135

missionaries. To-day it is the most widely distributed and diversified of all Mexican ceremonies. Part dialogue, part mime, part dance, the three ingredients are mixed in varying proportions. As done at Chalma it consisted almost entirely of dance figures, the Moors wearing grotesque and terrifying masks. In remoter parts the battles are often more serious affairs, with much clashing of *machetes* and sometimes a toll of dead and injured. At Totonac Mecapalapa I was told that when the battle results in one or two deaths the Indians say that 'it has been a good *fiesta*'. They regard the victims almost in the light of sacrifices, and no further legal or other steps are taken.

My pleasantest memory of *Los Santiagos*, as the Moors and Christians are often called, is at Santa Maria Acolman where the dance was offered by the villagers of Atlatongo. The village resembles countless others on the high plateau, its mode of life half-Spanish, half-Aztec, like its double-barrelled name. A tall church overshadows low houses of brown adobe brick, each with its little courtyard fenced in by organ cactus and shaded by feathery pepper trees. On this particular day Santa Maria Acolman was in full *fiesta*. Candles were burning before the church altar, and in the porch a little group of children carrying half-hoops adorned with artificial flowers were dancing and heying in honour of the Virgin. Suddenly a distant blare of brass brought people across to the far side of the churchyard, and a minute or two later *Los Santiagos* came into view, men in elaborate and brilliant costumes. Making their way round the side of the church they climbed on to an improvised wooden platform beneath two pepper trees, and took up their places for the dance.

The Christians, led by St. James the Apostle, Patron

Saint of Spain, were dressed in *charro* costume, their hats decorated with feathers and flowers. Each wore over his shoulders a little velvet cape with religious symbols embroidered in spangles and carried a cross in his left hand and a sword in his right. The Moors were less soberly clad in flowing robes of brilliant colours with linings of contrasting hues and strange mitre-like headgear. Pontius Pilate, who by immutable tradition is their leader, was distinguished by a crown, a theatrical wig, false moustaches, dark glasses and a costume of green, blue and pink. His General was the Roman Emperor Severus.

For the first hour or two of the five which the dance lasted the armies marched and counter-marched in a slow goosestep to martial music. Every time St. James and his men reached the edge of the stage they flourished their crosses and brandished their sabres. Next came the *relaciones* (speeches), a series of challenges and exhortations in which each side breathed defiance at the other and worked up its own martial ardour. In pairs a Christian and a Moor would stride up and down the stage gesticulating and breathing fire and slaughter.

Now a suggestion of action began to creep into the plot..

Pilate complains to the nobles of 'his Kingdom of Granada' of the insolence of the Christian General Ramiro who has refused to remit the recognised tribute of a hundred Christian maidens. His Ambassador goes to Galicia to protest to St. James. Santiago tells Ramiro that the ashes of Pelayo, first King of the Reconquest, call for vengeance. In a rousing speech Pilate now prepares his men for battle. In a last effort to avoid warfare Santiago in his turn sends an Ambassador to the Moors demanding the return of Pelayo's ashes and the payment of tribute. This scene was a piece of elaborately stylized miming suggesting the ballet rather than the legitimate stage. The blindfolded Ambassador was conducted in a sort of country dance figure threading his way in and out of the Moorish ranks. His message delivered he is condemned to death, and after a moving farewell to earth he is killed not merely once but over and over again by each successive pair of Moors who thrust their swords realistically up to the hilt beneath his armpits.

At last, after further parleyings, battle is joined. Here again, Indian patience and formalism will not allow the climax of the performance to be passed in a few brief moments. It must be spun out over an hour or more. Not only must each Christian and each Moor engage in single combat, leaping backwards and forwards in well simulated thrust and parry, but, though the Moors must of course be killed in the end, each takes an unconscionable time in dying. At last, however, they fall, each in his turn, and are laid out in a neat row, lying on their sides, each head resting on the thigh of the next. Mischievous children under the stage poke them through the cracks in the boards.

It was reserved to the smallest of the Santiagos, a little lad of six who had tirelessly gone through the whole performance with all its interpolated dances and parades, to despatch Pilate, and the quick tropical twilight was upon us before the corpses sprang to life once more and resumed their dance with a zest which made us wonder whether they were not quite ready to start the whole thing over again from the beginning.

In Europe, where it extends from Portugal to Dalmatia, the ceremonial battle of the Moors and Christians goes back to the middle of the twelfth century, and I have ex-

plained elsewhere[1] why I think it may have been grafted
on to some earlier ritual combat such as that between
Winter and Summer which survived until a century ago
in the Isle of Man.

Within less than twenty years of the Conquest it had
been implanted in Mexico, for as early as 1538 the city of
Mexico celebrated the conclusion of peace between
Charles V and François I at Aigues Mortes with one such
battle of which Bernal Diaz leaves a breathless description:

'Under two Captains the Turks lay in ambush, very
naturally dressed in the Turkish fashion with very rich
clothes of silk in crimson and purple, with much gold and
rich turbans such as they wear in their country, and all on
horseback, and they lay in hiding in order to spring out
and carry off certain shepherds with their flocks which
were pasturing near a spring, and one shepherd of those
who were guarding them fled and brought word to the
Grand Master of Rhodes that the Turks were carrying off
the flocks and shepherds. Then the Knights rode out, and
there was a battle between them and the Knights who
took away their booty of flocks, and other squadrons of
Turks fell from another side upon Rhodes and fought
other battles with the Knights, and these took many of the
Turks and loosed wild bulls on them to tear them in pieces.'

This pageant of the Siege of Rhodes by the Spaniards of
Mexico City apparently picqued the pride of the Indians
of Tlaxcala, who, anxious not to be outdone, represented
the Siege of Jerusalem on Corpus Christi Day in 1539.
Jerusalem was represented by a pasteboard stronghold
complete with keep, towers and crenellated walls, 'all full
of roses and flowers', says Father Motolinia in his *Historia*

[1]See Violet Alford and Rodney Gallop: *The Traditional Dance.*
London. 1935. Pp. 101-121.

de los Indios de la Nueva España. In the Spanish army all
the different provinces of Spain were represented. Ger-
mans and Italians constituted the rearguard, but the van-
guard was formed by Tlaxcala and Mexico.

When the army is ready to attack, God sends an angel
with a promise of victory and dispatches to their aid not
only St. James the Apostle but St. Hyppolytus, on whose
day the combined Spanish and Tlaxcalan army took
Mexico. St. James on his white horse puts himself at the
head of the Spaniards and St. Hyppolytus on his black
horse at the head of the Mexicans. The battle rages, and
the issue is in doubt until the moment when St. Michael
appears to the Moors and tells them that God forgives
them their sins for having respected the holy places, but
only on condition that they are converted and do penance.
The Sultan and the Moors suddenly see the light, surren-
der, pay homage to the Emperor and the Pope and are
publicly baptized.

It is from such performances as these that the rustic
Moros y Cristianos of to-day are descended, as well as
those other dances which represent the warfare between
Cortes and Montezuma, Spaniards and Chichimecs, and
even Mexicans and French. Some of them are still rehearsed from old texts preserved in thumbworn copy-
books. A few of these have been collected and printed, but
for the most part they have been neglected, which is to be
regretted, since they have considerable historical and
literary interest. In many cases the most amusing contra-
dictions and anachronisms have crept in. On the old road
to Cuernavaca I once heard Pontius Pilate addressed as
Presidente Pilatos and claim that 'all the ships of America'
were his, while his General referred to the 'sovereign
Congress of the Nation'. At La Gavia in the State of

Federico Ta, Yaqui Pascola

Totonac Men at Papantla

Tepoztlan: fireworks

Tepoztlan: the Sacred Drum

Village Church in the Mesquital

Otomi Volador

The Dancers

Totonac Volador at Papantla

Malinche in the Reed-throwing Dance

Thatching at Xoxocotla

Roofing at Xoxocotla

Taxco

Pilgrims to Chalma

Mexico my friend Don Pablo Martínez del Río listened to a Christian declaiming:

Señor San Carlomagnos	*Lord Saint Charlemagne,*
Gran Emperador pagano	*Great pagan Emperor*
Que quieres reinar en la	*Who wouldst reign in the*
República Mexicana,	*Republic of Mexico,*
Cuando nadie *há de reinar*	*When none shall reign in*
en Mexico	*Mexico,*
Más que la Virgen Guada-	*Save the Virgin of Guada-*
lupana.	*lupe.*

Passion Plays and 'Sieges of Jerusalem' have so confused the issue that in some texts Moors and Christians, Romans and Jews are all mixed up together in a glorious hotch-potch. Thus in the Milpa Alta text used at Iztapalapa on Whitsunday in 1937 Santiago apostrophizes 'the false gods of Olympus' and the 'hostile fury' of the *gente hebrea musulmana* (Jewish Moslem people). Jupiter is stigmatized as an adulterer and a homicide and Pericles cited as testimony to Christ's divinity. 'Defenders of Mahomet, adorers of Jupiter', the Moors are called, and in a passage of exalted lyricism the Moorish Captain describes the dawn over Palestine:

'Oh brillante aurora de la Tierra Santa, brillante como un lucero de la mañana, resplandeciente como una imensa sabana de espuma.'

(Oh brilliant dawn of the Holy Land, brilliant as a morning star, resplendent as an immense sheet of foam.)

Here, more than the breadth of Lake Texcoco separates us from Santa Maria Acolman and its Kingdom of Granada.

VIII. Yaquis in Tlaxcala

No one who has read the story of the Conquest of Mexico whether in Bernal Diaz, Prescott or any briefer summary can forget Tlaxcala and the rôle its people played in the defeat of Montezuma and Cuauhtemoc. The rôle of a traitor some would call it, and the younger Xicotencatl is held up to admiration to-day as the one patriot in Tlaxcala who consistently refused to help the Spaniards and who paid with his life for his independent spirit. Nevertheless, the attitude of Xicotencatl the elder and of that cacique whom Bernal Diaz calls Mase Escasi is easy to understand. It can hardly have been pleasant, even according to pre-Conquest standards, to feel that you were allowed to survive on sufferance by an enemy who would neither destroy you nor yet remain at peace with you, purely in order that by making ceaseless war on you he might be assured of a constant supply of prisoners for sacrifice so that his crops might prosper. Mars was a god of vegetation as well as of battle, but in no country was the strange connexion between war and agricultural fertility cults more pronounced, and be it added more logically put into practice, than in ancient Mexico.

One of the most curious things about Mexico is the

142

speed with which, thanks to modern means of conveyance, one can pass through what before the Conquest were virtually different countries. Speed to-day can almost be calculated in kingdoms per hour. Thus to go by car from Mexico City to Tlaxcala takes no more than a couple of hours, during which one passes through territories which once belonged to the ancient states of Texcoco, Chalco and Huejotzingo.

On the particular day that I have in mind, the wet season was not long past and the flowers had not yet all withered. Sky-blue lupin and scarlet Indian Paintbrush splashed their colour against the background of dark fir. At San Martín Texmelucan, we turned left from the Puebla road and were soon in the state of Tlaxcala, the smallest in the Union. Immediately the scenery changed. The high volcanoes fell away behind us, out of mind if not out of sight. Like the waves of the sea when the wind drops, the hills were smoothed out into swelling curves and assumed a placid air of fat and prosperous contentment. As far as the eye could see stretched green fields and meadows with little villages clustered round baroque churches diminishing in perspective back to the forest-clad slopes of Malinche. Even the once active volcano has taken on the lazy flowing lines of a couched panther which has sprung once and may spring again, but which for the moment is content to stretch its limbs in the sun.

Malinche, or to give it its older name Matlalcueyatl, dominates the state of Tlaxcala both physically and spiritually. It is believed by the Indians who dwell round its foot that the mountain is a beautiful woman who sits in a cave with her hair streaming down her shoulders. She is the protector of the peasants and sends the rain and the dew, though also the snow and the hail. It is strange that

she should have been identified with Malinche, Cortes'
Indian mistress and interpreter. The name in spite of its
appearance is not a native one but merely the best which
the Aztecs (whose language contains no 'r') could make of
Marina, the name assumed by the noble Aztec lady who
had been sold into slavery to the Mayas and who accepted
baptism when Cortes reached Tabasco.

It is a tragedy that Doña Marina never wrote her auto-
biography. Throughout the Conquest, she played the indispensable rôle of interpreter between the Spaniards and
the race which had cast her out. At Cholula she saved her
master's life by warning him of the great conspiracy to
massacre the Spaniards. In due course she bore him a son,
Martin Cortes, and on the expedition to Honduras, he
gave her in legitimate marriage to one of his officers, Don
Juan Jaramillo. Before this she had had a dramatic re-
union on the Isthmus with the mother who had sold her
into slavery to secure her inheritance to a younger
brother. According to Bernal Diaz, Marina seems to have
displayed a very Christian spirit on this occasion, publicly
stating that 'she was sure her mother knew not what she
did when she sold her to the traders and that she forgave
her', and presenting her with the jewels and ornaments
which she carried on her person. Moreover, lest the moral
be lost, she added that 'she felt much happier than before,
now that she had been instructed in the Christian faith
and given up the bloody worship of the Aztecs'. She survived to see the birth of her grandchild, and in recognition
of her services was presented by the Spaniards with a
house in Mexico City, gardens at Chapultepec and Cul-
hoacan and estates in her native province.

Tlaxcala, a little city of five thousand inhabitants, suns
itself in an amphitheatre of grey, limestone hills, Ocotlan,

Yaquis in Tlaxcala

Ocotelulco, Acxotla and others, over which Malinche's rocky summit peers down into a cross-word puzzle of rectangular streets, flat roofs and courtyards. It is well worth a visit if only for its historical associations. No city in New Spain received so many honours and privileges from the Kings of Castile, as testified by the initials of Isabel the Catholic, Charles V and Philip II embodied in its coat of arms. On the waters of the shady Rio Zahuapan which meanders round the outskirts, no wider than many a Scottish salmon river, were launched the brigantines which, to the cry of 'Tlaxcala! Castile!' were afterwards carried across country by eight thousand Indians to the shores of Lake Texcoco for the conquest of Tenochtitlan.

On a slope to the south of the town lies the first Catholic Monastery ever built on the American continent. Belonging to the Franciscan Order, it was of course dedicated to St. Francis. The square tower stands apart from the nave in which are preserved the first pulpit from which the Gospel was preached in New Spain and the font used at the baptism of the converted Tlaxcalan *caciques*.

Paradoxically enough, it was not primarily with the idea of seeing Tlaxcala itself that we went there for the first time. We had been invited to visit the regiment of Yaqui Indians which for some years has been quartered there. The true home of the Yaquis is in Sonora in the extreme north-west of the country, a wild and untamed region worthy of the splendid race which for several centuries defended it against all comers. There are Yaquis in Arizona as well as in Mexico. From Nogales on the border to Guaymas, the capital of the state of Sonora, the Southern Pacific Railway runs down to meet the coast. To the east, the wild cliffs and canyons of the Sierra Madre pile up into a storm-tossed sea of rock, into the recesses of

which the Yaquis have gradually been driven by the slow
tide of invasion. Throughout the nineteenth century and
even into the twentieth they fought independent Mexico
as they had fought the Spaniards who had come in search
of silver. Some compromised with the invader; others
resisted stoutly. Like bulls they came to be known respectively as *manso* and *bronco,* tame and wild. In President
Porfirio Diaz, they found an enemy as implacable as themselves. Conquered in appearance if not in spirit, many of
them were exiled to Yucatan. Not only in distance but in
climate, the flat jungle of the peninsula was the opposite
extreme to their mountain home in the Sierra Madre.
Many died in the tropical heat. Some few escaped and, like
the dog which guided by some unerring instinct returns
to his former home, made their way back on foot, 2,000
miles to Sonora. Only those who know Mexico, its tropical
forests, craggy mountains and wind-swept plateaux, and
above all its vast empty distances, can appreciate the
magnitude of this achievement and of the indomitable
spirit which prompted it.

The vast political upheaval of the last quarter of a century brought a turn of the tide. Plutarco Elias Calles and
Alvaro Obregón were both from Sonora, and one revolutionary wave after another swept down on Mexico from
the north-west, each carrying like the spume on its crest
the Yaquis who are universally recognised to be the finest
fighting material in the country. In due course, having
swept away all opposition, the waves spent themselves,
leaving like a rock-pool above the tidemark this little
Regiment in Nahua Tlaxcala: Yaqui from its Divisional
General to the humblest of its privates.

For me, this was the greatest stroke of luck imaginable.
I was never able to find time for an expedition to Sonora,

and had it not been for the courtesy and warm-hearted hospitality of General Amarillas I should never have had an opportunity of seeing the remarkable dances which, under a veneer of Christianity, the Yaquis have preserved from their ancestral heritage.

Like his men, General Amarillas has the immense breadth of shoulder and depth of chest which distinguish the Yaqui from the more slightly built Indians of Southern Mexico. We were accompanied that day by Don Julio Tello, the great Peruvian archaeologist who is himself an Indian, and by Mr. Bennet Greig who has joined him in some of his archaeological and ethnographical researches in the high Andean *cordilleras*. Both admitted that they had seen nothing in America to compare with the dances which we witnessed in a little courtyard behind the church of San Francisco.

These dances are generally done at Easter, but this was a special performance for our benefit, and had the advantage that we were able to see compressed into two hours what normally takes two or three days . . . and nights . . . of unending, monotonous repetition.

The dancers were oldish men who, more than the younger, have preserved the taste for the dance, and its tradition. One of them, Ramón by name, was nearly seventy years old, though so well-preserved was he and so springy his step that his age seemed impossible to believe. In one of the revolutionary wars, his leg was shattered by a bullet. Gangrene set in, and the surgeons wished to amputate. Ramón clung to his leg, and the General to his best dancer. Not for nothing is the General the descendant of a long line of medicine men who have been for generations the depositories of a lore unknown alike to church and to science. He will not say how he cured Ramón, but

147

it is whispered that it was with a mixture of organ cactus juice, herbs from Sonora and gunpowder. The fact remains that Ramón still has his leg and still dances. He is fat with a fatness which owes more to muscle and bone than to adipose tissue. In his broad face, deep-set eyes peep out with a sly twinkle. He lacks the high cheekbones, the hollow, lined cheeks and mask-like countenance which distinguish his companions Luis and Federico Ta. In the dances which followed Ramón was the Deer in the Danza del Venado, and Luis and Federico together with others whose names we did not catch were the Coyotes and also the Pascolas in the dance of that name.

Pascola, of course, is a post-Conquest word related to Easter, the season of its performance. But there is nothing Pascal or European about the dance except its music. This curiously enough is furnished by a harp and fiddle playing tunes which might have come out of an eighteenth century fiddle sonata. It is a solo dance. Federico Ta was the first to perform. His tall, gaunt frame was bare to the waist, which was girdled by a plaid shawl hung with little bells. His feet were bare. Round his calves were wound *tenabaris*, clusters of cocoons, emptied, filled with sand and strung together so that they looked like Morris Dancers' bell-pads and rustled drily as he danced. On the back of his head was a weird mask, like a tiny face, black daubed with white and fringed with straggling white hair and beard.

It is hard to convey in words his posture: head and torso motionless, shoulders hunched, knees and elbows slightly bent, hands grasping rose-brown gourd rattles to which he imparted a nervous, rhythmic movement, as his feet came alive with an independent life of their own in the unbelievable rapidity of the steps. He seldom moved far from his place. Occasionally he would retreat or advance a pace or two or rotate on his own axis. Then he would put one foot forward and drag it back along the ground, not smoothly but in a series of flexions seen only as a scarcely perceptible tremor. The dance did not seem designed to suggest movement but rather to hammer into the minds of performer and onlooker alike a merciless, hypnotic rhythm. Elevation in the choreographic sense of the word there was none, only a remorseless stamping which seemed to beat itself into the brain.

Presently the dance changed. The masks were shifted round to cover the face, and the performers turned from the harp and fiddle to an older music played by a pipe and taborer squatting on the ground. For a while we had been watching him tuning his circular drum to a definite pitch over a charcoal fire. Now he rested it vertically on the ground steadying it with his left arm. With his left hand he played the pipe, longer than the European kind, while with his right he drummed upon the tom-tom. Erna Fergusson was told that this new dance was called *Macho Cabrillo*, the 'He-Goat', but we could not confirm this. 'Why did you tell her so?' we asked. 'Because when we wear our dance-masks we are free to say anything we like', was the answer. Yet *Macho Cabrillo*, with its hint of black magic and witches' sabbaths, would have seemed just the name for this dance which was if possible tenser and more barbaric than the last. Gourd rattles had been discarded for a little sistrum, but its shaking was no less rhythmic and the steps were no less elaborate, while the masked head was jerked first to one side and then to the other with the spasmodic, darting movements of an animal and shaken from time to time like a wild beast worrying its prey.

149

To the vigour and intensity of these two dances, the Deer Dance added a real sense of choreographic beauty. Once again the music changed, and from the point of view of authenticity for the better. There were now three

more musicians cross-legged upon the ground. In front of two of them stood inverted gourd bowls which served to add resonance to a smooth stick which they drew in cross rhythms across a notched stick. The third had a similar gourd inverted in an earthenware bowl of water, on which he drummed with a hollow, booming sound. Above this rose a long, monotonous, improvised chant in the Yaqui tongue, half-heard through the racket of the percussion.

The Deer Dance was not like the Pascola a solo affair. There were four performers, Ramón being the Deer, and three of the others representing hunting coyotes or prairie dogs. Crouching low before the pipe and taborer the prairie dogs held long bows between their legs, on which they beat in time with little sticks. From the backs of their heads hung coyote skins stuck with eagle's feathers. Every now and then they raised their heads in an almost audible snarl and lowered them again. It was hard to take one's eyes off them, harder still to keep them from the Deer who danced in front of the gourd-drummers and, as it were, at them. Round his head was wound a handkerchief, on the top of which a tiny deer's head, stuffed and antlered, stood upright. Ramón danced softly at first, crouching low, almost touching the ground with his gourd rattles. In spite of the wonderful tattoo of the steps we saw in a flash that it was the deer's head which we must watch. Now the animal appears to be grazing peacefully, now a skilful flick of Ramón's head lifts its head from the ground, the light catching the liquid eyes as they move to right and left in evident alarm at some half-sensed danger. It is a triumph of choreographic mime.

Presently the hunt is up. One by one the coyotes run up with a snarling leap to the space before the musicians and displace in turn the deer and each other. There comes a moment when all four are dancing together, followed by the inevitable dénouement with the stricken deer outstretched upon the sand. This at least is how we saw it done that day in Tlaxcala, but the performance is by no means crystallized and varies in its details, much being left to the improvisation of the dancers. I have heard it said, though I can take no responsibility for its truth, that this dance caused more trouble to the early Jesuit fathers than any other obstacle which they met in Sonora where they long preceded the civil and military authorities. In those days the deer dancer, a chaste youth, was put to death after two or three days' dancing, not merely in mime, but in grim reality, as hunting magic and a sacrifice to the tribal gods.

151

IX. Tepoztlan

To the outside world Tepoztlan is known only as the little Indian *pueblo* where the American ethnologist Robert Redfield made a study of the 'works and days' of contemporary Aztec life. To those who live in Mexico City it is familiar as one of the most enjoyable excursions which can be made in a day from the capital, and one, moreover, which is equally rewarding to those interested in ancient archaeology, in colonial architecture and in the timeless Indian life of to-day.

Since February, 1936, it has been possible to reach Tepoztlan by road, but to those visiting the place for the first time in the true pilgrim spirit there is only one possible method of approach, the steep and narrow way by El Parque.

El Parque is the name of a station on the railway which runs southwards from Mexico City to Cuernavaca. It lies at about the same height as the capital on the southern slopes of the mountain range which separates the Federal District from the State of Morelos. From El Parque to Tepoztlan is a descent of 2,000 feet down a rough trail and, metaphorically, of two thousand years down the ages. The mountain side is prehistoric Mexico. It is a natural park of virgin woodland with no high trees or dense tropical forests but the low pines and scented shrubs of *tierra fria*, an aromatic hillside such as you might find in California or the Mediterranean.

152

Tepoztlan

Describing a hairpin bend, the railway line turns back westwards in its long drop to Cuernavaca, and the walker swings his pack on his back and strides off down the trail which leads to Tepoztlan and the Middle Ages. The path drops quickly, and soon on the left the first crags climb above the trail. A couple of Indians are riding down on brisk mountain ponies with box-stirrups and finely worked Mexican saddles. They must be Tlahuicas, like the Aztecs a branch of the great Nahua family. Farther on, two women in blue *rebozos* are picking their way down between the stones. One has white hair and a stern, lined face which might equally be that of a saint or of a witch.

Perhaps a third of the way down, we left the trail along an almost unnoticeable path, which assured the most dramatic as well as the most logical approach to Tepoztlan. Suddenly it emerged on a mountain-side which sloped away into a steep funnel, closed in front by vertical pillars of rock. Somewhere down there lay the hidden door to Tepoztlan. We could see the promised land beyond the gates: a vast green floor fifteen hundred feet below, stretching away to mountains on the horizon's rim. As the path wound down into the funnel this green land of faëry fell away out of sight. Then came a brief climb up a narrow chimney-like crevice in the rock, dark even in the noontide sun. At the top, in a storm-tossed congeries of crags, stands the Tepozteco, one of the smallest but one of the most remarkable of pre-Cortesian pyramids.

The temple is a small building of volcanic rock on the edge of a dizzy precipice. A short but steeply pitched stairway leads first to a little court with the remains of an altar and then to the shrine which, being of stone, remains partially intact. It consists of a single roofless

153

chamber reached by a door through a low wall, with a projecting bench-like course running along the back, carved
with Aztec hieroglyphics.

The temple was sacred to the god Tepoztecatl, also
known as Ome Tochtli or Two Rabbit from the date of
his festival. Tepoztecatl was one of the many gods of
pulque and intoxication and also one of the many mani-
festations of Quetzalcoatl. To-day the Indians call it 'the
house of Tepozteco', and of this Tepozteco, whom they
conceive as an ancient King of Tepoztlan, they have preserved many curious legends. He was, a small Indian boy
told me, the son of the Virgin of the Nativity. Also he
was the *dios del aire*, god of the wind. He never died but
was 'enchanted'. One Midsummer Day, not so long ago, a
villager was working high up on the side of the Chalchiuh-
tepetl or Cerro del Tesoro, 'Hill of the Treasure', when
Tepozteco appeared to him at the mouth of a cave. He
was like a little tiny child but beautifully dressed. To the
astonished Indian he expressed distress that his Holy
Mother was not clad in robes more fitting to her divinity
and bade the man stir the people up to furnish her image
with suitable raiment. So the people presented the Virgen
de la Navidad with a beautiful new robe.

Later I looked for that cave without finding it, although
a small boy called Agustín Rios who piloted me about the
slopes of the Hill of the Treasure confirmed its existence
on the rugged south side of the hill overlooking San
Andres de la Cal. His father had once seen it, he said. It
was *muy feo*, 'very ugly', as was the way to it, and 'full of
ancient things'. Tepozteco was very wild and could assume human form at will, when human beings were
powerless against him. When he was not asleep in the
cave, he was making wind all round the valley.

Tepoztlan

Another version of his origin, in which the lore of the old world and the new are equally mixed, runs more or less as follows:

A sacred fire used to burn in the temple, tended by a group of vestal virgins. While sweeping out the court-yard one of these found a seed lying on the ground, which with characteristic inconsequence she put into her mouth and unintentionally swallowed. Of this seed she bore a child in all secrecy, and cast him into one of the gorges east of Tepoztlan where he was found still alive by two old people who went there to wash their clothes. The child grew up to be Tepozteco.

At this time there lived at Xochicalco, a monster called Xochicalcatl, who terrified the district far and wide and exacted each day a tribute of human flesh. When it came to the turn of Tepozteco's foster-father to be devoured, the child insisted on taking his place. If his parents saw a white cloud in the east, he told them, they would know that he had killed the monster; if a black one, that he had shared the fate of the other victims. On his way to Xochicalco, the boy collected pieces of sharp obsidian glass in a little bag. On his arrival, the monster demurred somewhat at the smallness of his meal but eventually swallowed him whole. Once inside the vast belly, like Jonah in the Whale, Tepozteco opened his bag and cut his way out with his obsidian blades, emerging into the light of day to deal the monster a death blow. It is difficult not to compare the white cloud which the parents duly beheld with the white sail with which Theseus promised to announce his safe return after slaying the Cretan Minotaur.

There is a third legend which identifies Tepozteco with one of the Ambassadors sent by Montezuma to Cortes.

155

This Ambassador is said to have been converted and after
the fall of Tenochtitlan to have accompanied the Captain
General to Tepoztlan and brought about the conversion of
the natives. In reality, however, it is difficult to see in
Tepozteco anything but the deity worshipped in the outward form of the great idol which until the coming of the
Spaniards was revered in the mountain sanctuary. Of this
idol a story is told which may owe as much to fact as to
fiction, and which accounts differently for the conversion
of the people. Soon after the Conquest, Fray Domingo de
la Anunciación came preaching among the Tlahuica.
When he reached Tepoztlan it became clear to him that
the cult of Tepoztecatl was his greatest obstacle. So devoted were the Indians to their deity (and to the 400 other
pulque gods to which according to Seler the temple was
also dedicated) that, as appears from the manuscript, 'Re-
port of Tepoztlan', prepared by order of Philip II, they
used to celebrate a feast called *Pilauana* or *Pilahuana*,
'which means intoxication in children, because during
this feast the boys would dance with the girls and they
would give each other drink until they became intox-
icated . . . being already nine to ten years old.' Indeed, the
author of this manuscript saw in the statue 'the figure of
a great debauch which a village calling itself Tepoztlan
had as a rite. . . .'

To achieve his end, Fray Domingo resorted to a device
of somewhat Old Testament flavour. He prevailed on the
Indians to cast the image over the side of the cliff. If it
was truly divine, he said, it could not of course be injured
by the fall. If, on the other hand, it broke, it could not be
divine. There is said to be a providence which looks after
drunkards, and no doubt Tepoztecatl had as good a claim
as any to its protection. Be that as it may, the statue, to

the monk's dismay, survived the fearful fall intact. Nothing daunted, Fray Domingo fell upon it with an axe and hewed it into fragments, thus getting the best of the argument. Of the subsequent fate of these fragments there are varying accounts. In one form or another, however, they seem to have gone into the building of the monastery of Tepoztlan or of that of one of the neighbouring towns. Some say they were ground up for cement for that of Oaxtepec, but an Indian assured me with confidence that there were four pieces, one of which was built into the walls of each of the monasteries of Tepoztlan, Yautepec, Oaxtepec and Tlayacapan. It would have been characteristic of the Conquest to assure the attendance of the Indians at church by just such a subordination of doctrine to expediency.

The conversion and baptism of the first Indian Christians of Tepoztlan traditionally took place at a spot called Axitla (Aztec for 'where the water rises') at the foot of the split rock called Ehecatepetl or Hill of the Wind. A small spring gushes out in the shade of an *ahuehuete* tree so ancient that it has split into two parts and must certainly have witnessed the advent of Fray Domingo. The tradition is commemorated by a cross surmounting a stone orb.

Axitla lies on the path from the pyramid to the village. It is more like a stairway than a trail. To one side the triple pinnacle called Tres Marias, the Three Maries, claws into the air. On the left, a vertical wall rises sheer above your head. At its foot the gorge is bejewelled with the purple star of *pipitzahuatl*, the flecked earrings of *aretillo cimarrón*, the blue hoods of the *flor de pollo* and the nodding rosaries of wild dahlias, pink, yellow or vermilion. The town, which from the pyramid lay at your feet like an open map, is hidden by a spur of rock. The heat grows ever more intense, for the path takes you not from one place to another but, at the same geographical point, lowers you from *tierra fria* into *tierra templada*.

Where at last it eases from a stairway to a steep slope and the crags open out to right and left a spring bubbles forth among banana trees to the left of the trail. Here in the gathering heat one may rest awhile and slake one's thirst in the comforting knowledge that none save Tepozteco himself can have defiled the water. The light is strained of all its solid burning particles by the huge green banana leaves. Between them, lying on one's back, one sees the crags floating overhead, remote and insubstantial, void of menace as the very clouds. It is one of those spots where time, like the cliffs above, seems to hang suspended. A huge butterfly drifts past, dead white, like a fluttered handkerchief. A blue-grey centipede ripples across a stone. The bushes rustle. A lizard darts out on a sunlit rock and is still:

> '. . . *my pigmy crocodile,*
> *My sleeper on a lotus isle,*
> *My elongated curling smile.*'

From the slopes immediately above it, Tepoztlan is so submerged in foliage that not a single house is visible, only the slender towers of its seven parish churches and the long crenellated roof of the monastery. Under the vertical sun, the green sea reflects a brilliant metallic glint. The broad lanes of the *pueblo* are shadowed by mango, guava, mamey and other exotic fruit trees. Delicate ferns spring from the stone walls. In the gardens 'like golden lamps in a green night' hang ripening oranges, glowing among the varied colours of blue plumbago, morning

158

glory, bougainvillea, oleander, and scarlet and pink hibiscus.

Soon after the Conquest what is now the state of Morelos was divided into three spheres of influence running from north to south and apportioned respectively to the Franciscan, Dominican and Augustinian orders. Tepoztlan fell within the zone of the Dominicans, who built the massive monastery in the second half of the sixteenth century. In spite of the period of its construction, there is something reminiscent of the simplified, stylized lines of the Romanesque and early Gothic manner in the low reliefs of the west door.

Immediately above the doorway, the Virgin Mary stands on the crescent moon with the Christ Child in her arms, flanked by St. Catherine and St. Dominic in monkish garb. Above and on either side are two angel figures supporting a stone frame bare now of the inscription which it may once have borne. The cornice over the door and the spandrels of the arch are covered with symbolical carvings, among them the sun, the moon and sacred monograms. From the roof, the House of Tepozteco is clearly visible on the skyline, crowning one of a long line of precipitous crags: the Tlahuiltepetl or 'Hill of Light', Yohuatecatl the 'Night Watchman', Ocelotepetl the 'Hill of Tigers', Cuahnectepetl the 'Hill of Honey'; and Tlacatepetl the 'Hill of Man', most recent arrival, this last, to have played a part in this wild and grandiose amphitheatre.

The women of Tepoztlan (whom Bernal Diaz found 'very good-looking') have broad faces of the conventional Aztec type, but the men have thinner, more aquiline features than most Indians, with keen eyes which narrow and show their whites as the stranger passes. On the arrival of the Spaniards, they were reputed as farmer-warriors who esteemed bravery and killed off cowards. One aspect at least of their social organization dates from pre-Spanish days. Among the most characteristic features of ancient Aztec life were the *calpullis*, into which, as into parishes or wards, the community was divided for both religious and secular purposes, each with its animal totem and communal land. Something very similar persists in Tepoztlan's seven parishes, membership of which goes by heredity rather than by residence, so that although the boundaries are clearly defined a member of the *barrio* of La Santísima may live within the bounds of Los Reyes and so on. The principal functions of membership are cultivation of the communal cornfield which is regarded as the Saint's property and contribution to the annual *fiesta*. 'The barrio as a religious organization', writes Robert Redfield, 'the central religious building, the patron-god whose image is contained within it, and elements in the accompanying ceremonial are survivals from pre-Columbian culture.'[1] Moreover, the members of each barrio bear totemistic animal nicknames, those of La Santísima being called 'ants', those of San Miguel 'lizards', those of Los Reyes 'maguey worms' and so on.

One Sunday in early summer, as we stood on the pyramid of Tepoztecatl, the steady pulsing rhythm of a drum floated up from the village below. It was not the sharp tattoo of a parchment drum but a duller sound on two alternating notes, the thud of drumsticks on the vibrant wood of a *teponaztli*. Half unconsciously my eyes turned to the sanctuary and the hieroglyphics carved on its stones. On one in particular my eyes rested, engraved with the water-sign from which, like the tentacles of an octopus,

[1]Robert Redfield: *Tepoztlan*, p. 77.

radiated jade-signs, the conventional symbol of all things precious. Precious liquid, ran the message of the hieroglyph. No liquid is more precious than blood, and blood to the Aztec mind connoted human sacrifice. Even now the ancient sacrificial drum was resounding down below in the village with that 'most accursed sound' which Bernal Diaz heard when his comrades were being done to death. The thought sent a cold shiver down my spine.

Then I remembered that Tepoztlan is one of the few remaining *pueblos* in Mexico which still possess a carved, pre-Cortesian *teponaztli* drum. To the villagers this drum is not merely a precious relic of their past but an object almost of worship, the disappearance of which would be a personal blow to every member of the community. Throughout the year it is hidden away in the house of an Indian of whose identity the enquiring stranger will be met with professions of ignorance. Three times in the year it is brought out from its hiding-place for religious *fiestas*, and it was the first of these occasions, Trinity Sunday, which we had chosen for this particular visit. The *fiesta* is a small one observed not by the whole *pueblo* but only by one of the seven parishes, that of La Santísima, the Most Holy Trinity. The church of this parish is the first which you pass on the way down from the pyramid. It is also the oldest, said to have been built by Martín Cortes (the Conqueror's son by Malinche), a simple yet gracefully proportioned example of the Renaissance style.

There were no dancers at the *fiesta*, only a brass band, a *chirimia* piper and, of course, the inevitable fireworks. No priest was present. An old woman chanted prayers, and Indians were constantly arriving with offerings of flowers. The drumming by now had stopped, and the roof from which it had come was empty. Enquiries as to when

161

it would reappear were met with polite evasiveness. 'Towards nightfall', 'when the guardian of the drum returns': these and other answers were not so much replies to our questions as attempts to put us off. And sure enough,

when we were no more than five or ten minutes walk away, the sinister tom-tomming began anew. Returning hotfoot, we found the door to the belfry locked in our faces. Heads looked down upon us from the roof, round black shadows framed in sombreros white against the brightness of the sky. No one could come up without permission from the Mayordomo of the *fiesta*, they said. By now, however, the spirit of the chase had entered into us. Where was the Mayordomo? we asked. Entertaining the band to lunch in his house. Where was his house? Ten minutes walk up the hillside. Intended though they probably were to choke off our persistence, these answers were at least the truth, and Sr. Leobardo Vargas was, in his own good time, all hospitality and helpfulness. Giving us the curious, flaccid handshake of the Indian, he bade us be seated at the long table which nearly filled his hut of adobe brick and palm thatch. We must eat with him, he

162

would brook no denial, and course after course was served to us. As chicken *mole* succeeded rice, and *frijole* beans followed on the *mole*, each with its complement of fresh, warm *tortillas*, the company at the table gradually changed. Trombones and cornets tucked under their arms, the bandsmen wandered out with belches of courteous appreciation, and the seats were filled with persons of less distinction until, being slow eaters, we found ourselves under fire from a battery of dark liquid eyes, those of a row of little white-clad boys.

As it takes diamond to cut diamond, so Indian patience can only be vanquished by a patience greater than itself, and in due course ours was rewarded. Late in the afternoon, Leobardo Vargas walked down the hill with us to the church, where his services as Mayordomo were in any case required for Vespers. The roof once again was empty and silent, as instinctively I had known that it would be. Beckoning us round to the side, however, Leobardo knocked on a small door apparently opening into the sacristy. It was opened a few inches, and a dark, suspicious face looked out. Leobardo squeezed through, and once again the door was shut. We could only guess at the colloquy which followed. Presently he emerged again and asked if we would make a contribution towards the expenses of the *fiesta*. This we did willingly. Two pesos seemed to be his idea of a suitable sum, and I think that the demand was in no way mercenary in character, but due rather to a feeling that the drum should be produced only for those who had some part in the feast and who, even if they were not Catholics, were at least willing to make an offering to *La Santísima*. Now, however, even Leobardo had difficulty in obtaining readmittance. Several times he knocked and with whispered urgency called a

163

name, Felipe! When at last Felipe opened to him the
secret conclave was renewed inside, for, as we afterwards
learned, the majority of those responsible for the care of
the drum must pronounce themselves in favour before it
can be moved. I think now that our request must have
been a very real cause of embarrassment to Leobardo, and
it is all the more to his credit that when at last he came
out, the drum and the drummer accompanied him. In a
little hurried procession, seeking to avoid notice, we made
our way on to the roof, and were at last rewarded with the
sight and sound of this remarkable instrument. Carved
out of nut-brown wood and of surprising weight, it is adorned on one side with a dancing figure, holding in one
hand a bunch of flowers and in the other a gourd rattle.
The people of Tepoztlan firmly believe this figure to represent Tepozteco himself, but archaeologists identify it
as a representation of Xochipilli, 'Prince of Flowers' and
god of music, dancing and festivity.

Of its origin a curious legend is told. Apparently, it
once belonged to the King of Cuauhnahuac (Cuernavaca).
On a certain occasion this King invited Tepoztecatl to a
banquet, together with the Kings of Yautepec, Oaxtepec,
and Tlayacapan. Tepoztecatl arrived at the feast humbly
clad, but, seeing that no one paid any attention to him,
left the table and returned clad in a robe even more splendid than those worn by the other guests. At this, all those
present rose to their feet and offered him the place of
honour. To their astonishment, however, Tepoztecatl did
not eat the rich *mole* which was the first dish offered to
him, but deliberately spilt it over his fine raiment. To
their protests he answered only that it was not the man
but the clothes that they had honoured, and that he was
but giving the clothes their due. Having thus taught

them that 'clothes do not make the man' he escaped from their wrath with the assistance of a providential whirlwind, and with the inconsequence which distinguishes most Aztec legends carried off with him the *teponaztli* and the gourd-rattle depicted on it. The ensuing fighting was apparently of such violence that it rent the mountains into their present form, thus enabling Tepoztecatl to defy his enemies from his inaccessible bastions of rock. Here, the legend concludes, he chose to dwell. Picking up a handful of dust he threw it into the air. It fell to form the pyramid which was thus constructed by no mortal mason.

Towards the end of August, the *teponaztli* makes its second annual appearance when the last work is done on the *milpa del Santo*, the communal field of the *barrio*, the proceeds of which are devoted to the expenses of the annual *fiesta*. This rite, called *la acabada*, escaped Redfield's notice. It is an important occasion. Thenceforward until the harvest the crop must be left to take care of itself. Two days are set apart, invariably a Monday and a Thursday, although the dates on which they fall depend on the stage which the crop has reached. At  seven in the morning the men and boys go out with spades and *coas* to the *milpa* which lies nearly two hours on foot from the town. The whole day they work while the *teponaztli* throbs through the standing corn and pipe and tabor shrill their music to high heaven. Meanwhile, the women

165

are not idle. The church of La Santísima is decorated. Three tall maize stalks are adorned with flowers. Baskets are filled with dahlias, hibiscus, gladioli, roses and plumbago. In the afternoon we found the women waiting for their men near a little wayside cross high under the Cerro del Tesoro. As the men trailed in from the fields one by one, hot and tired after the long day, the little girls ran to meet them with nosegays which they fastened to their spades. When all had gathered and the *teponaztli* had been drummed once more on the base of the cross, we all started back to the village in a straggling, loose-knit procession to the bursting of rockets and a gay little tune on the pipe and tabor. The three maize stalks went ahead like banners, borne by the parish elders, in the middle the new Mayordomo, one Tranquilino Martínez, with a wreath of deep purple dahlias hung round his wrinkled neck. Down through the village we went and into the church where the maize stalks were laid before the altar. Here we paused for a few moments in prayer while deafening petards were let off outside and the drum beat its last tattoo. All had been done for the crop which human hands could do, and now it was commended to the care of the Almighty.

The *teponaztli's* third emergence from its hiding-place falls only about two weeks later, on September 8th, the anniversary of a legendary incident commemorated in an Aztec play written under the influence of early Catholic missionaries and performed annually on this day. When Tepoztlan accepted Christianity, runs the legend, the Lords of Cuernavaca, Yautepec, Oaxtepec and Tlayacapan came in arms against the converted Tepozteco in defence of the old faiths. Tepozteco, who was piously celebrating the Nativity of the Virgin, successfully defied them.

The play is known as *El Reto* (The Challenge) *del*

166

Tepoztlan

Tepozteco. All day the little town remained singularly quiet while beyond the mountains dancers and pilgrims thronged to Los Remedios, Cholula and many a smaller sanctuary of the Virgin. The play was supposed to begin at five, but twilight was falling before the crowd began to gather in front of a small stone stage just above the market square, with an ancient idol and two rings from the *tlachtli* ball-game cemented into it. On the stage stood the *teponaztli*, reverberating under the drummer's sticks with the monotonous rhythm in which the children pretend to hear the Aztec words: *Totonki, totonki, totonki, tamali, tamali, tamali* (hot, hot, hot, tamales, tamales, tamales). While we were waiting I was invited to try my hand at playing it, an honour which can have been paid to few strangers, least of all foreigners. It seemed that I had advanced in the *pueblo's* confidence since I had first sought out the drum sixteen months before.

All the light had gone from the sky when at last the performance began. Dressed in a very fair home-made representation of ancient Aztec costume with a bow, a shield and a plumed headdress, Tepozteco appeared on the stage supported by a number of his henchmen. Immediately, another figure sprang out from among the shadows, the Lord of Cuernavaca. Silhouetted against the flares, he struck an attitude before the stage and cried in a loud voice: *Tehtepetlan chane!* O Dweller in the Hills. Then in a challenging voice, he continued in the tongue of his forefathers:

> *Temolo in Cuauhnahuac;*
> *Amachi timomahtia*
> *In ticaqui noteyo notlahtol:*
> *Nican onihuala*

167

Tepoztlan

Nimitzpohpoloco
Tlalli huan tehtli
Nimitzcuepaco,
Nimitzcuepaz cemihcapan
Pampa huel niyolahpaltic
Ihuan ni yolohchicahuac
Ca noteyo ica nohuian
Nohnohuian moyectenehua
Nicchicahua noyollo.

'The Lord of Cuernavaca seeks thee. Why dost thou summon me? Fearest thou not to hear my voice and my words? I have come hither to encompass thy ruin. Into earth and dust will I grind thee. I am strong, I am powerful. Tell me where thou hast fame, and I will blot it out with this strong and warlike heart, so that it is lost for ever and ever.'

So saying, he shot an arrow over Tepozteco's head and was lost again in the darkness. In turn the three other Lords followed him, challenging Tepozteco in the same words.

When they had done, Tepozteco answered them in angry and contemptuous terms, yet with a somewhat gentler note in his voice as befits one who has embraced the teaching of Christ. Nevertheless, the four Lords returned to their challenge, reproaching Tepozteco for having abandoned the old gods and sold himself to the foreigner.

Tepozteco now answered each of them separately. Cuernavaca, he cried, is a coward to have come on a day of rest and pleasure, the day of 'Mary, Eternal Virgin, white and lovely Mother of God', to whom he owes his strength and wisdom. Has Yautepec not seen that Tepoztlan is protected by four steep hills, seven deep valleys,

168

seven chasms and four dark caves? How sad it is that Oaxtepec is still blind and will not see the light. Does Tlayacapan not recall how at Cuernavaca Tepozteco defied them all and wrested the *teponaztli* from them? As though to remind them of this humiliation the drum is heard and there is a brief interlude of dance. Then, in a long homily, with elaborately stylized pose and gesture Tepozteco expounds to them the mysteries of the Christian Faith. His eloquence has the desired effect. When he has finished, Cuernavaca exclaims that at last he has seen the truth. He expresses his gratitude, craves Tepozteco's forgiveness and states that he and his companions are ready to accept baptism. 'Oh happy day!' exclaims Tepozteco. 'May it never be forgotten. We will forgive one another like good brothers, like true believers. Let us all dance for joy and happiness.'

X. The Flying Game

The pursuit of *fiestas* was not always equally rewarding. Some, sought out at the expense of time and trouble, proved to have changed their date or to have been dropped altogether. On the whole, however, fortune generally smiled on us where the Otomis were concerned. True, when we went in 1937 to the Señor de las Maravillas at El Arenal, the most interesting feature of the festival was missing. In other years a group of Indians have been known in fulfilment of a *promesa* to fasten a cable from the belfry of the church and to 'fly' down it, holding with their teeth a handkerchief knotted round it, or, in the case of women, fastened by their hair.

On the other hand we were not disappointed of seeing the curious rite performed on Ash Wednesday at the sanctuary of the Santo Niño del Puerto, at Puertezuela near Ixmiquilpan. Like El Arenal, Puertezuela lies in the Mesquital, a waste of iron-grey hills and shallow valleys shaggy with cactus of every conceivable variety. Only a hundred miles from the capital, the Mesquital is a foretaste of the desert north. There is no water in the heaven above or in the earth beneath. To Puertezuela it has to be brought ten miles. We could see no maize-fields round the hamlet. There are no vegetables or fruit other than the prickly pear. Only of maguey aloes is there an abundance, and to the Otomis of the Mesquital *pulque* is food as well as drink.

Ten years ago this region held little or no communication with the outside world, and its inhabitants did not welcome those few strangers who found their way there on horseback. Now the Laredo Highway cuts straight through it, and Mexico has discovered the Mesquital and is taking steps to alleviate its misery. In time no doubt the whole lives and outlook of the people will be changed, but for the present they remain the most unkempt and uncouth even of the Otomi. From their tiny huts of aloe leaves they gathered at the church on that brilliant morning to receive a sprig of blessed rosemary and with it to asperge their heads with holy water. They then stayed to see the ceremony of the *corta gallos*.

The *gallos* proved to be *gallinas*, hens with miniature wreaths of golden cempoalxochitl blooms round their necks, and were carried piously by the young girls of the village. With them went two drummers; an old woman with a copal incense burner; a Standard Bearer, his banner a patchwork of square brocades; and two men with smaller flags, one red, one white. In the church, before the altar, they all knelt to the four points of the compass in turn and made the sign of the cross three times each with his or her burden. This they repeated at the church door, and again outside the church precincts before two organ cactus stumps at one end of what in less arid lands might have been the village green.

It was now more than clear that the hens were propitiary offerings, but nothing could have been more extra-ordinary than the manner of their immolation.

The drummers continued to beat a monotonous tattoo each at one of the beflagged cactus stumps. The Standard Bearer disappeared to have a drink, while the little knot of girls walked round and round the square in the manner

of passengers on a transatlantic liner conscientiously per-ambulating their daily mile. Suddenly a number of young men ran out, their cottons rolled up to the knee, and abruptly the whole spirit of the proceedings changed from religious piety to carnivalesque abandon. Where the boys ran, the girls pursued them, flinging the miserable trussed hens at their fleeing backs. When occasionally the missile reached its mark, the exploit was greeted with hilarious acclamations from the onlookers. Mercifully, the hens did not long survive this barbarous treatment, but their mere death was not enough. Through the whole long afternoon the fantastic game was kept up. Then the girls lined up once more and went in procession to throw the bruised and battered remains into the branches of a

Seven-Snake Mask

Tiger dancers

St. Dominic's Genealogical Vine, Oaxaca

Mitla

Mountain Zapotecs

Making Ixtle rope (Sierra Juarez)

Girl at Yalalag

Zapotec Sombrero

Mije Country

Lake Patzcuaro

Butterfly Net at Uranden

Bringing *petates* to Patzcuaro

mesquite tree against the churchyard wall. Here, I was assured, they would remain for days, untouched even by those voracious scavengers, the *zopilote* buzzards.

This extraordinary custom is repeated on the following day at the neighbouring village of Panales, where, by way of a change, it is the boys who attack the girls, and the hens are made into a dish of *mole*, on which the villagers, less squeamish than the buzzards, proceed to feast. It is difficult so much as to guess at its origin; less so at that of the infinitely more spectacular Flying Game.

When Mrs. Larsen discovered that Otomis of the Sierra

de Puebla still practised the ancient *juego de los voladores* it came as news to the archaeological authorities who were at first incredulous. It was known that this remarkable ceremony, depicted in pre-Spanish Aztec codices, still survived among the Totonacs, but that the neighbouring tribe had adopted it with certain modifications was a real discovery. Within less than a month of my first arrival in Mexico I was fortunate enough to have an opportunity of confirming it.

From Mexico City the high plateau continues for many miles eastwards at a mean height of 7,500 feet. Across the monotonous landscape of dusty mountains and wide plains diapered with maguey plantations a little train winds past Tulancingo to the station of Honey, named after the Cornish family who have mined in Mexico for several generations. To all appearances interminable, the plateau comes to an end with dramatic suddenness. Pine-woods clothe the brink. Emerging from them one looks down into a deep canyon, its bed vivid with the green of sugar-cane, banana, orange and coffee. To the north-east the valley opens out towards Tampico and the Gulf of Mexico, at which the disintegrated plateau points the long fingers of promontories shelving away until they are engulfed in the sea of tropical vegetation. Built in an amphitheatre on one such jutting spur is the town of Pahuatlan, attainable only on foot or on horseback.

It took us half a day winding backwards and forwards on the steep trail to reach the little *pueblo*. Gradually the ribs of the plateau climbed up into the sky, transformed in this inverted landscape into towering mountains cutting off valley from valley. In the brilliant afternoon light their shadows fell across Indian hamlets framed in green fields of maize and sugar-cane, Otomi on the far side of the valley, Aztec on the near. Interrupting their flow of vernacular speech with a friendly *Buenas tardes*, Indians passed us on the road while with a drop of hundreds of feet below we hugged the inside of the trail. The air grew warmer and lost the thin, sharp bite of the *meseta*. Flowers appeared in the undergrowth and flowering bushes beside the trail: wild begonias, yellow calceolaria, the white trumpets of the poisonous *floripundio* and others to which we could give no name. The sun had sunk behind the western wall, and a soft dusk was falling when at last we rounded a steep escarpment and came in sight of an amphitheatre of white houses, flanked and overhung by gardens and orchards climbing the hillside.

In a side street we found an anonymous *hotelito*, bare,

primitive in its sanitary arrangements but with clean beds. The proprietor was one Don Calixto of the *Barrio de Triana* grocer's shop. Its maid-of-all-work was Felix, a cherubic Indian boy of fourteen with a smile like a split calabash.

There was no special *fiesta* in Pahuatlan that week-end in mid-December. Through the kindness of Don Mario Abogado, the Mayor, we had been able to arrange for the Otomi Indians of Huehuetlilla (one of the villages which we had seen on the way down) to perform specially for our benefit in order that data might be collected and photographs and cinema films taken without the fluster and inconvenience unavoidable at any important festivity.

We had reckoned without the weather, however. On the day of our arrival it looked as though it could never rain again. Now, however, we were no longer on the rainless tableland but in *tierra templada* at about 4,000 feet where, on the Atlantic slopes, the weather is notoriously uncertain. During the night one of the dreaded 'northers' swept the Gulf, the valley filled with cloud like a seething cauldron, and we awoke in the famous *chipi-chipi*, a drizzle which not only dismayed the photographers but, by wetting the ropes on which the *juego de los voladores* depends and making them slippery and dangerous, jeopardized our chances of seeing anything at all.

After a dispiriting breakfast the *voladores* came to our lodging and discussed their chances and ours. There was nothing to do but to wait in the hope of an improvement in the weather, and I spent the time taking down from the musician one or two of the tunes associated with the performance.

After lunch the clouds swirling through the streets lifted a few hundred feet up the hillside. The rain stopped.

175

The Flying Game

On the roofs rows of *zopilotes* dried their drenched wings. The *voladores* gallantly expressed themselves ready to fly, and changed into their festal costume. Over their white cottons they pulled scarlet knee-breeches with lace fringes and fastened little aprons of the same colour. Round both shoulders they tied bandana handkerchiefs which crossed bandoleerwise on chest and back, and on their heads they wore scarlet bérets. Five out of six were dressed thus, one  carrying a three-holed pipe with a tabor slung over his arm, and the others *sonajas*, gourd rattles filled with pebbles like the *maracas* of a Cuban rumba band. The sixth represented Malinche and was dressed as a woman in a red skirt with a white *quexquemitl* and a head-kerchief. In his hand he carried a handkerchief and a painted gourd-bowl.

We gathered in the porticoed plaza of the village where a dejected little market was being held, the vendors protected against the wet by reed cloaks or by banana leaves spread over their heads and backs. In the middle the *palo volador* towered into the sky, a stripped pine trunk eighty feet high, buried eight or ten feet in the ground, its base supported by boards and wire. A long liana had been freshly wound round the pole to afford a foothold, and the *tecomate* (literally 'gourd'), the name given to the apparatus on which the

176

performance depends, had been newly placed in position. Of this a careful description is necessary in order that the reader may understand how the *voladores* fly. It consists of a wooden, mortar-shaped cap, about a foot high and two feet in diameter, hollowed out so that it fits on to the top of the pole. This cap forms, as it were, the hub of a hexagonal wooden frame which hangs from it by cords fastened to the angles. Round the top of the mast, just below the cap are wound six ropes, each long enough when unwound to reach almost to the ground.

When all was ready the six *voladores* climbed up the pole and ensconced themselves on the six sides of the frame, facing inwards. The pipe-and-taborer struck up a thin, rhythmic little tune, and one of the others clambered on to the top of the cap. Then, on that miniature platform, he proceeded to execute a stamping, jumping dance of unmistakably Indian character, shaking his gourd-rattle in time with the music. He must have danced for nearly ten minutes at that dizzy height, as, each in his turn, did the four others, the musician handing over his instruments to another player when his turn came. Last of all, Malinche, though hampered by 'her' skirt, clambered up like the rest and danced for fully twice as long, moving her gourd and handkerchief rhythmically from side to side. The last part of her dance included a perilous movement in which, at intervals, she stooped down on one knee and passed her kerchief over the head of each of the others.

Now all had danced, and the moment came for the climax of the whole performance, the descent. Carefully the *voladores* fastened round their waists the ends of the ropes wound round the pole. Gingerly they stepped backwards and outwards over the frame, grasping it with their hands and resting their feet against the pole. For a moment they paused, looking like some great white and scarlet tulip bud. Then the bud burst into flower. At a given signal its six human petals flung themselves outwards and downwards into space. Their weight set the cap slowly revolving on the top of the pole, and as its revolutions unwound the ropes the *voladores* were whirled round in ever-widening circles. As they swung clear of the framework all except Malinche grasped the ropes between their feet so that they continued the flight head downwards, the musician never ceasing for an instant to play his pipe-and-tabor or the others to shake their gourd-rattles.

Lower and lower they flew. Except for the music and the menacing creaks of the pole, all was still in the market square. In the crowd broad Indian faces were upturned, framed as in a halo by wide *sombrero* brims. Obsidian eyes concentrated in a stare. 'Now there's no fear the pole will snap', said an appraising voice when they were more than half-way down. A moment or two later their blood-suffused faces were swept only a few feet over our heads. Then, when it seemed that they must be dashed against the ground, they let go the ropes with their feet, righted themselves and landed lightly as children on a Giant Stride. The flight had taken just about two minutes.

The weather remained dull and lowering, but on our way back to Honey we had the opportunity of seeing another Indian ceremonial dance at the Aztec village of Santa Catarina, called the Acatlaxque or Reed Throwing Dance. The dancers, a dozen or so in number, were dressed like the *voladores* but with conical headdress. They carried bundles of ten or a dozen reeds adorned with coloured feathers and lightly fastened together with slip knots, the purpose of which only became apparent as the

178

dance progressed. They, too, had their Malinche, a small boy dressed in a pink skirt and white *quexquemitl* embroidered in red in a pre-Spanish design. In addition to the kerchief and gourd bowl he carried in his hand a skilfully articulated silver snake.

First, the reed-carriers danced in a row facing the open church door, alternately advancing and retreating with a clumsy hopping step punctuated by a little reverence and a right-about turn. This concession to Christianity completed, they formed a circle round Malinche, and it was to 'her' and her silver snake that they danced and addressed their reverences. Next came a figure in which, in ones and twos, they danced out from their places and round the little Man-Woman. Finally, two of them fetched a sort of wooden stretcher on which they hoisted the dancing Malinche. The purpose of the reeds was now revealed. Each in turn the dancers deftly threw out their bunches so that these extended like telescopic fishing rods and formed a sort of crown or arbour over the central figure, which rotated as the dancing circle slowly moved round. Of the significance of this act of obvious worship they have not conserved the slightest notion, but it appears to me to be almost certainly bound up with the fact that the great fifty-two year cycles of the Aztec religious calendar were called 'sheafs' or 'bundles' and were represented hieroglyphically by a quantity of reeds bound together by a string.

To return to the *volador*, information which I was able to obtain in Pahuatlan, coupled with the generous hospitality of Mr. Cecil James at Apulco, enabled me to see the performance again two months later in brilliant sunshine at Metepec, just over the border of the State of Hidalgo. It was the *fiesta* of the Cristo de Metepec, and there was plenty to distract us, so much so that we spent two whole days within the scalloped walls of the churchyard, fascinated by the unending procession of shaggy men in cottons and sarapes; of dark women in *quexquemitls*, scarlet and white from Otomi Santa Ana or embroidered with the flowing patterns in red and blue of the Aztec villages; of grave children whom their parents crossed with holy water in the church porch. The flying game, here, was not, like the last, an arranged performance, but a purely spontaneous act in fulfilment of a vow, attended by one or two features which had been omitted at Pahuatlan. Thus a new character in ordinary clothes but with a sooty

face, called the Negrito, was there to protect the pole from evil influences. With this object he carried a whip and a stuffed *cacomixtli* skunk, the former conceived no doubt as operating by the power of noise and the latter by that of smell.

Three or four hours down the valley from Pahuatlan is Santa Maria near Tlacuilotepec, the first village inhabited by Totonacs, a big tribe whose territory includes part of the Sierra de Puebla and the lowlands of northern Vera Cruz. A branch of the great Maya family they have the small stature, the oriental appearance and the spotless cleanliness of that race.

180

The Flying Game

Our first contact with them was at Papantla in the state of Vera Cruz on the day of Corpus Christi when they perform the *juego de los voladores* in a manner even closer to the ancient original than the Otomis. The usual way of getting to Papantla is to make one's way by road or rail to the edge of the tableland and then to ride for three days dropping all the while to *tierra caliente*. This is how I should have liked to do it, for to my mind you cannot properly appreciate the spirit and character of a place if you have skipped all that leads up to it. But in that month of June 1936 I was too busy to be able to leave Mexico City for more than twenty-four hours, so our trip was a flying one in every sense of the word.

The alternative to the three-day journey to Papantla is one lasting precisely an hour, the time it took Herr Fritz Bieler to cover the 135 miles between the two landing-grounds. We could scarcely have had a less auspicious start. It was a grey, cheerless morning, the kind that ushers the rainy season in or out with low scudding clouds driving in from the east and likely to be thicker on the coast. A friend in Papantla Sr. Ramon Castañeda had actually telegraphed to us not to come, but, fortunately as it turned out, the wire did not arrive in time. After bumping over Lake Texcoco and the pyramids we rose steeply through the clouds and at 13,000 feet were in sunshine and blue sky with calm cirrus, looking down on a white woolly sea through which we caught only an occasional glimpse of blue-brown plain or, once over the edge, of deep canyon with the great cascade of Necaxa to give us our bearings. As we approached the coast the weather cleared. Below was rolling country, covered with dense vegetation, with occasional clearings here and there where six or eight huts marked a lonely Totonac *rancheria*.

181

The Flying Game

Following the windings of a river, we were soon swinging over the little white *pueblo* lost in a sea of green, and falling as it seemed like a stone on to a landing-ground, no bigger than a pocket-handkerchief, hewn out of the living jungle.

Cars met us. With the aid of chains, and then only with difficulty, had they got through on tracks deep in mud from the town several miles away. Once again we heard the same sad story. The torrential rain which had fallen in the night had soaked the ropes of the *volador*, and the flight would only take place in the late afternoon if at all.

We made the best of matters by spending the middle of the day in visiting the Tajin pyramid, one of the most remarkable archaeological remains in the whole country. The way led through fairly open country with lush vegetation, tree-ferns and a thousand tropical plants which were unknown to us. As for the tracks, only a 'flivver' with chains on its wheels could have got through. The site of the Tajin is a remarkable one. Hills a few hundred feet high, covered with undergrowth, surround it. On one side of this natural bowl, as though to emphasize the contrast between the old and the new, the gaunt framework of a solitary oil well points to the sky, like a skeleton picked bare by *zopilotes*. All around are little green mounds with the unmistakable lines of pyramids as yet uncovered. In the centre stands El Tajin, with its seven superimposed tiers and its 365 niches, corresponding to the days of the year. A few hundred yards away new excavations were on foot, and the drums of stone columns carved with an Eagle warrior, a serpent, a priest, or a sacrificial scene had been thrown up to the earth's surface.

All this while, the day had been clearing. The sun was now shining, and by the time we reached Papantla the ropes had dried and the *tocotines* as they are here called, were preparing for their performance. Their costume did not vary greatly from that which we had seen among the Otomis, except for the headdress which was pointed, adorned with mirrors and artificial flowers, and surmounted by fan-shaped crests, a faint reminder no doubt of the bird costume worn by their ancestors, the wings of which have probably shrunk into the bandoleer kerchiefs.

We had, of course, missed the preparations for the ceremony. Whereas the Otomi pole, of some kind of fir, stands for two or three years until it rots, the Totonac pole, made of a tree known as *palo volador*, is planted anew on each occasion. A few days before, five hundred Indians had gone into the jungle and chosen as straight as possible a tree of the necessary height. To measure the height they had paced off the required length along the ground, turned their backs on the tree and looked at it between their legs. Selecting one of which the top just showed from this unconventional viewpoint they had felled it, lopped off the branches and using no other gear than liana ropes had hauled it with songs and shouts into the town. There it had been planted in a deep hole in the ground into which, with a ritual more pagan than Christian, a strange assortment of sacrificial objects had first been thrown; hard-boiled eggs, sugar-cane brandy, tamales, pieces of cloth and a dead hen, all to propitiate the pole lest it should 'devour men'. (Among the Otomis a live turkey is buried in the hole as an offering whenever a new pole is set up). They had danced before it, and finally, lest propitiation should be insufficient, had used a sterner form of persuasion and sought to intimidate it by a public whipping.

When they made their appearance the *tocotines* directed their steps to the church and danced first in a line and then in a circle before the porch. There were nine of them, and it was evident that not all would fly, for the frame of the *volador* here had only four sides and not six. They had no Malinche but were accompanied by a character called Pilatos (Pilate) who, in spite of his change of name was clearly the equivalent of the *Negrito* of Metepec. He wore a nigger mask, ordinary clothes and a battered straw hat of the 'gent's boater' type, and straddled a horse-headed stick. His clownish antics attracted to him the gibes and the stones of all the small boys.

Making the pole the next object of their dance, the *tocotines* paid homage to pagan as they had to Christian symbolism. Then four of them, including the pipe-and-taborer, scaled the pole, which was less high but whippier and more crooked than those of the sierra. The musician clambered straight on to the cap, here called *manzana* (apple) and no more than a foot in diameter. His place on the fourth side of the frame was filled by Pilatos. Then, while the remaining *tocotines* circled ceremoniously round the foot of the pole, the musician, seated on the cap, began to play and at the same time to sway backwards and forwards eventually leaning back on his perch till his head was level with his feet and it seemed that he must fall head over heels to destruction. Not content with this, he climbed to his feet and danced as the men of Huehuetlilla had danced, but continuing to play his instruments. When the moment came for the flight he seated himself once more and resumed his gymnastics on the rapidly revolving cap, as his four companions, flinging and lunging about in the air, were carried in spirals down to the ground.

It was with a feeling of relief that we saw him at last climb down the pole and reach safety. People in the crowd had criticized him for not leaping high enough during his dance. Two years before, the man who took his part had leapt a good ten inches into the air. It was true that he had fallen from the top and been killed. But then the *voladores* were expected to take their lives in their hands. Eight or ten years ago the pole snapped during the flight and all five were killed. The dancer-musician is chosen a year in advance, and during that whole year he is treated with special consideration, overwhelmed with attentions and granted his slightest wish. This is done in order that if he is killed he may not die with any desire unfulfilled and it equates him with many an annual sacrificial victim who died in the person of the god, that of Tezcatlipoca, for instance.

So fascinating is the *juego de los voladores*, and so obviously a purely pagan ceremony except in the occasion of its performance that some account of its history and probable meaning must be given. In two Aztec codices, those of Porfirio Diaz and of Fernandez Leal, both dating from about the time of the Conquest, it is clearly depicted. Surrounded by date-signs and other hieroglyphics the pole stands straight up with a four sided frame hanging from the top. Since the ancients had no notion of perspective the frame is depicted vertically instead of horizontally, in order that its shape may be apparent, and in the second of the two codices the *voladores* themselves are shown with bird-like headdresses ready to fly. Bernal Diaz saw the flight and Durán briefly mentions it, but the first connected account and explanation comes from the pen of Fray Juán de Torquemada who wrote his book *De la Monarquía Indiana* in 1612. His description shows that at Papantla the performance has changed scarcely at all, the only differences being that the flyers used to clothe them-

185

selves as 'various birds, that is to say some assuming the
form of eagles, others of griffons and others of other birds
representative of greatness and nobility'; and that some
eight or ten other dancers accompanied them to the top of
the pole and slid down the ropes when the flight was near-
ing its end.

It is when he comes to consider the meaning of the custom that Torquemada is most illuminating. 'I think this
contraption was invented by the Devil', he writes, 'to
keep these his false servants and devotees in fresher and
more continuous memory of his infernal and abominable
service; for it was a reminder of the fifty-two years which
they reckoned to their century, at the end of which cycle
of years they renewed with the new fire which they took
out their pact and agreement which they had made with
the Devil to serve him as many years in the time to come.'
It would be difficult to find a better illustration of the
principle that the deities of one age of belief are the devils
of the next, for the fifty-two year cycle known as the
xiuhtonalli was closely bound up with the complex Indian
religion, and, as Torquemada points out, the four flyers
made up this number by each describing thirteen circles
round the pole.

'This flight', he continues, 'did not cease at the time of
the Conquest and Implantation of the Faith in these
Indies; rather did it continue until the monks, ministers
of God, discovered the secret and prohibited most rigorously that it should be done. But after the death of the
first idolators who had received the faith, and the sons
who followed them having forgotten the idolatry which it
signified, they have returned to the flight and performed
it on many occasions; and . . . no longer care whether the
palos voladores are fourfold, and thus they make them

sixfold . . . and hang from them six ropes . . . not caring whether the circles are only thirteen in number for according as the poles . . . are great or small so are the circles many or few which they describe round them.'

From the eighty-foot pole of Pahuatlan the total number of circles described was twenty-two, and even at Papantla they exceeded thirteen. But whether indeed the Indians have quite forgotten the significance of the custom may be judged from a remark made to us by one of the flyers at Pahuatlan: 'We fly six nowadays to make a better show, but we should really be four, for we are the sacred birds who fly with the four winds to the four cardinal points.' Not only does this remark show that the tradition of four flying instead of six has been remembered among the Otomis as well as preserved by the Totonacs, but the association of the flyers with the four points of the compass throws further light on the religious implications of the custom. Like the fifty-two year cycle the cardinal points or 'world directions' played an important part in Mexican religious symbolism, thirteen of the years in each cycle being apportioned to each of them. It may be added that in some cases the pre-Conquest Indians reckoned not four but six world directions, including the zenith and the nadir.

Torquemada witnessed the ceremony in Mexico City, where a square near the Zócalo still bears to this day the name of Plaza del Volador. For reasons into which it is unnecessary to enter here its originators were probably those same Totonacs who still practise it most assiduously to-day. In their language it is known as the game of the *lakas* (macaws), though it seems more likely that the bird originally represented was the *quetzalcoxcoxtli* or Crested Quetzal (*Gallinae Penolepe Purpurascens*) sacred to

187

Xochipilli, god of music, dance and revelry, which is often represented in ancient Totonac sculpture and still frequents parts of the Sierra de Puebla.[1]

Neither Torquemada nor Clavijero, who described the *juego de los voladores* in the eighteenth century, make any mention of extraneous figures such as Malinche, Pilatos and the Negrito, who may, to adopt the simplest explanation, owe their presence in it to a confusion of ideas. The Negrito is clearly no more than the Folk Fool or Devil who accompanies countless Indian dances. Pilatos appears to combine the Negrito's role with a name taken from one protagonist of the Dance of Moors and Christians and with a hobby-horse stick taken from the other. Even Malinche may only have strayed from the Dance of the Conquest in which her presence can so much more reasonably be explained.

Yet, I am not so sure about Malinche. In Europe, where the Man-Woman character is universal in ritual dance from Greece to the British Isles,[2] she has generally a name, such as Maid Marion, which does not so much account for her presence as seek to explain it away, and is obviously less archaic than its bearer. What if the name Malinche had only been given after the Conquest to a Man-Woman who had existed for long before? In another part of this book I have mentioned some of the associations which seem to cluster round the Malinche volcano and the historical figure from which it is named. In Aztec belief each of the four world directions was connected with certain of the gods, the west being, as Mr. T. A. Joyce points out in his *Mexican Archaeology*, 'the home of the female

[1] See Dr. Walter Krickeberg: *Los Totonaca*. Mexico. 1933. p. 73.
[2] For numerous examples of the Man-Woman in Europe, see Violet Alford and Rodney Gallop: *The Traditional Dance*. London. 1935. pp. 86, 98 etc.

188

deities, especially the fertility goddesses.' This alone might suffice to explain the presence of a female figure among these 'sacred birds who fly with the four winds to the four cardinal points'.

We have yet to account for the handkerchief, the gourd bowl and (at Santa Catarina) the silver snake which Malinche carries. By a stroke of good fortune Papantla yielded the missing clue. Although the *volador* had no Malinche, one accompanied another dance which was going on at the same time, the *Danza de los Negritos*. Dressed as a bride with a veil and wreath this Malinche carried the same three objects, but the snake was inside the bowl and the handkerchief covered it. At the end of the performance, the bowl was uncovered, the snake fell out on to the ground, and the Indians made pretence to beat it to death. In the very similar *Danza de la Culebra* at Huehuetla it is Malinche herself who kills the snake.

Throughout Central and South America the serpent is the emblem of the lightning, rain and rain gods. The circular eyes which are the distinguishing mark of the Tlaloc rain gods are themselves symbolic of coiled snakes, though they are generally stylized into plain rings. Of this association of ideas there are some fascinating survivals in modern Mexico. In many regions, for instance, the people believe that every natural spring is inhabited by a serpent, generally horned, which keeps the water flowing and which resents being disturbed.

When it is remembered that a high male official at the religion-dominated Court of Montezuma was known as the 'Serpent-Woman' and when the Serpent-Goddesses of far-off Minoan Crete are recalled one begins to have some inkling of the ideas for which a pre-Conquest 'Malinche' may have stood.

XI. Morelos and Guerrero

In the 290 miles of its length the highway from Mexico
City to the Pacific at Acapulco crosses seven mountain
ranges. The first, naturally enough, is that which en-
circles the Valley of Mexico. The road runs out through
the gardens of Churubusco and Tlalpam, skirting the
Pedregal and climbs swiftly beneath the shadow of Mt.
Ajusco to a broad, undulating upland of pines, tufa rock
and dry, tufted zacate grass. Like the Puebla and Toluca
roads, it attains a height of 10,000 feet.

These lonely mountain tops long enjoyed an unenvia-
ble reputation for brigandage, practised less by outlaw
bands than by local Indians who resumed their appearance of peaceful peasants as soon as the soldiers appeared
on the scene. Sometimes, too, the soldiers took to brigandage on their own account. Tyler who travelled to Cuernavaca eighty years ago, describes his feelings on passing a

spot 'from which forty men had rushed out and plundered the Diligence just ten days before'. His worst fears appeared to have been realized when he caught sight of 'some twenty wild-looking fellows in all sorts of strange garments with the bright sunshine gleaming on the barrels of their muskets'. They turned out to be only the guard, however, 'and such a guard! Their thick matted black hair hung about over their low foreheads and wild brown faces. Some had shoes, some had none, and some had sandals. They had straw hats, glazed hats, no hats, leather jackets and trousers, cotton shirts and drawers, or drawers without any shirt at all; and . . . what looked worst of all . . . some had ragged old uniforms on, like deserters from the army, and there are no worse robbers than they.' To-day things have changed, and in order that the casinos, bathing-pools and pleasure-gardens of Cuernavaca may be safe for democracy, the road is patrolled by spruce little Indian soldiers in neat khaki uniforms.

Just before the village of Tres Marias the road begins to drop, slowly at first, then rapidly, and not far beyond the village, the traveller is vouchsafed his first breath-taking glimpse of the wide valley of Morelos.

I have seen that view many times in every variation of season and weather, but I shall always remember it one day early in the wet season. As so often happens at that time of year, a pall of cloud lay on the mountains, and it had been drizzling at the top of the pass. Suddenly, as the car swept downwards in wide curves, the curtain of cloud lifted to reveal the bowl of Morelos far below, bathed in brilliant sunshine, pin clear to the far *sierras* away in Guerrero and Oaxaca. Cutting out the high light from the sky, the cloud curtain gave the land a jewelled brilliance,

191

blue and green and gold, which no words could hope to convey.

In about fifteen miles the road drops over four thousand feet to Cuernavaca, twisting and turning along a wooded hillside yellow in winter with Alpine mimosa and with the cistus-like blossoms of the *tronadora*, an infusion of which is said to kill a man or make him mad six months later, when he can no longer recall whose was the hand which administered the potion.

Of Cuernavaca, the ancient Cuauhnahuac of which the Spaniards could make nothing better than their equivalent of 'cow-horn', I do not find it easy to write. It is attractive, too attractive for a place so easily accessible from Mexico City, and it has become the Mecca of week-enders, devotees of a cult which spells death to the *genius loci*. Outspread at the foot of the mountains on a broad valley-floor gently tilted towards the south, it enjoys the perfect climate of Mexican *tierra templada*. In consequence, the golden sixteenth century cathedral, Cortes' Palace, the Borda gardens, the old colonial houses embowered in purple and crimson bougainvillea and misty blue jacaranda trees, have been swamped by what the Mexicans call *tijuanización*. Tijuana is a place just across the border from the United States in Lower California, which has been developed as a Mexican resort for Californians to the point that the word has become synonymous with that somewhat meretricious and self-conscious cultivation of the picturesque which accompanies the development of tourist traffic all over the world. Cuernavaca's villas are good Santa Monica, but what place has Santa Monica in Morelos?

I may sound ungrateful to the place which has yielded me many hours of rest and recuperation from the strain of life at 7,500 feet. But that is not so. In fact, what I have most enjoyed at Cuernavaca have been the week-end houses and gardens of my friends, their deck-chairs, swimming-pools, detective novels and iced drinks. Paradoxically, I have gone to Cuernavaca not to find Mexico but, on the rare occasions when I have so wished, to escape from it, to lotus-eat in luxury and to contemplate the palms, the blue mountains, the flaming sunsets, with the aloofness of a theatre-goer confronted by a drama in which he has no part.

From Cuernavaca, the main road slopes down towards a brown range of mountains, wrinkled with age and erosion. Now winding down the side of an undivined canyon, now running free across wide, empty stretches, it drops steadily but so imperceptibly that it is with surprise that the traveller learns at Puente de Ixtla, three quarters of an hour further on, that he is only 3,000 feet above the sea, in *tierra caliente*.

Bordered by blue hills, the slanting plain of Morelos assumes in winter the colour of stubble after harvest, broken only by occasional touches of emerald where a precious thread of water runs along the bottom of a cactus bordered ravine. The first rains of summer blacken the volcanic soil, and bring the vivid young green sprouting through, with white clad figures scattered over the face of the land to hold the composition together. The villages are invisible, their presence betrayed only by the orchards of mango, guava, zapote and mamey in which they are hidden. These villages vary extraordinarily in atmosphere as though the few miles which separate each from the next formed an inviolable frontier. Some, like Xochitepec breathe an atmosphere of dejection and decay. A ruined sugar refinery suggests that for generations its people

193

worked under the broiling sun in the sugar-cane fields, slaving for the hard taskmasters depicted by Diego Rivera in the frescoes bequeathed by Ambassador Morrow to the Palace of Cortes in Cuernavaca. No less ruined are many of the houses of the little *pueblo*, wrecked by the revolution which redeemed it. The 'Hill of the Flowers' from which it took its name bears every appearance of having been an artificial pyramid, but on the day I scrambled up, it boasted no flowers but the scrawny *zopilote* buzzards, scavenging in the municipal rubbish dump which crowns the eminence. Down in the *plaza* a *pulquería* bears the name of *La Ilusión del Sueño*. Is even sleep only an illusion here, to be painfully attained through intoxication? A tragic place, whose sorrows are reflected in the faces of its people.

Only a few miles away stands Xoxocotla, an arcadian paradise where Aztec is still spoken and the people lead unchanged the tranquil lives of their forefathers. I have watched them building their houses, white figures against the deep blue of the Morelos sky. Trimmed branches form the uprights and the roof-tree, on either side of which a criss-cross fabric of canes supports the thatching of *zacate* grass. In a corner of each courtyard stand one or two *cuexcomates*, granaries. These are great bowls of dried mud stiffened with a little straw, swelling out from a narrow base to a height of six feet and about the same in diameter, sheltered by a steep conical roof of thatch. At one side beneath the eave is an opening into which as into a letter box are dropped the maize cobs, white or rose-pink when they have dried in the sun on the beaten earth.

The people of Xoxocotla have the blend of quiet dignity and open friendliness which characterizes the village Indians as opposed to those of the *haciendas* and those of the

194

mountains. The people of Tetelcingo lying barely a mile off the highway to Cuautla are unaccountably shyer and more retiring. With their unkempt hair, and skirts and cloaks of blue home-spun, the women have misled many into taking them for Otomis instead of *mexicanos* speaking the Tlahuica dialect of Aztec. The schoolmaster knew their language and was using it to teach the little boys the Spanish names of animals. The schoolmistress did not, and was finding it uphill work to induce the tiny children to join in her games and dances.

Driving along the roads of Morelos, you may be fairly sure that anyone you pass on foot has many a weary mile to trudge before reaching his destination. The men walk immense distances in search of work. Nature in Mexico is merciless, and the local drivers, perhaps understandably, are not generous with free lifts. So at least I should judge from the many Indians who would not accept an *aventón* of thirty or forty miles in the hot sun until it had been made clear beyond any doubt that there was no question of payment.

The conversation of these 'foot-sloggers' was always entertaining, and their curiosity insatiable. Their questions revealed only the haziest notions of the outside world. The United States always meant something to them, but England generally meant the United States. Then we had to explain that our country was nearly three weeks by sea from Vera Cruz, a statement which was generally greeted

195

with a long-drawn *Caray*! of astonishment. There was
room to sleep in the ship, they assumed, never having
seen anything much larger than a duck-punt, but what
did we do about food? Was there room for cows and chick-
ens? And anyhow, what happened when the boat met a
shark? It all reminded me, albeit in a kindlier, more
courteous form, of that Don Melchior de Velasco of Chiapa
who 'in the best, most serious and judicious manner and
part of his don-like conference', asked Thomas Gage
'whether the sun and moon in England were of the same
colour as in Chiapa, and whether Englishmen went barefoot like the Indians and sacrificed one another as formerly did the heathens of that country; and whether all
England could afford such a dainty as a dish of frijoles;
and whether the women in England went as long with
child as did the Spanish women; and lastly whether the
Spanish nation were not a far gallanter nation than the
English'.

The main road turns west at Puente de Ixtla and follows the river up towards its source near Cacahuamilpa,
running along the foot of hills which have the bare, prim-
eval look of a relief model for geological students. The
river is crossed, and with it the border between Morelos
and Guerrero, at the village of Huajintla embowered in
yellow *tronadora* and fiery *flamboyant*. A steep climb up
the second of the seven ranges, regaining all the height
lost since Cuernavaca and a little more besides, brings the
traveller to Taxco, one of the loveliest towns in the whole
country, but unfortunately in danger of becoming one of
the best known and most visited.

The road approaches Taxco along the side of a lofty
mountain, thickly wooded. Sheer, naked precipices peer
here and there through the trees, with the consciously ro-

mantic exaggeration of an early nineteenth century engraving. Round a bend there suddenly appears the pink and white cascade of Taxco's houses looking as though they had been swept down the slope by some cloudburst in the mountains and were struggling to save themselves from slipping into the abyss.

The town takes its full name of Taxco de Alarcón from a Spanish writer who is believed on rather insecure evidence to have been born there. This was not Pedro Antonio Alarcón, the genial nineteenth century author of *The Three Cornered Hat*, but the Golden Age dramatist, Juán

Ruíz de Alarcón, author of the neatly turned comedy *La Verdad Sospechosa*, and of the vigorous *El Tejedor de Segovia*. Except in name, however, it is not to Alarcón that Taxco is dedicated but to the great Borda, to whom it owes all that it is and almost all that it has.

Like Taxco itself, Borda owed his fame and fortune to the silver mines discovered on the spot in 1534 by Spaniards in search of iron and tin. The site had not previously been inhabited, and the name was transferred to it from the old Aztec city which has dwindled into an Indian village, known to-day as Taxco Viejo, some eight miles further down towards Iguala. It is derived from *tlachco* the Aztec ball-game, a representation of which served as Old Taxco's hieroglyphic.

The mines had their ups and downs. Gage, passing in 1626, does not mention them but describes Taxco as 'a town of some five hundred inhabitants which enjoyeth great commerce with the country about by reason of the great store of cotton wool which is there'. It was not until the eighteenth century, that the mines yielded their riches, principally to José de la Borda. *El Fenix de los Mineros Ricos* (The Phoenix of Rich Miners) as he came to be called, was born at Jaca in Aragon, in 1699, possibly of French Béarnais parentage, and joined his elder brother Francisco at Taxco in 1716. Here, in 1720, he married one Teresa Verduguillo Aragonés by whom he had two children named Ana Maria and Manuel. He had had no technical training in mining, but his energy and business ability enabled him to strike one *bonanza* after another, not only in Taxco itself but at the famous Real del Monte in Hidalgo and further north in Zacatecas. He amassed three huge fortunes and lost them all, less through extravagance than through generosity, both to the church and to those around him. 'I owe three hundred thousand pesos', he is alleged once to have declared, 'but to me they are no more than a *real* and a half.' To him the people of Taxco owed not only new roofs for their houses, provisions in time of famine and the water-supply brought by an aqueduct which still spans the main road, but also their splendid parish church, still to-day the pride and glory of the little town. For this munificent gift, Borda was publicly thanked in a Papal Bull by Pope Benedict XIV, and from it came the saying attributed (probably apocryphally) to the man himself: 'God gives to

198

Borda, and Borda gives to God.' The Phoenix was so far in advance of his time that he abolished in his undertakings the iniquitous system of the *tienda de raya*, not yet fully obsolete in Latin America to-day. By this system, the workman was tied to his plantation or mine by the debts he ran up at a store run by the management at extortionate prices. However hard he worked, he could never rid himself of his burden of debt, which in some cases was passed on to his children.

Borda's fortune reached its apogee half way through the eighteenth century. Yet in 1772, he was compelled to obtain the authority of the Archbishop of Mexico to sell to the Cathedral of *Mexico de Yndias* for 110,000 pesos, a number of jewels and sacred vessels which he had bestowed on Taxco church, but of which he had prudently retained the legal ownership. Chief of these was a golden monstrance, part of which has found its way to Notre Dame in Paris. In 1778, he died at Cuernavaca, in relative poverty.

Against his great qualities must, for the sake of truth, be set some slight faults. He was, it seems, obstinate, passionate and at times violent. With his biographer, Jiménez y Frías, we may try to gloss over these by the discreet remark that 'if he sometimes argued with heat it was not to impose his own convictions, but rather that the truth might prevail, and if he was greatly addicted to his own ideas he was so from conviction and not from contrariness'.

Two portraits have survived of this great figure. One hangs in the Sala Capitular of Taxco parish church. In this he is seen in the prime of life, dressed in a French coat of the middle of the eighteenth century, with embroidered sleeves and jabot, a powdered wig with a black bow, and white stockings. The features are bold and imperious, the eyes dark and flashing beneath heavy eyebrows. He has the high cheek-bones, tight-lipped mouth and thin, hooked nose, straightening at the tip, of the Basque, and these, coupled with his name, make it probable that Basque blood ran in his veins. A later portrait in the National Museum shows him in profile, dressed in sober black, with a sword at his side and taking snuff. He looks older and more drawn, but the hawk-like gaze is, if anything, intensified.

The great parish church which 'Borda gave to God' and to Taxco stands in the centre of the town athwart a ridge running down from the steep and wooded Mount Huisteco. Dedicated to San Sebastian and to Santa Prisca, an obscure Roman martyr, it is one of the jewels of Mexican churrigueresque architecture. It was designed by Diego Durán, and completed in the seven years from 1751 to 1758. Many of the materials were brought from abroad, the tiles for instance from Spanish Talavera as well as from Mexican Puebla, but the exquisite rose-coloured stone which gives the building its principal charm, came from no further away than Mount Huisteco. In the light of dawn, Santa Prisca's church has a delicate shell-pink translucence. Under the high noontide sun, it takes on the sheen of burnished copper which the late afternoon warms to ruddy gold.

It was only in 1922 that a motor-car reached Taxco for the first time, and the motor-road followed some years later, bringing with it a more or less residential cosmopolitan colony, of some of whose members it remains uncertain whether they are painters who have gone there to drink or drinkers who have gone there to paint. Yet Taxco has preserved its spiritual integrity. It remains to-day

what it has always been, a congeries of white walls and
red roofs clambering up the hillside and slithering down
the ravines; of arcaded loggias, balconies of open, maur-
esque tile-work and wrought iron grilles over narrow
windows; of hidden patios and gardens betrayed only by
purple bougainvillea, scarlet hibiscus, pink *rosa mantana*
and the tattered pennants of banana leaves.

Besides Santa Prisca, Taxco counts several churches and
chapels: the solid convent of San Bernardino de Sena; the
chapels of Ojeda and Guadalupe perched like falcons'
eyries above the town; and, on the ridge below Santa
Prisca, the chapel of Nuestro Señor de la Santa Vera Cruz,
Our Lord of the Holy True Cross, whose miraculous image
attracts crowds of Indians to his *fiesta* on the fourth
Friday in Lent.

We were there in 1937. In the tiny *atrio* stood a *castillo*,
a tall pole hung at intervals with hoop-shaped frames
strung with crackers and fireworks linked by a thin train
of powder. When this was lit the fire slowly travelled up
the pole, setting each hoop dizzily spinning and flinging
off little rockets in the shapes of men and animals. The
top ring consisted of six or eight dolls which danced round
in a grotesque, agonized rigadoon as the crackers scorched
their papier mâché legs. White against the deep blue sky
they were like a cruel burlesque of the *juego do los voladores*. I wondered whether there was not some atavistic,
sadistic memory of the *auto da fé* in the crowd's laughter
at their tortured, writhing antics.

At the foot of the pole the Dance of the Moors and
Christians was being performed.

We had hoped, however, that this *fiesta* would bring
out Guerrero's speciality, the *Danza de los Tecuanes* or
Tiger Dance. Unfortunately, this did not appear, and for

my account of it I am obliged to rely on a performance by dancers from Chilpancingo which I saw in Mexico City.

Although it has lost any choreographic virtuosity which it may once have had, the Tiger Dance, like the Yaqui Deer Dance, is a survival of hunting magic, and its theme is the pursuit and death of a tiger, or rather of its Mexican equivalent a jaguar. The *tecuan* was played by a dancer in a spotted and striped overall and a big tiger mask, its features frozen into something between a snarl, a gape and a grin. The other dancers took the parts of hunters and their servants. The hunters were magnificent figures in broad sombreros, grotesque black or red masks and clothes of sack-cloth, with whips in their hands. They and the tiger skipped backwards and forwards in various dance figures. Then one of the hunters was caught and mauled by the tiger, and a Doctor was produced who cured him in the best tradition of our English mumming-plays. Finally the tiger was killed and, after a brief moment recumbent on the floor, recovered 'to fight another day'.

That *fiesta* night at Taxco, another speciality of Guerrero appeared, the *Torito*, obviously a near relative of the Spanish St. John's night *toro de fuego*. He was a man carrying on his head a small figure of a bull, like his namesake in the Vaqueros' Dance. From it rose a flimsy frame of bamboo, strung like the *castillo* with squibs, crackers and catherine wheels. To the music of a brass band, he ran about among the crowd with a queer loping step, scattering the small boys and, like a fighting bull from San Mateo or La Laguna, charging the improvised cloaks with which *aficionados* sought to play him. Then light was set to his train and the bull-man was transformed into a flaming monster, crackling and spitting fire. Before his onrush the screaming crowds broke and fled, only to return the moment his back was turned. Coloured flares fell from his frame and flooded him with light in the surrounding darkness or from behind threw him into sinister silhouette. The scene had the fantastic, nightmare quality of a Goya.

To me the most fascinating spot in all Taxco is the little *plaza* before the great west front of Santa Prisca. The other three sides are filled with white houses, the highest of them Borda's, three stories lower on this side than on the other. In the middle, round the municipal bandstand, runs a tiny garden with evergreen American laurels clustering so thick above their bare trunks that the intertwined branches form a canopy casting a green shade on even the hottest day. By day or by night the *plaza* has the heightened colour of a stage setting, dark green of laurels against the rose-pink stone of the church. You want to relapse into your stall and wait for the actors to come on and play their parts. There is an atmosphere of suspense. Something, you feel, must happen soon. Then you realize that the actors are there before you. All who walk across the stage, *mestizo,* Indian or even American tourist, become somehow endowed with a new emotional significance. For a moment they have become fragments of a pattern. Then they are gone and the kaleidoscope is shaken up anew.

Here for centuries there used to be held each Sunday the most picturesquely set market in Mexico. From the untouched hinterland of Taxco the Indians came in the night before, spread their wares out on *petate* mats and sheltered them with white awnings which, alternating under the sun or the moon with pools of shadow, made the square look from above like a chessboard. Up the steep narrow lanes the market used to overflow, past the baroque drinking-fountain and down towards la Vera Cruz. Now to make way for tourists and their traffic the *tianguis* has been tidied away, relegated to a cement platform built up in a *barranca* below Santa Prisca. I shall always treasure its memory as one which composed and condensed into a veritable work of art the elements of Indian markets all over the country.

A description of a Mexican market is apt to degenerate into a wearisome catalogue, yet some account must be given of that institution which plays so vital a part in the lives of the inhabitants. Long before the Conquest the *tianguis* was an essential feature of life, and Bernal Diaz has left a vivid description of the great variety of wares exposed for sale in the great market of Tlaltelolco.'Each kind of merchandise was kept by itself,' he begins, 'and had its fixed place marked out. Let us begin with the dealers in gold, silver and precious stones, feathers, mantles and embroidered goods, slaves, pieces of cloth and cotton. In another part, there were skins of tigers and lions, of otters and jackals, deer and other animals and badgers and mountain cats, some tanned and others untanned, and other classes of merchandise. . . .' So he goes on with a list of wares many of which it would be difficult to find in a modern market. The arrangement is the same, however, and the variety as great, in any rural market to which the Indians flock to-day. Grudging neither time nor effort, they come unbelievable distances to sell their few surplus products, bartering them for others or expending the proceeds on the factory goods of which they stand so greatly in need.

Maize, seed and beans are exposed for sale on *petates* in heaps of varying colour and texture. Fruit, vegetables and chiles are neatly arranged in little pyramids of five. To the amateur of gastronomic tourism they offer wide scope for experiment, seldom entirely satisfactory in my own case, I must confess, for exotic fruits are often a sad disappointment. Juicy pineapples from *tierra caliente* and golden, melting mangoes earn unqualified approval. Equally unqualified is my dislike of astringent persimmon and of the rugous-skinned mamey. Passion fruit, despite its name, is a sad deception with a mouthful of brittle seeds to a trickle of gelatinous, gooseberry-flavoured juice. Between the two extremes lies the whole gamut of *zapote negro*, its dark flesh delicious when mashed up with a little orange juice; the purplish *camote* or sweet potato; the *papaya* or paw-paw, rich in pepsins; the knobbly *chirimoya* or custard-apple; the *jícama* root, in consistency like a flavourless apple yet quenching to the thirst; and the tasteless *tuna*, fruit of the prickly pear. Scarcely to be counted as a fruit, but as fresh to the taste as its purplish-green enamel skin is a delight to the eye, is the *aguacate* or alligator pear.

So much for the fresh, natural foods. Cooked ones sizzling at innumerable booths are as savoury in smell as they are perilous in appearance. Viscerous meats, *tamales* and *tacos* filled with unknown ingredients must take unending toll of digestions weakened by hot chiles.

Pulque flows from inflated pigskin or wooden tub. At the soft-drink stall, mineral waters have not entirely displaced the fruit essences of a more innocent age. In their tall glass containers, they are as vividly coloured as Rosamund's Purple Jar. Orange, lemon, tamarind, crimson *jamaica*, opaque white *orchata* made of barley, and *chia*, dyed arsenic-green by the little black seeds which float in it. No less lurid are the sweets, *jamoncillo* of brown sugar and coconut from Juquila, *chongos* of violent pink cream from Oaxaca, and a hundred others, enticing to the children, alarming to their parents.

At Taxco and throughout Morelos and Guerrero, colour is supplied less by the women than by the men. Here, the soul-destroying blue dungarees which are making such inroads into the native costume on the high plateau have scarcely penetrated to displace the clean white shirt and loose trousers whose twisted cut at the waist makes them appear to stay up of their own volition. In this part of the *tierra templada* there is a great vogue for shirts of coloured satin in every possible hue: crushed strawberry, sky-blue, yellow, pea-green, tangerine, eau-de-nil, old rose, cyclamen and wine. The white *cotones* reflect, the straw *sombreros* refract, a diffused light on the brown faces giving them a golden glow like light shining through alabaster. Often the men gather round some itinerant minstrel with a guitar, singing to a thin, threadbare little tune *corridos*, ballads about the heroes of the Revolution or the latest crime in the capital. He does not pass round the hat but relies for his earnings on the sale of broadsheets with the words of the songs. It is these men who have carried the same popular ditties into every corner of the vast Republic, making Mexican folksong national rather than regional.

Threatened though it is by factory production and by a rising standard of living, the handicraft tradition is still very much alive in Mexico. Arty-crafty shops abound in Mexico City and in the larger tourist centres, but on the whole they cater for the undiscriminating visitor to the point that among Mexicans the term 'Mexican curios' has acquired almost a derogatory sense. Nevertheless they drive a lively trade in pictures in inlaid wood or straw, bird pictures made of real feathers which are no more than a hollow memory of the lost art of the Aztecs and Tarascans, lacquered gourds from Olinalá, black, purple or green on a ground of orange-red, embroidered *faja* belts from Milpa Alta, life-sized men in *petate* wicker from Lerma, Oaxaca sarapes in the wrong colours and the wrong designs and a host of other objects, to-day mostly made for the tourist. There is practically nothing you cannot buy, from a *charro* suit to a cake of soap, with the Aztec calendar stone emblazoned upon it.

In the rural markets, on the other hand, handicrafts may be seen fulfilling their proper function, faithful to the true canons of Indian taste. Textiles, pottery and basket-work offer a fascinating range to the collector who will be satisfied only with the authentic and is prepared to take his time and to travel far in search of it.

Sarapes, for instance, must not be judged from the crudely coloured specimens, fit only to adorn the piano of a suburban parlour, into which the wonderful eighteenth century weaving of Saltillo has degenerated. Those of Oaxaca, or to be precise of Teotitlan del Valle, are traditionally correct in sober grey, black and white, and aesthetically pleasing when they preserve the Zapotec designs of deer and tiger with flowers growing from their backs. The plain of Toluca weaves attractive stepped patterns in brown and cream, the natural colours of the wool. These are probably pre-Cortesian as are the diamonds and zig-zags of San Miguel Chiconcuac near Texcoco. San Francisco Xonacatlan has misguidedly taken to weaving, at infinite trouble, *charros* and *chinas*, eagles and serpents in place of the graceful floral designs in blue, red or maroon on a white ground which, with luck, you may buy off the back of one of its inhabitants.

Earthenware, with certain exceptions, is rather disappointing when compared, for instance, with peasant Portugal or for that matter with pre-Cortesian Mexico. Decoration is apt to be restricted to a brown glaze with a few rather haphazard stripes of black. Form, too, is undistinguished, though unglazed water jars, tall in the Mesquital Valley, rounded at Yalalag, are often effective in their simple curves.

Two villages near Oaxaca have each a well-defined tradition of its own. San Bartolo Coyotepec produces a so-called

black ware the colour of which is in reality something between gun-metal and pewter. Azumba specializes in a rich green glaze. Both are seen to better advantage in little toys than in utilitarian objects. Coyotepec makes jars in the shape of monkeys and vampires, bells in which the head and torso of an archaic-looking female figure form the handle and her flared out skirt the bell. At Easter time, Azumba produces jars in the shape of angels or animals with glazed heads and roughly corrugated bodies in the interstices of which seeds are placed. Watered through the porous walls of the jar, the seed puts forth a hirsute growth of cress-like shoots appropriate to the season of renewal.

Morelos and Guerrero

At Taxco, or better still at Iguala, you can buy jars of all sizes in a ware made in the hot country of Guerrero at San Miguel Huapan and other villages. The ground is pale, almost colourless, unglazed and painted freehand in reddish brown. Loops of clay serve as handles and as feet. The designs, stylized floral patterns, birds or animals, strongly recall the geometrical ornament of the Aegean civilization and even include the spreading tentacles of the octopus so closely associated with Minoan Crete.

*   *   *

There is something about Taxco which suggests an island town running down to a sea-shore which is not there. These ridges and ravines, one feels, should lead to storm-beaten promontories and sheltered coves with boats drawn up on the sand, nets spread out to dry and the strong tang of the ocean. Instead there is a deep abyss overhung only by the few houses which have, as it were, rolled over the edge of the Acapulco road. Beyond are bare, lonely hills, cut by a trail which winds over the horizon into the unknown. This marine feeling is to some extent explained when one climbs up along the hillside to the west of the town, and the vast panorama of Guerrero's *tierra caliente* is gradually unfolded. This is indeed a sea, though not of water but of vapours rising from a tangle of age-wrinkled hills and wide valleys stretching away to the heaving, broken horizon of the Sierra Madre.

I have seen this view many times, pin-clear in the rain-washed light of the wet season or reduced to its essential outlines by the heat-haze of the dry, yet I can never grow weary of it, not so much for what it is as for its implications, the spur which it sets to the imagination. This, I never tire of telling myself, is *tierra caliente*, what

Morelos and Guerrero

William Spratling calls 'the country's physical unconscious . . . vast and fecund, forbidding and promising,
practically unexplored and difficult of access'. These are
the bad lands with their fevers and their strange, dis-
figuring, tropical diseases. Through them winds the
great Rio de las Balsas, symbol of unknown Mexico. As I
look out upon them from the healthy mountain air and the
civilized security of Taxco, I feel as though I am gazing
out over the 'dangerous and combustious seas' from the
safety of a cliff-fortress, or looking down on a riotous
street-crowd from the sanctuary of a lofty balcony.

As you walk or ride up the trail behind the town the
view grows ever vaster. The near landscape has something
of a Japanese quality, with steep rocks among the trees.
These are dumpy little cedars or the curious *cucharillo*
which I have seen nowhere else, with big velvety leaves,
rather broader than horse chestnut, which, reversing the
ordinary process of nature, are scarlet when they unfold
at the tip of the branch and then, shedding their rust-
coloured pollen, turn to a vivid green. The Mixteca
country climbs up beyond the iron-grey hills. Away to the
left, Popocatepetl soars into the sky, its lower slopes lost in
the mist, the streaked cone floating in the air, sundered
from earth, borne aloft by white-winged clouds. To the
left, a side trail leads deep down into a lonely valley,
where tropical undergrowth has swamped the bleached
bones of an *hacienda*, San Francisco Cuadra, picked bare
by revolutionary wars as a carcase by *zopilote* buzzards,
more heart-breakingly desolate in the brilliant sunshine
and rank vegetation than ever it could be under our cold
northern skies.

From Taxco, the main road drops down to Iguala in
wide circles, dropping 4,000 feet in twenty miles. Here

one is in *tierra caliente* with a vengeance, steaming hot at all seasons of the year. The road skirts the little town where on a sultry day in 1821, Morelos made his famous Plan of Independence and designed the Mexican flag. A curious legend has it that, happening to eat a water-melon he chose its colours, green, red and white, but another explanation is that white stands for purity and religion, green for independence and red for understanding with the Spaniards. So deeply embowered in trees is the little town, that from the highway scarcely a house is to be seen.

Not for many miles does one climb again into cooler air. Dropping even lower, the Rio de las Balsas is crossed by a fine bridge at Mescala, full of turbid water as I saw it one September day and flowing with a quiet and sinister purposefulness, out of the unknown and into the unknown, between steep hills which soon hid it from view.

This must be one of the low points of the road. Thereafter, one follows up the bed of a shallow river between wooded hills which gradually close in to become the dreaded Cañon del Zopilote or Buzzard's Gulch, a place of such stifling, oppressive heat that it is easy to believe that none but the croaking carrion-bird finds a home there. To obtain the full effect of the canyon you should be going the other way, dropping from the cool heights of Zumpango ever deeper into this inferno, so that you expect round every corner to come upon Charon and his dark river.

Zumpango and, a little higher, Chilpancingo furnish one of those brusque transitions of climate which are the hall-mark of Mexico. After the first a crest is passed and one finds oneself in a shallow green valley reminiscent, of all things, of Wales. A long ridge cuts the western sky. The road borders on a broad expanse of pasture through

211

which trickles a stream with grassy banks, and Chilpancingo, when it is reached, has an atmosphere of small-
town characterlessness which might belong to almost any
country.

It is beyond Chilpancingo that the road, narrow and
tortuous, attains its full majesty. The four remaining
mountain-passes crowded into the last ninety miles can, at
a pinch, be distinguished and told off on the fingers, but
the impression is rather of a continuous tangle of mountain. The thin ribbon of road, never visible for more than
a hundred yards or so ahead, threads its way through the
Sierra Madre Occidental, the Pacific *cordillera* which
runs almost unbroken from the Canadian Rockies to the
great Andean volcanoes. Following a route traced out in
colonial times (when the treasure of the *nao de China*, the
China galleon, had to be conveyed from Acapulco to Mexico City), the road twists and turns, rises and falls with
bewildering rapidity. In retrospect one sees it not with
the continuity of a cinema film, but as a series of brilliant,
kaleidoscopic snapshots; a group of palm-huts by a stream
among the flame-like acacia blooms of the 'Pride of Bar-
bados'; the firs and cloud-enfolded distances of Agua del
Obispo; the broad waters of the Rio Papagayo and the
peripatias of the road first down and then up its tumbling,
cascading tributaries; a high waterfall dropping out of a
feathery hillside; a glimpse of glistening, brown bodies in
the tawny waters of Xaltianguis; and that last steep rise of
all, from the crest of which,' in a wild surmise', the Pacific
is first seen and the blue horseshoe of Acapulco Bay lies at
last at the dusty feet of the traveller.

Acapulco is exactly what you expect of the small tropical harbour. The houses of wood or palm thatch lead down
to an untidy, ill-defined water-front. In one-storied ship-

ping offices, perspiring clerks work in their shirt-sleeves, at a temperature which seldom falls below 80 or rises above 90 degrees Fahrenheit. Zopilotes, so noble in flight, so repulsive at rest, roost in rows on the cocoanut palms, and the astonished northerner discovers that cocoanuts growing on the trees are more like clusters of great green cow-bells than the round, hairy skulls at which he has so often shied at village fairs. Overhead, in dignified, streamlined beauty, passes the shadow of a frigate-bird, and off-shore, another lesson in natural history to the Londoner, the pelican which he deemed such a monster of clumsiness behind the railings of St. James' Park, fishes with swift dexterity.

Of the many sandy bathing-beaches, the most popular are the sheltered Caleta and the Playa de los Hornos beyond the sixteenth century fort, where the Pacific combers come rolling in, their violence tempered by the long arm of land which half closes the bay. More beautiful but infinitely more dangerous is the great expanse of Pié de la Cuesta, on the open sea to the north-west, an unbroken line of white, seething surf as far as the eye can see. The road to Pié de la Cuesta winds corniche-fashion along a mountain-side with glimpses of little rocky coves suggesting a tropical Devonshire. Where it drops down to the sea there is a small fishing hamlet of palm-huts inhabited by Indians and *lobos* (wolves) or Indian-negro half-breeds. At the far end of the beach is another village where naked men, their skins tanned to a rich mahogany, harpoon great fish in the surf with two-pronged fish-spears.

The intervening ten miles form a long, narrow spit of land, never more than a quarter of a mile wide, separating the sea from a wide freshwater lagoon, the Laguna de Coyuca, fringed with impenetrable vegetation, a paradise for naturalists and sportsmen. At early dawn, the mud-coloured caimans may be seen before they hide away from the intense light of the sun. Bird-life of all kinds abounds. Graceful egrets, delicate little stilts and sand-pipers, duck of all kinds, fishing pelicans, flocks of green parrakeets and, as once I saw, a great black and gold kingfisher pursue their avocations almost heedless of the intruding stranger.

Behind it all, like a painted backcloth, hang the sultry mountains of the tropics, overgrown with low feathery thorn-trees nameless to all but the naturalist. They are empty of human habitation, of cultivation even, in-distinguishable from one another and preserving a sullen, brooding anonymity strangely disconcerting to those ac-customed to our individualized northern hills.

XII. Oaxaca

On a clear winter's evening we took the Inter-oceanic Railway for Oaxaca. It was one of those rare days when there is no trace of mist or haze in the Valley of Mexico and the great volcanoes stand out pin-sharp. As the sun went down behind the Sierra de San Francisco, their snows caught the Alpine glow, while the lower slopes took on hues of amethyst and sapphire. Then they faded and the colour deepened in the west. The serrated outline of the Nevado de Toluca was etched against the afterglow. We had scarcely passed Texcoco when the swift twilight of the tropics deepened into dusk.

When we awoke next morning the sun was already slanting down into a narrow gorge. It glinted through the white blossoms of the *casahuate*, the morning glory tree, traced against the dark background of the hillside with the delicate precision of a Persian miniature. Then the train climbed to a watershed, and at Las Sedas the panorama of Oaxaca was unfolded, line upon line of sierras which fell away again as we dropped in wide curves past Etla to Oaxaca City.

215

Oaxaca

The capital of the state was founded by Aztec conquerors in the fifteenth century at a strategic spot where three valleys meet. It has charm, character and, earthquakes apart, the perfect climate which one finds at 5,000 feet in this part of the world. At first sight there is a hint of Castile in the massive stone doorways, the cloistered patios and the ironwork adorning windows and balconies.

There was, indeed, more Spanish than Indian philosophy in the remark of a small *mestizo* boy to a little girl which I overheard near the market. He knew he was ugly, he said, but that was as it should be, for men ought to be ugly, strong and wicked. I thought of the Spanish phrase '*muy macho*'. But a climb to the Cerro del Fortín, the hill on which Juarez's statue stands, dispelled this impression by revealing an even flatness of roof broken only by church towers which is wholly Mexican. From here the westering sun colours the escarpments of the Sierra Juarez and gilds the baroque façade of Santo Domingo. For forty years in the troublous nineteenth century this lovely church was desecrated and used as a stable for army horses. Impious hands scraped the gold from the *retablos* and hacked down the carved altars for firewood. At the turn of the century it was restored in all the wonder of its baroque gesso work; the pairs of angelic musicians in the organ loft, the Dominican martyrs in skilful perspective leading up to the cupola over the west gallery, and above all the genealogical vine springing from the body of Don Felix de Guzmán, father of St. Dominic, in the branches of which appear rulers of Spain and members of the Guzmán family associated with the development of the Order, including St. Ferdinand, Isabel of Castile, Joan the Mad, and Philip II.

Oaxaca

It is not known who were the primitive inhabitants of the Valley of Oaxaca. They may have been the ancestors of almost any of the sixteen Indian tribes who are to be found in the state to-day. Its present inhabitants are Zapotecs and Mixtecs, closely related tribes who may be the descendants of Toltecs driven southwards from the Valley of Mexico a thousand years ago. The Zapotecs lived in the valleys and the Mixtecs, as their name implies, in the hills.

To-day the border between the two races runs through Monte Albán, a high hill across the valley from Oaxaca, four miles away as the crow flies but six or eight as the *forcito* (flivver) crawls. Monte Albán will always remain in my mind as the Mycenae of Mexico. Both sites were obviously chosen for their defensive strength, Mycenae placed inconveniently far from the Gulf of Nauplia but with its back to a wall of rock, Monte Albán set at an inconvenient height but impregnable on all sides. Its Zapotec name of Danni Depaa meant 'fortified hill'. The Mixtecs, who conquered it in the fourteenth century, called it Yucundusan which in their tongue means 'the hill of the tombs'. This name recalls another parallel with Mycenae, the revelation to the excavator's spade in the now famous Tomb No. 7 of a golden treasure of hitherto unexampled excellence and delicacy of workmanship. In the Museum of Oaxaca City one may admire diadems, pendants, masks and other jewelry of gold, objects of jade, pearl and turquoise, and bone tallies with exquisitely carved but indecypherable hieroglyphics. The Mycenean parallel even extends to the Zapotec (and Mayan) false arch. If Monte Albán has no beehive tombs or Lion Gate it has the carved stone reliefs known, without perhaps much justification, as 'the dancers' and an ordered array of stepped

217

pyramids, some uncovered, others still tantalizingly draped in brushwood and greenery.

Finally, the Mycenean parallel may be extended to the loneliness and natural beauty of the spot. The very light is Greek in quality, and so are the contours and texture of the mountains. Two months of drought had parched the countryside, but in the deserted courts there still bloomed the yellow bells of the *cascabelilla* flower, the tiny scarlet trumpets of the *doncelita*, the purple *palito de San Pablo*. Lizards scuttled through the undergrowth; undaunted, a great emerald grasshopper let us open out the scarlet and black lining of his folded wings; a blue-black swallowtail butterfly drifted aimlessly by. Over the empty sierras, white clouds hung suspended. Only the hand of man had rescued from complete obliteration man's handiwork of another age.

From Monte Albán one may clearly see three wide valleys leading away from Oaxaca. One runs back to Etla, one westwards to Zaachila and Zimapan and a third southwards through Tlacolula to Mitla. Along this last has been traced the Pan-American highway destined to unite the two Americas by motor-road. A few miles outside Oaxaca City the road leaves to one side the biggest tree in the world, the famous *ahuehuete* of Santa Maria del Tule, standing in the yard of a church built on the site of an ancient temple. Statistics vary slightly, but it must be about one hundred and fifty feet high and the same in girth. Its age is estimated at two thousand years or more, and it takes twenty-eight men touching finger tips to encompass it.

Tlacolula boasts a church with a barrel-vaulted chapel dedicated to the Santo Cristo de Tlacolula, the silver and gold workmanship of which is one of the loveliest things of its kind in Mexico. It is soon forgotten, however, at Mitla, where Zapotec art reached its apogee. A Christian church sits awkwardly straddled among the ruins of these palaces which have paid the penalty of neglect but have never required excavation. They are decorated with no less than fourteen variations of the stepped key pattern, derived originally from textile motifs and closely paralleled in Peru. The designs are picked out in mosaic relief, each piece separately made so that it could be fitted into its appointed place in the pattern. In one of the cruciform underground chambers stands a pillar, to which, according to tradition, condemned priests or nobles were bound and left to starve to death, food and drink being placed just out of reach while the people passed and upbraided them. Probably, too, this was the entrance, sealed up in horror by Spanish monks in the sixteenth century, to the passages and caves where those who had resolved upon votive suicide vanished to die of starvation. To-day the Indian guide claims to be able to foretell with the aid of the column the number of years which the visitor has to live. You clasp the pillar with your arms, and he measures off the number of finger-breadths separating your two hands. Nineteen years was my allotted span, but I took comfort in the thought that if I returned in a few years' time it would be unlikely to have much diminished.

The thought of death is ever present at Mitla. The Aztec name is a form of Mictlan, the abode of Mictlantecutli, Lord of the Dead. The Zapotec name of Yoopaa, meaning 'resting place' has a similar implication, and it was actually believed that this was the entrance to the underworld. Even to-day the death cult associated with All Souls is observed with special intensity at Mitla, and at the end of it the whole village is 'dead to the world' in a manner reminiscent of pre-Spanish ceremonial drunkenness. At a wake it is regarded as cold-hearted callousness  not to get gloriously drunk. The Indian attitude to death will never be comprehensible to the white man. A friend of mine attended the funeral of a child at Mitla and was astonished at the apparent lack of feeling shown by the mother. He asked her how she could bear to join in the revelry at the wake of her own child. '*No murió la fábrica*', was the disconcerting reply. 'The factory's still alive', and the bereaved mother gave herself a self congratulatory pat.

Ancient Zapotec tombs are generally found to contain earthenware funeral urns of remarkable workmanship in the form of human figures representing the deceased, a divinity or a masked priest. Sometimes the features are shown, as in an example in my own possession depicting a warrior standing with sword and shield in his hands. Time and again I saw his double among the Zapotec Indians, who have fine profiles with bold, curved noses and large well-shaped eyes in contrast with the flattened, slant-eyed features of the Aztecs. More frequently the figure is squatting in the Indian reverential position, and a death-mask covers either the face or the brow. The head is often crowned with a plumed headdress of which the equivalent may be seen in the famous Plume Dance of this region.

The *Danza de las Plumas* survives to-day in four or five

Nets at Janitzio

Nets at Janitzio

The duck-hunt

Tarascan fisherman

Francisco cutting out paper dolls

The teponaztli and its guardian

The paper dolls in the *oratorio*

Riding to Huehuetla

Crossing a river

Pancho of Huehuetla

The teponaztli of Xico

The teponaztli of San Juan Acingo

villages of the valley, both Zapotec and Mixtec. We had
our first sight of it at a 'Mexican Night' held on Lake
Chapultepec as part of the celebrations for the inaugura-
tion of the Laredo Highway in July 1936. The dancers'
heads were surmounted by great fans of feathers, blue,
red, orange, green and white springing out from small
mirror-faced crowns. Holding gourd rattles they danced
at great speed in a crouched attitude with bent knees and
long bounding steps. Yet the huge headdresses never
touched as they intertwined in the mazy intricacies of the
dance. We were naturally anxious to see it in its proper
setting, when it is done for hours at a time in the intervals
of a play representing the Conquest, in which Montezuma,
Malinche and Cortes play their respective rôles. Cortes
has a special connexion with the region, for he was made
Marqués del Valle de Oaxaca, although, contrary to the
general impression, he never visited his domains. An
occasion seemed to present itself on December 8th, when
the dancers of Zaachila generally perform in honour of
Our Lady of Juquila. Full of high hopes we went out to
the little *pueblo* hidden in tall evergreen trees in the
western arm of the valley.

Zaachila took its name from the Zapotec King who
transferred his capital from Mitla to what was then an
island in the lake and by discovering and developing a
natural process of erosion emptied the valley of water at
the end of the fourteenth century. His descendant, Señor
Pérez, still lives in the village where, incongruously
enough, he is the head of a flourishing Methodist community.

By a cruel stroke of luck there was no dance in 1936.
The church was full of people, and some sort of service
seemed to be going on without a priest. The Indians were

going in and out with flowers and lighted candles in their hands and were strewing the altar of Our Lady with scarlet Poinsettia blossoms and the white cascade of the yucca flower. The silence was broken only by the wailing of a woman swathed in a blue rebozo. Eerie, almost animal in quality, it seemed to lack all emotion and poignancy and came as a sharp reminder of the deep spiritual gulf between the white races and the brown. For the missing dance there was some slight compensation in a performance of the ball-game of *pelota mixteca* in which some have seen a survival of the ancient sacred ball-game of pre-Cortesian times.

Of this game, called *tlachtli* or *tlachco*, only a very vague idea can be obtained from the accounts of early Spanish writers, and no living tradition survives among the Indians as to how it was played. The ball, according to Padre Motolinia, was made of 'a certain gum which comes out of certain trees found in very hot country, and pricking this tree thick white drops come out and then solidify and when treated go as black as pitch'. (The Spaniards, of course, had never seen rubber before.) The court was five times as long as it was wide, with low walls at the end, higher sloping walls at the side and seats for the spectators. The ball was struck not with the hand or foot but with the hip or knee. The spectators waged jewels, mantles, plumes, arms and slaves on the outcome, the object of which was to carry the ball to the farther end and score something like a try in rugby football. Still better was to make the ball pass through a narrow stone ring set high on either side-wall. So difficult was this that it was very rarely accomplished, as rarely perhaps as a goal in the Eton College Wall Game. Any player scoring thus had hymns sung to him and was entitled to claim the clothes and portable property of all the spectators. This caused a regular *sauve qui peut* among the latter, for the other players helped the victor to catch and strip them, an innovation which may be commended to the Provost of Eton as a way of livening up St. Andrew's Day. Between the two rings a line was marked with a certain herb, which, says Padre Durán, smacks somewhat of superstition. Any ball which failed to cross this line even along the ground was bad.

Like every other feature of pre-Cortesian life the ball-game was bound up with religion. It was used for purposes of divination or for settling tribal disputes. The night before a match the players placed in a bowl the ball and the loin-cloth and pads which they wore, and squatting down prayed to them, burned copal incense and made offerings of food. They then felt as sure of victory as any manager of a heavyweight champion. By a pretty conceit the northern sky was known to the Aztecs as *citlaltlachtli* 'the ball-game of the stars'.

The ball-court at Monte Albán differs in construction from the type prevalent from Mexico City to Yucatan and in particular lacks the stone rings, which has given rise to the supposition that the Mixtecs played a game under different rules, of which the *pelota mixteca* of to-day is a survival. This is a little difficult to believe owing to the close resemblance which the modern game bears to the old *longue paume* (as distinct from *courte paume* from which tennis is derived) played in the mediaeval courts of Europe.

As we saw it that day at Zaachila the game is played on an unenclosed space on which are marked two side lines eleven metres apart and two transversal lines eight metres apart. The ball of either rubber or leather (the latter at Zaachila) is four inches in diameter and is struck with the bare hand on the volley or first bounce. There are two teams of four players, taking it in turn to attack and defend. The server places himself between thirty and forty yards from the nearer of the transversal lines, and his service must fall within the quadrilateral which these form with the side-lines. Scoring is as in tennis, 15, 30, 40, game, with two advantage points if deuce is called. A set consists of the best of five games. If the ball is completely missed by one side or is hit out the point is definitely lost. If, however, it is hit down and crosses the central transversal line along the ground, the other side attempt to touch it as far forward as possible. A *raya* (chase) is scored, and a new line is drawn where the ball was stopped. When one side reaches 40, or two *rayas* have been scored, the teams change ends and each chase is played off, the defenders seeking to stop the ball before it crosses the new line. The suspended point is thereby decided if it has not been actually won outright. A *raya* is also scored if the ball crosses a side-line along the ground. The game closely resembles not only the old *jeu de paume* but the archaic form of Basque pelote called *rebot* still played in the French Basque country[1]. My own feeling is that it must have been introduced into Oaxaca by Spanish or Basque clerics or conquistadores to replace the ancient Mixtec game with which it can scarcely have had more than a few fortuitous resemblances.

Market day is Saturday at Oaxaca and Sunday at Tlacolula. Just outside the city is a ford across the River Atoyac, flowing here between green trees and meadows. I never tired of watching the passage of lumbering ox-waggons

[1]See Rodney Gallop: *A Book of the Basques*, p. 238.

with solid wheels, covered with nets or awnings of petate mats, pausing for a while to let the oxen drink and then going on their way laden with the fruits of the hot country from the coast down by Puerto Angel and Pochutla. Indians from the valleys come in on donkeys, the women with their *rebozo* shawls wound turbanwise round their heads. Those from the sierras come on foot, sometimes two or three days journey, bearing their produce on their backs and bartering them for the few necessities which they do not produce in their own villages. The sight of the Mijes in their full white trousers, the queer little men in the pointed black hats of the Sierra Juarez, and the white flowing robes of the Yalaltec women fired us with the desire to see something of their mountain homes, and we mapped out a five days' ride from Mitla far into the sierras and back by a different route to Tlacolula. We left Mitla at ten o'clock on a hot morning, a party of seven with two guides representing six different nationalities. One of the guides was a Zapotec Indian named Daniel. The other, nicknamed *Biché*, was the son of an Indian mother and a Cornish father. He was a remarkable character, combining the endurance of the one race with the reliability of the other. Our mounts were sturdy creole ponies, well-used to the sort of work which they would have to face. Mine was a little grey. He had the three essentials of endurance, sure-footedness and stolidity. But he was desperately slow, even for the trails which seldom allowed the horses to break into the triple known in Mexico as *paso de cura* or priest's gait. He had no name when I took him, but I had called him by many, each less flattering than the last, by the time we parted.

The route lay first across an arid, baking valley-floor with no vegetation but organ and candelabra cactus. A range

225

of bare limestone hills rose ahead, apparently unbroken, and it was only at their very foot that a gap appeared leading into a narrow, rocky gorge. This proved to be the gate to the sierras, and from the moment when a sharp turn cut it off from the outside world, the trail began to zig-zag up the hillside into cooler air. The sun shone brightly. Distant sierras climbed up the horizon, range upon range, until in the clear air the view extended at least a hundred miles to the south. The higher hillside was clothed with pine and holm-oak. Orchids grew from their branches, some cyclamen-hued, others with tiger markings, and parasite maguey-aloes hung their blossoms down in pink festoons. Along a ridge the trail dropped more gradually than it had risen, and the brilliant afternoon light threw into high relief the escarpments of the Mije mountains, home of one of the most primitive tribes in Mexico, rising to the summit of Cempoaltepetl, literally the 'Twenty Mountains'. They lay only a single valley's breadth away, but so wide was the valley and filled with such a welter of lesser mountains and gorges that it would have taken two hard days' riding to cross.

Down a trail which was more like the bed of a water-course we came in the swiftly falling twilight to San Miguel Albarradas where we were to spend the night. It is an unforgettable experience to arrive at dusk in an Indian village. On either side of the trail steep-pitched huts merge into the hillside, whisps of smoke curling from their thatched roofs. Women and children hide at the approach of strangers. Only the men stay outside their doors, motionless figures huddled in sarapes, their faces pools of ambiguous shadow beneath wide straw sombreros. There is neither welcome nor hostility in their attitude, only an inscrutable aloofness.

Oaxaca

The scattered huts run down the steep ravine to the centre of the village, an improbable interval of horizontality supporting the church and the school. At the moment we had greater need of the latter than of the former,

for in such villages a straw mat on the schoolroom floor is the best bed for which the stranger can hope. Outside the school, therefore, we halted, and awaited the arrival of the Municipal President. Presently he emerged from the shadows, an Indian like the rest in poncho and white cottons, and kissed our hands with a gesture which owed as much to Indian courtesy as to Spanish feudalism.

A bottle of cane brandy broke the ice, and from that moment our reception could not have been more cordial. The school, closed for the holidays, was flung open, and the packs unloaded from the tired animals. Maize was forthcoming for the horses, and straw *petate* mats for ourselves, followed at a short interval by coffee boiled with sugar in the Indian fashion, dark brown *frijole* beans and *tortillas*.

When we had eaten we sat for a while on a wooden

227

bench in front of the school. Under the stars the Indians had lit a bonfire. Daniel, one of our guides, had disappeared with a relative, for this was his native village, but the other, the faithful Biché, was watching the horses lest they should trample the fodder underfoot and refuse to eat it.

The firelight flickered and leapt on the dim outline of the church, on the horses contentedly munching their maize stalks and on the little group of Indians who stood or crouched beyond the fire. In their eyes, fixed upon us in a quiet unwinking stare, the flames were held in glittering reflection. Their statuesque immobility melted into talk and laughter, intermittent and subdued, with the curiously indolent, deprecating intonation of the Zapotec tongue.

When the fire died down, we retired into the school, but for the Indians the spectacle was not yet over. They crowded into the door, a wedged mass of heads and bodies. Driven away by the President they peered through windows and ill-fitting shutters. It was fortunate that undressing was in any case out of the question, and my last memory before I fell into the deep sleep begotten of sun and air and a long day in the saddle was the lulling murmur of their voices outside.

Next morning we were up with the first light and away before the sun had struck down into the coombe. The trail wound up hill and down dale, through enchanting woods empty of life both animal and human. The most we saw was the white breast and bright blue wings of the *huarate* bird, an occasional strange-hued butterfly and green and gold spiders with bodies an inch across whose webs spanned the trail. At one place the rock had been carved into the rude semblance of a serpent, barely

228

distinguishable with age. The Indians have a legend that this serpent bit the horses of the Spaniards coming over from Mitla to colonize in the valley, and that it is for this reason that there are no haciendas there and the Indian stock has remained pure. This, at least, was what they told us at Santo Domingo Albarradas, a village embowered in feathery *tepeguaje* trees, which we reached at one o'clock. We could have gone on in the afternoon, but in that empty country of vast distances the next village was seven hours away which would have meant an uncomfortably long day. It was pleasant, too, to have an afternoon to watch the men spinning rope of maguey fibre and the women deftly weaving with unbelievable rapidity *petates* of palmetto leaf, and to hear more of the Zapotec tongue with its queer aspirates. As near as I could transcribe it, *ihipe, tjope, chone, tape, kahi* meant 'one, two, three, four, five'. In addition to these attractions Santo Domingo offered eggs, a chicken and tortillas sixteen inches in diameter.

Before leaving next morning we stumbled on a curious bit of folklore. In the portico of the school half the young male population of the village were sleeping rolled up in *sarapes* each with his hat and clothes in a neat little pile at his feet. They explained that it is the custom for unmarried men and boys not to sleep in the huts with their sisters but outside in some communal dormitory.

On the third day we completed a good day's ride before lunch, for we were anxious to reach Yalalag in time to photograph the costume of its women. We rose in the dark and rode from half past six to two with scarcely a halt. The scenery was, if anything, more dramatic than the previous days. The trail followed a long ridge terminating in a promontory just in Mije territory. Then for an hour and a half it wound downwards into a deep canyon where the sun scarcely penetrated. At the bottom was a river twenty-five yards wide, the Rio Hamaca so named from the remains of one of those swaying bridges of liana used in this country, which had been destroyed in the revolution. Luckily it was the dry season, and fording was not difficult. Steeper even than the descent was the climb out of the gorge, a good two hours, for the first part of which we had to let the horses stop for breath every forty or fifty yards. When at last Yalalag came into view it appeared quite a metropolis after San Miguel and Santo Domingo. Its houses were of stone or adobe with pillared porticos and tiled roofs, but this did not mean that we slept anywhere but on the schoolroom floor or found anything to eat but beans, eggs and tortillas. It was the eve of Our Lady of Guadalupe, and at night the women crowded into the church with candles in their hands. All were dressed in white *huipiles* of homespun linen, flowing robes

cut like a sack with a hole for the head and a little twist of coloured silk at the neck.

On their heads some wore white woven shawls and others a remarkable turbanlike headdress called the *rodete* made of skeins of black wool sewn together, which unfortunately is beginning to go out of fashion. No suggestion has ever been put forward as to the origin of this headdress, but I have been greatly struck by the resemblance

230

which it bears to one representing thirteen intercoiled serpents worn by the figure adorning one of the funerary urns found by Sr. Caso at Monte Albán.

In the evening a vicious little wind set the dust swirling and brought up clouds from the east. The next day, our longest, was the only one on which the weather was not perfect. It did not rain, but the clouds settled down on the mountain tops and for two hours we were in them, for after recrossing the Rio Hamaca, the trail climbed steadily over steep rocks slippery with mud and wet until it must have risen a full 4,000 feet. After ten and a half hours in the saddle we dropped down to Santa Catarina Albarradas, the third of the Albarradas trinity, facing San Miguel across the valley. The *Presidente Municipal* came out to greet us, not with a handkiss like his colleague over the way but with staggering steps and extravagant gestures. He was grandly, gloriously, uproariously drunk, delighted to see us and ready to oblige in any way he could. As a mark of special esteem, he announced, he would honour us with the *grito a la policia*. This summoning of the police filled us with vague apprehension. He walked across to the edge of the little rocky spur on which the church and school are built and curving his hands round his mouth let out a weird, long-drawn call across the valley to the amphitheatre of huts opposite. Such methods of broadcasting are not unusual in the mountains. The previous night at Yalalag we had heard a drum in the middle of the village 'speaking' to the community in a language of complex rhythms. At Santa Maria del Tule the primitive conch-shell is used for the same purpose. The Presidential summons was not without its effect. A few minutes later three Indians in cottons and sombreros came trudging up the path and stood in a sheepish row before the

231

Mayor who to our relief instructed them to help us prepare for the night.

Lest there should be any anti-climax the last day brought the most dramatic part of the trail. It took nine hours from Santa Catarina to Tlacolula, consisting practically of one climb up and one drop down, each of three thousand feet. We rode out of Santa Catarina while the stars were still in the sky, and it was nearly midday before we reached the top of the pine and oak clad mountain which lay between us and the Valley of Oaxaca. Here began the last and worst part of the trail, a place known as *El Campanario*, 'the Belfry'. So precipitous was it that only the bells were lacking to make the name completely a fitting one. The path is cut in steps out of steep rocks which in places have been worn smooth by centuries of Indian feet to a gradient of one in one. You can ride neither up nor down, so dismounting we watched the horses delicately pick their way down and tried in vain to take photographs which would give a true idea of the steepness of the trail.

After 'the Belfry' Tlacolula is reached in two or three hours across the plain by way of Santo Domingo del Valle. Civilization seemed curiously superfluous as we went to meet it, and it was with a feeling of distaste that we changed our horses for Ford cars and returned to Oaxaca. The trail to Yalalag had been rough and arduous, hard alike on mount and man, but it had given us five of the best days of our lives.

XIII. Jalisco and Michoacan

Fourteen hours journey by rail westwards from Mexico City lies Guadalajara, capital of the State of Jalisco and second city of Mexico. Perhaps it was because I had heard so much about it that I found the reality a little disappointing. People had said that in contrast to the Castilian austerity of Puebla on its high uplands, the *Perla del Occidente* (Pearl of the West) lying 5,000 feet above the sea had all the grace and charm of Andalucia. This applies no doubt to its inhabitants and to the life they lead behind closed doors. It is not the impression produced on the newcomer by the streets, from which fine colonial buildings stand out as exceptions rather than as the culminating expression of a uniform whole. Of the Cathedral, the less said the better. Tasteless restoration has so deformed its earthquake-shattered fabric that it is difficult to believe that it was not built in 1860. Most pleasing, on the other hand, are those of Guadalajara's several hundred churches in which a sober Plateresque style has been carried out in a fine sandstone ranging in colour from bistre to rose and recalling Spanish Salamanca and Ciudad Rodrigo. The buildings which remain in my memory after the briefest of visits are the little church of Aranzazu near the station, the Governor's Palace in which curling scrolls mark the transition from Renaissance to Baroque, and the Convent Church of Santa Monica, a gem of pure Plateresque.

On the corner of Santa Monica stands a giant statue of St. Christopher known owing to his size by the affectionate augmentative of San Cristobalazo. The long, gaunt figure, with its vast, potent thighs has almost a Gothic quality.

Around this Saint a special cult has grown up. Candles are lit before him at night. Porters pray to him for the strength which they deem inherent in his stature. In order that their prayers may be the more efficacious, they couch them in verse:

Dichoso Cristobalazo,	*Happy St. Christopher,*
Santazo de cuerpo entero,	*Full-bodied Saint,*
Y no como otros santitos	*Not like other Saintlets*
Que ni se ven en el cielo,	*Who are scarcely seen in Heaven,*
Herculeo Cristobalazo,	*Herculean St. Christopher,*
Forzudo como un Sansón,	*Strong as any Samson,*
Con tu enorme cabezón,	*With your huge head,*
Y tu nervudo pescuezo,	*And your brawny chest,*
Hazme grueso y vigoroso,	*Make me big and lusty,*
Hombrazo de cuerpo entero,	*A full-bodied man,*
Y no como esos tipitos	*And not like those miserable creatures*
Que casi besan el suelo.	*Who almost kiss the earth.*

Nor is the cult limited to men, for the Saint is also the 'advocate' of despondent old maids and of unhappily married women. The first exclaim with a wealth of augmentatives aimed no doubt at operating by sympathetic magic:

234

Jalisco and Michoacan

San Cristobalazo,	*Great St. Christopher,*
Patazas grandazas,	*Huge great feet,*
Manazas fierazas,	*Fierce great hands,*
Cuando me casas?	*When will you find me a*
	husband?

The latter, substituting diminutives for augmentatives, seek a diminution of their troubles by exclaiming:

San Cristobalito,	*Little St. Christopher,*
Patitas chiquitas,	*Tiny little feet,*
Manitas bonitas,	*Dainty little hands,*
Cuando me lo quitas?	*When will you rid me of*
	him?

The foundation of Guadalajara dates from colonial not from pre-Cortesian times. Several sites were tried before the final choice fell upon a spot a few miles from where the Rio Verde and the Rio Grande de Santiago mingle their waters and fuse the canyons which they have gouged two thousand feet out of the level plain.

One of these earlier sites was Tonalá, to-day a village of Indian potters with a decorative tradition handed down from father to son. We watched them at work at San Pedro Tlaquepaque, to which many of them have moved, a few miles nearer Guadalajara. The clay, a grey dust which goes black when mixed with water and bistre when fired, is painted in various colours, all, with the exception of the blue, found in the immediate neighbourhood. True to Indian tradition no implement, not even the potter's wheel, is used in its fashioning. With deft movements of his fingers, a man shaped a little bull before our eyes. Within less than five minutes the seeming miracle was complete, and a final twist to the head gave it the authentic posture of the charging *toro bravo*. Another man was outlining designs on plates and jars which his companions filled in with colour. His touch was no less swift and sure. Never a moment's hesitation did he show in deciding where to begin, yet his freehand designs, many of them of astonishing complexity, invariably revealed a fine sense of composition within the space at his disposal. He worked without any model, painting not towards but away from himself with a home-made brush of pig's bristles. In drawing an animal, whether deer, bull or donkey, he began with three legs, completing the head and body before putting in the fourth, 'lest it should run away before it is finished.'

The designs seem to reflect more European than pre-Cortesian influence. The lines have the supple, flowing rhythm of the Persian miniature, and the balance of masses carries the mind back to Persia through the Hispano-Moresque and Asia Minor ceramic schools. At times one senses something Chinese in feeling, which gives the impression of having filtered through the Near East and Europe rather than of having crossed the Pacific from west to east.

The potters of Tonalá and Tlaquepaque are all young, for their work requires a steadiness of hand of which advancing years soon rob them. They are as temperamental as any ballerina, working two or three days a week and only when they feel like it. They have forgotten the significance of such Indian motifs as they have incorporated into their style. Yet an old man in Tonalá remembered that one apparently abstract design symbolized rain, another crops, a third the stars and so on.

An hour's drive to the south-east brings one to Lake Chapala, a great stretch of opaque water, glinting with opalescent light, sixty miles long and from eight to

twelve wide. Here D. H. Lawrence chose to set some of
the scenes of *The Plumed Serpent*. Cloud-topped mountains slope down to its western and southern shores, some
of them in Jalisco, others in Michoacan, where one hears
stories, never properly investigated, of Indian tribes with
fair skins and grey eyes.

In Ajijic, at least, we found no lighter colouring, but
golden skins and the features which one would expect in
Indians who, though they have lost their language, belong
to the great Nahua family. They fish with seines in long
dug-out canoes, cultivate the slopes rising steeply from

the shore and carry merchandise across the lake in heavy
square-sailed craft well able to ride the seas whipped up
by Chapala's sudden storms. From Spain by way of Guadalajara, they have borrowed the custom of *el coloquio en la
reja*, the lover's tryst at the barred window. The young
man who wishes to honour both the custom and the lady
of his choice is required to present himself at the *Pres-
idencia Municipal* an hour before his tryst and at the cost
of a peso to take out a license showing that he is sober.
This does not mean that the Mayor thinks he must be
drunk to wish to serenade any girl in Ajijic. On the contrary, it is a practical measure aimed at preventing brawls,

and the high charge not only brings money into the municipal coffers but increases the value of the compliment to the lady.

It is difficult to understand why Lawrence did not choose Lake Patzcuaro rather than Chapala for the scene of his imaginative phantasy reviving the ancient Mexican cults. Of the two lakes, Patzcuaro, though smaller, is far richer in native life and customs. It is indeed one of the shrines of Indian Mexico which no true devotee can fail to visit. Perhaps Lawrence never went there. If so, the loss is his, for few eyes can rest without pleasure on the glittering surface of the lake and on the green, wooded slopes mirrored in its waters.

As if to emphasize the Indian character of the lake, the town is withdrawn a mile or so from its shores, out of their sight. But then the town is colonial, as its churches and fountains proclaim. It was largely colonized from Biscay, and the fortress-like church of San Francisco and the wide eaves which shelter its pavements bear testimony to its debt to that rain-swept Atlantic province.

Only on Friday, the weekly market-day, does the Indian reverse the conquest. Then, at dawn, the dug-out canoes, hewn from a single pine-log, bring in soft-voiced Tarascans from Tzintzuntzan, Cucuchucho, Purenchecuro and many other villages with sonorous Tarascan names, embroidered on the shores of the lake and on its tiny islands.

The meaning of Tzintzuntzan is 'humming-bird', and like a humming-bird the village appears to hover at the foot of the hills. It was once the capital of the pre-Cortesian Tarascan kingdom. The Tarascan was one of the marginal cultures of ancient Mexico, like the Totonac and the Zapotec, which, without attaining the splendours of the Toltec, the Aztec or the Mayan civilizations, nevertheless

had its own well-defined character. Ancient Tarascan artefacts are crude and primitive like those of the Archaic
strata, and it has been supposed that there may be a connexion between the two. To-day, upwards of forty-five
thousand Tarascans speak their own tongue, in which the
tribe's name for itself is *purepecha*. The men wear the
uniform white cottons of all Mexico and drape themselves
in great sarapes, red and black or brown. The women are
distinguished by white blouses, embroidered on the neck
and sleeves, and by skirts of scarlet or black homespun,
bunched in pleats, not at the front like the Otomis but at
the back. As much as thirty-three metres of material used
to go to the making of these skirts, but hard times have reduced their length to twenty metres on the lake and a
mere twelve in the sierra. The blouse, too, is turned up in
pleats at the back, so that where the two waves of pleats
meet and break against each other the women have the
look of fan-tail pigeons.

To-day Tzintzuntzan is no more than a tiny *pueblo*, a
few lines of unwashed cottages, their sun-baked bricks a
richer and less dusty brown than usual from the red loam
of the earth hereabouts. Once only in the year the village
awakes to unwonted animation. On the Wednesday before
Ash Wednesday, the whole region throngs in pilgrimage
to the Señor del Rescate (the Christ of the Redemption).
The church, all that is left of a sixteenth century Franciscan monastery, stands in a vast grass-grown churchyard
lined with a double row of gnarled and ancient olive trees.
The Señor del Rescate is no carved image but a dark oil
painting hanging in a side-chapel. In artistic merit it is
considerably inferior to a bigger canvas, the Descent from
the Cross, which hangs beside a giant fresco of St. Christopher on the left hand side of the nave. This picture

has been ascribed to Titian and is undoubtedly an Italian picture of his period, perhaps even of his school. To the festival come all the lakeside dancers, the *Moros* of Janitzio and Ihuatzio, the *Viejitos* of Jaracuaro and Cucuchucho, and the *Borrachos* (Drunkards) of Erongaricuaro carrying bottles inside each of which a tiny altar has been erected with infinite skill, like those bottled models of sailing ships in which seamen delight. For a day or two, all is noise and animation with the braying of brass bands and the bursting of innumerable rockets and petards. Then the crowds melt away, and Tzintzuntzan dozes off again to slumber for another year and dream of its royal memories.

Tarascans meet and gather not only in Patzcuaro market or at the *fiesta* of Tzintzuntzan but in the many other markets held on different days round the lake, for commercial exchange is promoted by the specialized crafts carried on by the different villages, many of which enjoy a monopoly of their particular product. Thus, only the people of Nahuatzen hollow out canoes, while paddles must be sought in Pichataro. Cucuchucho produces reed petate mats, and Santa Fé de la Laguna green glaze pottery. By an unwritten law the white fish of the lake, which it is said will take no bait, are still reserved in great part to the nets of Janitzio, whose fishermen barter them for the firewood of Erongaricuaro and the corn of Jaracuaro.

It was the great Bishop Vasco de Quiroga, one of the finest Spanish clerics in the history of Latin America, who after converting the Tarascans, taught them the benefits of specialized production and exchange. To each village he himself allotted its trade or craft, laying down that those of Cocucao, now named Quiroga after him, should fashion and paint the wood cut by Capula, that Patamban should

240

devote itself to pottery and San Felipe de los Herreros to the ironwork which gave it its name and fame throughout New Spain.

Don Vasco de Quiroga was born in 1470 in a little town in Old Castile, the name of which, Madrigal de Altas Torres, rings like a line from one of the old *romances*. He did not enter the church but studied law, and it was in the lay capacity of Oidor of the Audiencia that he came to Mexico in 1531 at an age at which many men's careers are at an end. Distinguishing himself by his charity and kindliness he was entrusted in 1533 with the task of pacifying Michoacan. The peaceful Tarascans had at first given the Conquerors no serious difficulty but had been goaded into revolt and into a return to the old gods by one Nuño de Guzmán who, among other cruelties and injustices, had put to death the converted Tarascan King Caltzontzin whose statue now overlooks the lake from a pillar in Quiroga market square. It speaks much for the Christian spirit in which Don Vasco accomplished this task, that he, a layman, was both ordained and consecrated Bishop of Michoacan at a single step in 1538. Like all great men he had his critics, and he came into conflict with Gasca and Fray Bartolomé de las Casas through his defence of the *encomienda* system by which vast tracks of land and their Indian inhabitants were handed over in trust to individual Conquistadores. Las Casas could see no good in a system which had been so gravely abused. Quiroga, on the other hand, thought it preferable that the Indians should not be at the mercy of the changing whims of Viceroys and Governors. That he knew what was best for his own diocese, if for no other, is shown by the deep affection in which the Indians held him. Tata Vasco, as they still affectionately call him, was buried in the Cathedral of

241

Patzcuaro (now the Church of La Compañia) on his death
in 1565, and the mere suggestion that his ashes be taken
to Spain was enough to threaten an insurrection among
the people to whose welfare he had devoted more than
thirty years of his life.

The tale goes that it was Vasco de Quiroga that the
gigantic statue which crowns the island of Janitzio was
first intended to commemorate, and that not until the
neck was reached was the liberating priest Morelos substituted for the missionary Bishop. To most visitors that
statue is the one blemish on the lake. It simply will not be
ignored. Like a white finger it points to Heaven as though
imploring its own destruction. I do not know its exact
measurements, but an American who stood with me at its
base told me that it was three feet higher than New
York's statue of Liberty. 'I suppose', he added, 'that's to
show there's just that much more liberty in Mexico than
in the States.' From the ample cement folds of the skirts,
the monstrous figure narrows to the squat head and up-
raised hand. The effect from near is that of a lighthouse.
This is intensified inside by the spiral stair which leads
the visitor to an opening at the base of the palm where,
from outside, his head looks like a flea biting the liber-
ator's wrist. The statue might be tolerable in a modern,
urban setting. In the centre of Lake Patzcuaro it is, to say
the least, ill-placed. The Indians, who have to live with it,
betray a most regrettable lack of appreciation of modern
art, and have tersely dubbed it *el gran mono* 'the big
monkey'.

It is all a great pity, for Janitzio is one of the most idyllic spots in Mexico. Its charm seizes the traveller from the
moment he leaves the landing-stage of Patzcuaro where
the Indians moor their canoes. The first time I went there

was on a brilliant day in late July. Vast white clouds towered into the sky, steeping their mirrored silver in the
blue of the water. In the late afternoon, they would thick-
en and blacken and discharge their rain in a shattering
deluge. Now it was early morning and the sun shone
brightly. Yellow butterflies with black mourning borders
fluttered across the lake. What tempted them so greatly
on the northern shores, I wondered, and would they ever
reach their goal? Or would their tiring wings bring them
ever lower above the water until some wavelet higher
than the rest flicked them with spray and brought them
heavily to disaster? The snakes inspired greater confidence, shearing their way across the lake like miniature
sea-serpents and showing their forked tongues with a
vicious hiss as our outboard motor-boat pencilled a wake
across their track. We divined their purpose when we
reached the island and saw the water alive with serpents
twenty or thirty yards out, waiting for the scraps of fish
which the fishermen throw out of their boats.

Janitzio rises out of the water in a steep, green slope,
its southern shore lined with fishermen's huts. Here, by a
merciful dispensation of providence, the statue is out of
sight, hidden away behind the curve of the hill. Above the
houses, the church and presbytery face one another, the
belfry tower rising for some strange reason from the latter.
The church contains a remarkable image of St. James
which, an old fisherman told me, had been presented to
it by President Cárdenas in gratitude for his safety after
being caught in a storm on the lake. The whitewashed
balconied presbytery has been turned into a school and
bears the charming inscription *Tzitziqui Urapiti* which in
Tarascan means 'Little White Flower'.

I had been told that the Indians of Janitzio were the

most disagreeable in the Republic, and their charm and friendliness came as a pleasant surprise. True, they will not let themselves be photographed without payment, but American tourists have taught them their photogenic value, and one would be churlish indeed to grudge them the penny which is generally all they ask.

The previous night they had been fishing, and now in the morning all the nets were drying in the sunlight; long seines, draped and festooned from tall wooden poles the whole length of the narrow alleys, softly veiling the houses of whitewashed adobe with tiles mellowed by age to a golden brown. Through their gauzy mesh we watched men and women coming and going or crouched at their doorways making nets. Down by the water's edge the long dug-out canoes were drawn up, tilted at an angle at the bow and stern. Two small boys in white and a dusky little girl in deep rose were playing with the paddles, their blades like ping-pong bats on the end of long handles.

Fishing goes on all the year round, except when the moon is full. Some four or five years ago the lake was further stocked with trout. Against these the celebrated 'white fish' have continued to hold their own, but the invaders have devoured the *thiru, chegua* and *cuerepu,* and have thereby almost killed the picturesque 'butterfly' nets used by the islanders of Uranden to catch these smaller fry. Soon, it will no longer be possible to see, as we saw, the men of Uranden put out in small canoes, each with his plunge net shaped like a butterfly on the end of a pole twelve or fifteen feet long. With the pole laid flat and the 'wings' projecting in front the canoe looks like a gigantic dragon-fly. At the appropriate moment each fisherman grasps his pole where it meets the net and plunges it deep into the lake.

Jalisco and Michoacan

From Janitzio we went across to Jaracuaro, a mile or two to the west. If Janitzio looks rather like a rock-cake in its configuration, Jaracuaro may better be compared to a drop-scone. Teams of oxen, each with its ploughman frozen in the age-old gesture of the man with the goad, were cutting deep furrows in the red-brown earth. We made our way to the house of the schoolmaster, Sr. Nicolas Juarez, whom we found composing little waltz-tunes to Tarascan words for the village band and super-intending the manufacture of straw *sombreros*. Thanks to

his kindness, we had the good fortune to see a special per-formance of the *Danza de los Viejitos* or Old Men's Dance.

The 'Old Men', most of whom were in point of fact youths and boys, wore ordinary Indian dress with sarapes and sombreros. Their faces were hidden behind grotesque masks of earthenware twisted into leering, toothless smiles. Standing in a semi-circle and supporting their bent figures on little sticks, they began their dance with legs quite motionless and heads waggling rhythmically from side to side.

Once their feet came into play, however, the effect of senility vanished and they conveyed the impression of frisky old men indeed. Seldom moving more than a few inches to the side or lifted more than an inch or two from the ground, the sandalled feet beat such rhythmic tattoo, that they set one's own toes tingling. Some of the steps were on the ball of the foot, others on the heel and toe, and there were various figures, some danced in a line, some in a circle, others in solos, pairs or heys. At one moment they were drawn up in two lines each of which in turn stamped out what appeared a petulant challenge to the other. The only music was a tiny guitar carried by the leader and thrummed on a couple of chords in complex rhythms so as to produce almost the effect of a percussion instrument.

*   *   *

It was eighteen months before I returned to Patzcuaro. On this second occasion, in the dry season, I was lucky enough to be present at one of the periodic duck hunts in which the people of the whole lake take part. These duck hunts begin just before All Souls' Day and continue through the winter. On Sundays, the Indians hunt one or other of the two eastern arms of the lake, on Wednesdays the western end. Exceptionally, however, the particular *feria de los patos* which we attended fell on a Tuesday, the eve of the Feast of the Assumption of the Virgin, December 8th, when all the dwellers on the lake congregate in Patzcuaro for the *fiesta* of Nuestra Señora de la Salud. This *fiesta* is popularly known as *los cacahuates* from the monkey nuts which are on sale at every corner of the market square at a hundred or so for a penny.

In spite of the time of year it was a typical wet season day, with a fresh breeze blowing up great clouds from the sierra and rainwashed, west-wind colouring. Early in the morning, before the drying nets had been taken in, a white figure climbed on to a steep bluff on the eastern slope of Janitzio, and, silhouetted against the sky, hailed

246

the mainland villages to announce the hunt. Faintly, answering cries were borne across the water. An hour or so later, as we skirted round the island, canoes were putting out from every fisher-house at the water's edge, and soon we were heading westwards in the van of a fleet which gradually began to assume a half-moon shape. The broad lake surrounded by green hills and mountains, the throng of swiftly moving canoes filled with white figures reflected in the blue water, conjured up in the mind a picture of Tenochtitlan as it must have appeared before its lake was dried up and its native life eclipsed by the conquerors.

We were heading towards Jaracuaro. Off the eastern shores of this island lie extensive shallows, thick with water-weed, where the duck love to feed. As we approached we could see them clearly, dark grey waterfowl almost black to the eye, with bright white beaks, winter emigrants from the great lakes on the Canadian-United States border. Some rose into the air at our approach and wheeled about uneasily; others scarcely interrupted their feeding to scud a few yards across the water, trailing a white wake with their webbed feet. In order not to disturb them too soon we sheared off to the left and hid in a thick bed of reeds. Here we waited for about a quarter of an hour until all the canoes had assembled and the circle was complete. Then we stealthily emerged and moved in towards the middle of the circle. The duck were seriously alarmed now. Many of them flew high into the air and, wheeling, were soon out of sight in safety. Others sought refuge in the reeds, or, less easily scared, continued to swim about in apparent unconcern.

Now the great circle began to break up into little groups, each intent on hunting some few scattered birds. While their companions continued to paddle, the hunters

247

rose to their feet holding their duck spears ready to throw. Now at last I should see in actual use the Indian spear-thrower, *atlatl* in Aztec, or in Tarascan *tzipaqui*. The wooden throwing-stick is about two feet long, grooved along the top, with two small holes near the front through which the fingers grip the *patamu* or spear. The latter, seven or eight feet in length, is of cane with three metal barbs at the end like a harpoon.

Soon I caught sight of a duck only about thirty or forty yards ahead and a little to the right, bobbing up and down on the wavelets. In the next canoe an Indian stood poised, expectant. Suddenly, with a whirring of wings, the bird took flight and rose from the water. At the same moment the spear flew through the air, glistening in the sunlight, the tip slightly lofted. But the duck climbed too steeply, and the spear passed harmlessly beneath it, entering the water at an acute angle and continuing its course like a torpedo below the surface. Then, its energy spent, it lay aimlessly floating, to be recovered a few moments later by its owner.

The next bird was less lucky. In its innocence it waited until the canoes were scarcely twenty yards away, and the hunter, before throwing his spear, had to startle it with a shout and a fling of his arms, not from any sense of sportsmanship but because a 'sitting bird' is harder to kill than one which is just leaving the water. This time there was no mistake. With unerring aim, the hunter made just the right allowance for forward speed and lift, and the quivering spear brought the bird down. A few moments later a dark bunch of feathers, fluttering in its death spasm, was thrown down into the stern of the canoe.

All around us the hunt continued. Spears were cast in a far-flung parabola, hit or missed, were picked out of the water or torn out of their victims. When at last we turned homewards, the total bag was still relatively small, for the stiff breeze had not only made the spears more difficult to control but by whipping up waves on the lake, had made the birds harder to hit. Instead of the eight or ten birds with which each canoe is rewarded under good conditions the day's hunt had yielded only four or five.

*   *   *

For the railway journey, if for nothing else, it is worth while to go on to Uruapan, some forty or fifty miles to the south-west. The motor-road makes a wide détour to the north, but the line faces its problems squarely and after crossing a low rise at Ajuna and skirting the aquamarine waters of little Lake Zirahuen winds down steep, pine-clad slopes opening up ever wider views over the *tierra caliente* of Michoacan, the Sierra de la Tentación and those mountain ranges of Guerrero which on the map are marked as unexplored. Bracken springs up among the pines, giving an illusion of Surrey belied only by the maize fields, by the wild lavender which takes the place of heather and by the distant blue shades of the sierras.

Uruapan lies tucked into a sheltered amphitheatre of hills some five thousand odd feet above the sea. The name in Tarascan means 'Eternal Spring'. No Tourist Bureau could have devised a better one. A bird's eye view at dusk from the Cerro de la Charanda reveals a neat little town of small, white houses and gently inclined streets, the whole wreathed in softly curling smoke and surrounded by a thick rampart of fruit trees and banana groves, sheltering the coffee for which the place is famed.

The secret of Uruapan is water. Everywhere it flows and ripples, and many a time in the night I awoke to

think it was raining only to find that I had been misled
by the trickle of a stream or the plashing of a fountain.
Every house has its garden, and looking through the doorways as one walks down a street, one has the impression
that the walls enclose not stuffy rooms but airy fragments
of the countryside.

At the top of the town in a thicket of guava, mango,
ahuacate and liquidambar trees the River Cupatitzio
wells up from beneath the earth in a shallow pool among
rocks. The name means 'river that sings'. Heavy in December with the scent of guava fruit, the place is called *la
rodilla del diablo*, the devil's knee. One of those small
boys who inevitably attach themselves near any place fre-
quented by tourists told me the legend of the name. In
1914 (he was very precise as to the date), the Devil took
possession of the spring from which the town derives its
water, and the inhabitants, in danger of dying of thirst,
invoked the aid of St. Michael. The Saint offered to play
the Devil for the water at *rayuelas* (a Mexican form of
shove ha'penny). The Devil agreed, lost and then tried to
evade his bargain. St. Michael insisted, and the Evil One
made off, leaving the imprints of his knee and foot in the
rock where they are clearly to be seen. It was a little disconcerting to find that my foot exactly fitted the Devil's
imprint.

At the risk of spoiling a good story, I will add what is
more probably the true origin of the legend. Early in the
sixteenth century, soon after the foundation of Uruapan
by Fray Juan de San Miguel, the water failed, owing to
some subterranean disturbance. The monks tried the only
possible remedy known to them, namely, blasting the
rocks with gunpowder. Before they did so, however, they
were careful to tell the people that the drought was the

work of the Devil and adjured them to pray to God that it might be brought to an end. While the people were busy with prayers and litanies the charge was exploded, the waters flowed once more, and the smell of sulphur from the charge convinced the faithful that the Evil One had been present in person.

The pool where the water rises is so clear and limpid that every stick and stone can be seen on the bottom. This appearance of tranquil innocence is not long maintained, however. If the Cupatitzio is born in the odour of sanctity, St. Michael's influence scarcely extends beyond the source. Only a few yards down stream the Devil reasserts himself, and the river is off like a thing possessed, carving its way through the tropical undergrowth in a series of rapids, falls and whirlpools, no longer singing but shouting in exultation.

Uruapan has long been known for its lacquer industry which is concentrated in the *barrio de San Pedro* not far from the Devil's Knee. The industry, indeed, is pre-Cortesian, but was established at Uruapan by Vasco de Quiroga. In many a hut or tiny courtyard, the Indian artists are at work. The ground colour, generally black, is first rubbed on to gourds or wooden plates. Next is applied the *aje* or lacquer derived from an insect found in large quantities in the hot country on the borders of Michoacan and Guerrero, about a week's journey away. The insects are gathered in the rainy season and thrown into hot water where they give out a gummy scum which is skimmed off, washed and mixed in a certain secret proportion with linseed oil. When a high lustre has been brought up by rubbing with a cotton pad, the designs previously traced on the surface are chipped out and filled in again with a variety of colours.

251

Jalisco and Michoacan

Behind Uruapan, to the north and west, rise the forest-clad slopes of the *sierra*. It has no name, just *la sierra*. Even its peaks have no proper names of their own, being called after the villages at their foot, thus Cerro de Paracho, Cerro de Patamban, Cerro de Tancitaro and so on. Two or three hours ride brings the traveller to San Lorenzo, the first of the Tarascan villages, lying among its *milpas* in a lonely bowl in the hills. The village is almost a prolongation of the forest. The houses are all of weather board, many of them lifted off the ground on stones set under each corner. To the village street, they present windowless flanks, the front with its carved portico facing the courtyard. The graceful shingles of the steep-pitched roofs catch and reflect the sunshine in fan-shaped patterns. Neither the municipal building nor the jail, only the church, is of stone. With a box of matches, it looked possible to burn the prison down over one's head and escape.

Our glimpse of San Lorenzo tempted us to see more of the *sierra* and we spent a week in riding twice across its breadth, from Uruapan to Chilchota by way of Paracho and back again by a more westerly route through Patamban and Parangaricutiro. It was the first time for a year that I had been off on horseback for more than a week-end and it was a deep satisfaction to feel the whole rhythm of my being slow down once again to the steady jog of a *sierra* pony and my mind gradually empty itself of anxiety and preoccupation, of all thought even, and become void of everything save physical sensation.

The principal interest of Chilchota, and an extrinsic one at that, is that it marks the end of the *Cañada de los Once Pueblos*, the Gorge of the Eleven Villages. These villages have long preserved a sense of their communal unity and a reputation for being the home of the purest

Tarascan Indians. It used to be said that they could be visited only in their strict order, though whether for reasons of custom or geography I am unable to say. Now, the main road from the capital to Guadalajara is being driven remorselessly through them, leaving some to the right hand and some to the left, and breaking down in more ways than one their ancient traditions. With the exception of Etucuaro, which stands a little apart to the north of Chilchota, the *Once Pueblos* are contained within the six miles between 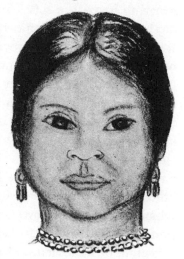 the latter and Carapam. The names of the others are Uren, Tanaquillo, Acachuen, Santo Tomas, Zopoco, Huancito, Ichan and Tacuru. Each with its little church standing apart from the belfry of crumbling adobe, they are almost continuous, Tacuru and Ichan actually running into one another while Chilchota and Uren are separated only by a dyke and Acachuen and Santo Tomas by a small ploughed field.

We visited all the eleven villages with the exception of Etucuaro, but fate decreed that of them all we should become most closely acquainted with Zopoco. Our stay coincided with a period of bad weather quite exceptional in December. For thirty-six hours it rained without ceasing, not the abrupt torrential rain of the tropics but the steady ceaseless downpour of more northern latitudes. We had just reached Zopoco when it began in earnest, and there seemed nothing for it but to shelter in the portico of the village school. Here, the whole village, prevented by the weather from working in the fields, gradually gathered, greeting us with a soft Tarascan *Nareranskoushki* (Good day). We ate our picnic lunch under the concentrated stare of innumerable unwinking eyes. With their dark brown sarapes draped round them and wound round close under their eyes, the men had the look of *zopilotes* huddled dejectedly in the rain. They were very friendly and, in the afternoon, we were invited into many of their huts and engaged in innumerable conversations. Among other things, I recall, we were asked whether we were Otomis, and also whether we 'divined medicine'. One man wanted to know of a good cure for deafness, while another had a child which could not swallow. One of the most useful qualifications for travelling off the beaten track in Mexico would, we reflected, be a modicum of reliable medical knowledge.

Next morning dawned without a cloud in the sky, nor did we see one during the three days of our ride back to

Uruapan. Patamban, where we spent the night in the Mesón de San Francisco, is chiefly distinguished by its pottery industry. One of its two *barrios* specializes in great round water-jars, the other in bowls and jugs adorned with a high green copper glaze. Both products are decorated with floral designs, and with birds and rabbits executed with that swift virtuosity which comes only from an ancient inherited tradition.

Jalisco and Michoacan

From Patamban to Parangaricutiro was our longest day, ten and a half hours over the mountains where until noon the frost stood stiffly up in minute knife-edges under the shadow of the pine trees. As in Oaxaca we were struck by the absence of wild life. Once or twice in a week's riding we saw the blue flash of the guarate bird, and more often smaller birds, blue, red or dun-coloured. Once a big sandy coyote loped across the trail and was swallowed up again by the forest. Once, too, we put up a *correcaminos,* a bird like a lanky, crested cock-pheasant which, true to its name, did not take to its wings but scuttled along the path in front of us.

As we rode down towards Zacan in the late afternoon, the view suddenly opened to the West, and over nearly a hundred miles of tumbled country, the southern part of Jalisco, a snowy range was etched against the sky; the volcano of Colima with its two peaks, the rounded Peak of Fire and the conical Peak of Ice.

In a lurid sunset light Parangaricutiro welcomed us at the end of the day. To the right, the smoke from Parang-aricutirimicuaro curled upwards against the snow-flecked pines of the Cerro de Tancitaro. A dozen little Indian girls came running out of the *milpas* and whooping down the trail behind us, belying the legend of the 'sad Indian' and making us feel like palefaces pursued by Redskins. The feeling must have been mutual, for when they were only fifty yards away, they suddenly paused in a little startled knot. Then one of them cried to the others 'Don't be frightened', and they dashed past us with baby brothers and sisters bouncing up and down in their *rebozos* and looking as though they must inevitably be flung out on to the boulders.

Parangaricutiro's welcome was a mixed one, for the

255

mesón where we slept was indescribably filthy and full of what Gage picturesquely described as those 'busy guests and individual mates and companions as . . . intruded themselves upon us'. But then Michoacan is famous for its fleas, and it is told of a theatre in Morelia that in the olden days a flock of sheep used to be introduced into it before its annual opening to attract to themselves the insect life which it harboured. Fragments of starlit sky were to be seen through the gaps in the rickety roof like the stall at Bethlehem in a Dürer Nativity. The night was a cold one, too, and we saw no signs of the bedding the making of which has earned Parangaricutiro its alternative name of San Juan de las Colchas (St. John of the Quilts).

It is surprising that Parangaricutiro has no better accommodation, for it is the Chalma of Michoacan and attracts innumerable pilgrims from great distances to the annual *fiesta* on September 15th. The pilgrimage is apparently of no great antiquity, and the Santo Cristo of which it is the object has neither artistic merit nor antiquarian interest. A curious belief has sprung up, however, that the image 'likes to see' dancing. Accordingly, every single soul who enters the church on the great day, candle in hand, keeps up a curious shuffling, stamping step until he leaves it. It must be an extraordinary sight to see the vast press of people bobbing up and down. The church looks somewhat askance upon the pagan flavour of this tradition. Once a priest stricter than the rest is said to have locked the church doors to keep out the dancing multitude. That night, pale with fright, the Sacristan woke him and bade him come down into the church. Empty of people, the great nave was nevertheless alive with little lights jigging up and down and with the echoes of invisible stamping

256

feet. Next day the church was open again, and has never since been closed.

On one side of the aisle are grouped the inevitable *retablo* pictures testifying to the miracles wrought by the Christ of Parangaricutiro. Two of them particularly interested me because of their connection with the U.S.A., to which many people emigrated from Michoacan when the worst years of the Mexican revolution coincided with the boom north of the Rio Grande. One of these *retablos* is by a man whose life was saved in the floods of 1918. The flooded area in his picture is distinguished from the dry ground by the simple expedient of depicting houses, railways and so on upside down with heads bobbing about among them the right way up and one man being rescued by a boat. At the top of the picture is the Crucified Christ with a candle on either side and the donor kneeling in adoration before Him.

The other *retablo* tells a long story of a young man of Patzcuaro who fell in love with an Irish American girl, called Catherine Mars. When Miss Mars proved faithless, the young man followed her about with threats and soon found himself first in court and then in the lunatic asylum at Akron, Ohio. If he is to be believed, he owed his release from the latter to the vow he took to dance for six hours in the sanctuary of Parangaricutiro on its *fiesta* day and to approach the church of Nuestra Señora de la Salud in his native Patzcuaro from within 'about 500 metres' on his knees. The picture, remarkably well drawn in pencil, shows him with rumpled hair and distraught features in a cell realistically endowed with 'all modern conveniences'.

XIV. Earth Magic

More than a year after the first *volador* we found ourselves again at Pahuatlan. It was Easter, the time of year when by all rights the weather should have been set fair. Once again we rode down from Honey on an afternoon of enamelled brilliance. Once again the cloud drove up the valley during the night, clinging to the hills, so that the *voladores* flew over the Easter market in a chilling Scotch mist.

On Easter Saturday we went to one of the Otomi villages across the valley from the Honey trail, which for the sake of convenience I will call San Cristobal. As usual we were accompanied by Antonio, our muleteer, with Capulina, his flea-bitten grey, and Chucha, the surest-footed mule I have ever ridden in the *sierras*. Antonio is a great character. Some white blood flows in his veins, but not much. His round, smiling face reflects his natural good humour. Any little joke will keep him chuckling for half a day. He neither smokes nor drinks, an admirable quality in a muleteer. His favourite parlour trick is an anecdote in which he imitates the speech of the *gachupín*, the Spaniard, strongly flavoured with the physiological expletives of the Peninsula.

Earth Magic

It was Antonio who first took my friend Herr Weitlaner to San Cristobal some years ago. Then the Indians
all ran away and hid in their houses at the stranger's
approach. Successive visits by Herr Weitlaner, Helga
Larsen and others have accustomed them to visits from
the outside world, but except with those whom they know
they remain reserved and uncommunicative. Yet San
Cristobal is no great distance from Pahuatlan, and its
women come in to market in their skirts edged with blue
and their cotton *quexquemitls* elaborately embroidered in
red and black with a broad border of scarlet or purplish
serge.

The trail drops steeply to the bottom of a gorge where
a river flows between rocky banks. The Indians fish this
river with a technique all their own. They build a barrage
of stones and branches and some way above it squeeze
into the water the juice of a plant called *mexal*. So bitter
and astringent is this liquid that the fish flee downstream
to escape from it, only to be caught at the barrage, where
those too small are allowed to escape.

At the river we crossed a dozen or more white-clad
figures whom we had seen coming down the opposite
slope in Indian file, pausing and drawing up every now
and again like a caterpillar on a twig, then extending once
more as they moved forward. It was only when they passed
that we saw they were bringing a wounded man in to
Pahuatlan. Two men had been drinking in the village.
Suddenly one of those abrupt, unaccountable Indian
quarrels flared up. Machetes flashed, and the victim was
badly cut about the head and wrist. So they had bound
him upright in a chair, his hands crossed on his breast, a
piece of sack-cloth over his face and the blood slowly drip-
ping on to his knees. Chair and all was loaded like any

259

other burden on a man's back, the weight taken by the usual *mecapal* or tump-line from the bearer's forehead.

From the river the trail zigzags steeply upwards a thousand feet or so to the village, of which all that can be seen from a distance are two stone buildings, one the church, and the other, twice as large, the prison. As we drew closer the bamboo huts became visible against their protective background of bananas. From the fields Indians returned our Otomi greeting of *teshki ha'tzi*.

We went first to Manuel's house, a tiny store which was doing a flourishing trade in *refino*, sugar-cane brandy, at 25 centavos a bottle. Manuel was most helpful in our quest. It was not only the landscape and the Indian life which had brought us to San Cristobal. In a region thick with superstitious practices the village enjoys an unrivalled reputation for witchcraft and ancient magical cults. Its *brujos*, sorcerers, are respected and feared more than those of any other. They hide their rites and beliefs behind a deep veil of secrecy, to pierce which, even but a little, it is necessary to find a go-between. This part was played by Manuel, who almost alone of this village has been to Mexico City and seen something of the outside world.

So far as I know San Cristobal has no stone idols. The cult centres round *muñecos*, paper figures. Of these *muñecos* there are two kinds, some cut out of manufactured coloured paper, others from paper home-made from the bark of trees by an ancient pre-Spanish process as simple as it is effective. In the door of one of the huts we saw a woman making this paper which, once used for codices, to-day serves none but magical purposes. From the bark of the *moral* and *jonote* trees a light-coloured paper is made, from that of *xalamal* a dark, the former for white magic, the latter for black. Beside the woman lay strips of *moral* bark soaking in a basin of water in which they had been boiled. On her knees lay a flat, wooden board, and in her hand she held a stone shaped like a cake of soap. Laying a piece of the wet bark on the board, she pounded it with the stone until it had spread into a rough oval so thin as almost to be transparent. All it then needed was to dry.

With Manuel's help we were able to obtain not only some of this paper but to have the magic figures cut out for us from it. With great caution and secrecy a *brujo* came into Manuel's hut and set to work. His name was Francisco. Doubling the paper in two, he cut it with deft fingers into the shapes of a man and a woman both with arms uplifted, the latter distinguished only by her smaller size and by the hair which zigzagged straight up from the top of her head. Three slits for eyes and nose gave their faces a curiously sinister expression.

Next, the sorcerer set to work on the coloured paper of which he superimposed two or three pieces one upon another before folding and cutting them. Though made of more ordinary material, these figures were even more remarkable. From their sides sprouted little excrescences in the shape of the crop whose growth they were intended to promote, maize, sugar-cane, chile pepper and so on. Moreover, to each crop corresponded a definite colour-scheme. Thus the maize-doll was compounded of green and white, the banana of purple and green, the chile of green and white and red, the coffee of red and green. There was even a honey doll, white for the wax and yellow for the liquid, with bees flying out from the figure's sides. As he snipped away, a sly twinkle played in the *brujo's* eyes.

Presently I wandered away from the others out into the grey mist. Chance guided my footsteps to a building to which, I think, not even Manuel would otherwise have led us. This was the principal *oratorio* or temple of this strange cult. It had nothing to do with the church which lay further down the hillside where even now its bell was clanging and rockets were being let off to celebrate the hour of noon on Easter Saturday.

In the oratory all was silence. Two doors led through the side of the long, narrow shack. On a shelf running along the opposite wall stood a row of religious images, framed in festoons of white strips cut from the heart of the sago palm. From strings hung *muñecos* of cut paper, some of which also lay in a heap on a chest, the size of a child's coffin, which occupied the central position in the row. What was in this coffer I could only surmise.

On a row of small stands separated from the images by a narrow passage-way stood vases of flowers, in which hibiscus, *colorín* and orchid struck a predominant note of scarlet. Candles burned, and hierophants walked in and out, bearing smoking vessels of copal incense. I feared that they might resent my presence, but at first they did not seem to do so and crowded round me asking for cigarettes. Presently I went back and fetched my friends. For a few moments all was well, but suddenly the atmosphere changed. A long discussion started with Antonio in which, if any Spanish words were used, they were so deformed as to be unintelligible to me. Gradually, however, the sense emerged. The *mayordomo* in charge of the ceremony resented our presence. We had entered 'without respect', he said, and we were to go out, unless, that is to say, we were ready to purge our offence with a couple of bottles of brandy. Fifty centavos changed hands, and all was well, but I was left wondering what might have happened if the celebrants had not been so easily appeased.

It is axiomatic that one should never visit an Indian village for the first time. Perhaps I should explain the apparent paradox. The Indian has suffered so much at the hands of the white man, that the first time you visit him you can seldom fully overcome his reserve. If you return after an interval, the atmosphere is changed. He will remember that on the previous occasion you were as polite to him as he to you, that you offered him cigarettes, gave him perhaps ten centavos *para su pulque*, sent him the photographs you had taken. He will now be ready to welcome you as a proven friend.

Rewarding as our first visit to San Cristobal had been it was as nothing to the second. In the meantime, moreover, I had obtained certain clues which were to prove invaluable in probing the mysteries of the village. They shall be told in their proper order.

In January 1938 I went with Herr Weitlaner and Dr. Ecker to the two Otomi villages of Santa Ana Hueytlalpan and San Pedro Tlachichilco between Tulancingo and the edge of the plateau. Here Herr Weitlaner had discovered the existence of a genuine Indian tradition of song, of which I was anxious to collect the music. It is only the women who sing, and they only when they are drunk, the words of the songs being of an unbelievable triviality. We went first to the hut of a woman called Maria Ignacia. She was friendly and hospitable, but she needed more coaxing than the most temperamental prima

263

donna before she would sing. First she said she had no time, as she had some pots to make to sell in Tulancingo. Then she said she couldn't sing because she wasn't drunk. This argument was met with a bottle of cane brandy, but it merely made way for the next which was the familiar one of *vergüenza*, or 'shame'. It would be too shaming for her to sing before us, she said. For an hour we waited patiently, trying to defeat her bashfulness. Every now and again she would seem to overcome her inhibitions. Then at the critical moment, vanquished by shyness, she dissolved in a fit of girlish giggling, and we had to start all over again from the beginning. At last, however, a song rose to her lips, sung in a high, thin little voice to a pentatonic, unmistakably Indian tune, mouth half shut and words scarcely audible. When she had finished and Herr Weitlaner wanted to take down the text, she was quite unable to repeat in a speaking voice what she had sung. Her twenty-year old son undertook to do so, but when we made her sing again in order to fit the words to the musical phrases, the words which she sang proved to be quite different. The following, therefore, may or may not be what she sang the first time:

> *This is how the song goes,*
> *The one that I sang*
> *Because I had taken brandy*
> *Which made me drunk,*
> *And I don't remember what I said,*
> *This is what I said,*
> *This is why I am singing,*
> *And I am singing*
> *The same song which I am singing.*
> *It says:*

Earth Magic

Whether my song be good or not
Pardon what I sang
Because I was drunk.

It was Maria Ignacia who furnished the first hint of a
very strange custom observed in her *pueblo*. The village
has a number of *oratorios* like those of San Cristobal, the
cult of which similarly centers round a mysterious coffer.
The devotees used to go in procession to a cave about an
hour away on the slopes of a hill called *nts'ont'hö*. This,
they told us, meant 'Good Hill', but in reality it means
'Bad Hill'. There they danced, feasted and sacrificed turkeys. With them went a woman who had chewed and
swallowed with wine a dozen or so seeds of a plant called
pâts'iyêthi in Otomi or *rosita* in Spanish which are obtained from the sierra. Literally translated the Otomi
name means 'bound witch'. The seed must contain a very
powerful drug. Under its influence the woman fell into an
ecstatic condition, raving so that she had to be kept under
restraint lest she injure herself. Her eyes were half closed
and she had a kerchief bound round her forehead.

Crouched on the ground at the entrance to the cave,
she pronounced oracles. First a male 'diviner' interpreted
her words into a forecast of the year's weather. Next, those
present asked her direct questions, such as the whereabouts
of lost objects and the remedies for their ills. All these she
answered truthfully, or so they declared. After about three
hours she recovered her senses, apologized for anything
she might have said and added that it was probably all lies.

This ceremony has not been performed for about twenty
years and Maria Ignacia and her aunt, who herself used to
have charge of the coffer and play the rôle of the oracle,
were both agreed that the crops had never been the same

since. The seed of the 'bound witch' is still used at San
Pedro in cases of illness. The sick person is stretched out
on the floor, and the drugged woman is sat on a tiny household altar, decorated with flowers for the occasion. From
her words a diviner diagnoses the disease and prescribes
the cure.

This information was to prove invaluable at San Cristobal to which I returned the following month. This time,
the Indians were infinitely more forthcoming than they
had been before. Discreet enquiry revealed that the seed
of the 'bound witch' was known also to them, and used by
the sorcerers for divination purposes. If, for instance, you
thought that you had been bewitched you consulted Santa
Rosa (as it is called there) who told you that in a certain
spot, on a certain day, such-and-such a person had cast a
spell over you in such-and-such a manner. Then you
would pay a sorcerer to undo the spell by reversing the
ritual. We were actually able to arrange for a practical
demonstration of the ceremony for our special benefit.
It could take place only at night, and such was the respect
in which the sorcerers held Santa Rosa that none of the
details of the ceremony could be omitted. Needless to say,
we were delighted that this should be so.

That night, therefore, we foregathered in a stone building which had once been an *oratorio* but was now used as
a barn, with one or two of our Indian go-betweens, a
couple of musicians armed with a violin and guitar, and
two sorcerers, a thin, sly-faced man called Mariano and
Juanita a white-haired, expressionless old woman. The
seed was produced for our inspection, a tiny packet
wrapped round with *cempoalxochitl* flowers. It looked not
unlike coriander. Elsewhere I was told that it was in fact
the seed of *marihuana*, that Indian hemp whose leaves

produce the same effects as hashish. At San Cristobal they denied this and maintained that the plant was a tall shrub with a mauve flower and a feathery leaf. Chocolate was buried at its roots that it might grow the better.

The little packet was placed in a dish and covered with *cempoalxochitl* and pink hibiscus, beneath which we were bidden to place the sorcerer's fee. Then, while the musicians played the opening tune associated with the ceremony, Mariano uttered a brief incantation. Next he

placed over his head a square white cloth delicately embroidered in the corners, one of which hung down over his breast, completely hiding his face. While a woman censed him with copal, he carefully took a handful of the seeds and swallowed them with a mouthful of cane brandy. Both his hands disappeared behind the cloth, one of them holding a wooden stick splayed out fanwise and stuck with *cempoalxochitl* blossoms. The musicians continued to play.

After a few minutes his arms and knees began to tremble violently. The first intimation of Santa Rosa's presence was a curious noise behind the cloth, vaguely like the hooting of an owl. Then the sorcerer began to sing in a thin, incredibly high little voice, the voice not of Mariano but of Santa Rosa herself. Even if we had been fluent in

Otomi it is doubtful whether we could have understood what she sang, which was interpreted by a woman sitting close to Mariano, straining to catch the words of the oracle. Santa Rosa, she told us, was very glad to have been summoned and was at our entire disposal. Each pronouncement ended with the same curious sound, followed by a deep sigh. Presently we were told that we might ask questions. The replies were sometimes tactful, sometimes evasive. We asked, for instance, whether we would have rain on our two days' ride to Huehuetla, on which we were starting the next day. The reply was oracular in every sense of the word. We should have no care; we should go and nothing would happen to us. We then asked whether Refugio's mother would live long. No, was the answer, she would die soon. This was scarcely surprising, for the old lady was approaching her 109th birthday. Would there be war in Europe? we next enquired. There was already. So San Cristobal knew what was happening in Spain.

When we had exhausted our curiosity, the musicians played the *Despedida*, and Santa Rosa politely took her leave.

We were all expecting Mariano now to emerge from his trance, when it was suddenly announced that the *Dueño del Cerro* would speak through his mouth. The Lord of the Hill (a rocky eminence rising behind the village) had a deep voice, infinitely old and infinitely weary. I did not gather clearly what he said, except that he, too, was very glad to be with us. He did not stay long, and presently, in the dim candlelight, Mariano lifted the cloth from his head, and sat blinking sleepily until he had recovered consciousness sufficiently to ask for *refino* and a '*graciosa*' (*gaseosa*: fizzy lemonade).

Earth Magic

Juanita's performance was in every way similar, except that the Lord of the Hill did not honour her with a visit. Mariano had changed his tune so often that I had never been able to transcribe one in full. Juanita had a less extensive repertoire with the result that I was able to note one or two melodies, of which the most characteristic was the following:

It was unfortunate that we had chosen that particular night to consult Santa Rosa, for it coincided with a no less remarkable occasion. On the previous day we had been to see our first sorcerer acquaintance, Francisco, whom we discovered cutting out bark paper into the shape of sprouting maize. It was needed, he said, for *el papango del muñeco del maiz*, the dance of the maize doll, to be held on the following night. Paper dolls had been buried with the seed at planting time. Now that the maize was shoulder high, homage was to be offered to the Earth in order that it might continue to prosper.

Next morning we went to see the preparations. One of the smaller *oratorios* was open, and the music of violin and guitar issued through the door. Now we were to learn what was inside those mysterious coffers. Coloured paper dolls representing all the different crops, stiffened with sticks, had been taken out of them and were being dressed for the ceremony by a grave young Indian woman. The most meticulous care had gone to the making of their

269

diminutive clothes, which were complete down to the earrings and embroidered blouse-fronts of the female dolls
and the boots and wide brown hats with scarlet ribbons of
the male.

We returned to the *oratorio* at dusk. Now the dolls were
all dressed up for the party and were arranged round the
inside of four baskets covered with clean white cloths so
that only their heads showed. Four young girls with the
baskets in the crook of their arms were dancing with
grave, downcast eyes, facing to the east, where Francisco
was waving a copal burner. Presently the musicians rose
to their feet and broke into a new and sprightly tune:

Francisco leading, we all filed out of the door, with candles
in our hands. The procession wound between the huts and
out into the fields, an old man firing rockets into the
standing corn, and a small boy following with a basket of
cempoalxochitl.

Presently we paused, and the tune changed again. We
were now approaching the scene of the ceremony. In an
open space among the maize fields, a small arbour had
been made of banana and sugar-cane branches and leaves,
arranged so as to form two small niches about three feet
above the ground. In front of the arbour stood a little
cane cross wreathed with the sacred golden flower.

The baskets were ceremoniously placed in the niches
with much burning of incense. Their hieratic task accomplished, the vestal virgins became ordinary little girls
again and broke into laughing chatter.

Francisco now settled down to cut out more paper and to
string it along the top of the arbour. Older women arrived

with jars, bowls, *metates* and everything necessary to prepare a ceremonial meal. It appeared that nothing in particular would happen for a while, so we returned to keep our tryst with Santa Rosa. Unfortunately the consultation of the oracle took longer than we had expected, and it was not until after midnight that we returned to the fields. We had missed the ritual chants and the oblations including a hen offered alive to the dolls and then consigned to the cornfields. But the musicians were still playing rhythmically, and the sacred dance was in full swing.

Four or five tousle-headed youths with *cempoalxochitl* fans held to their breasts were dancing in file, their knees bent, their rounded shoulders heaving to the rhythm of the music. Francisco led them with his inseparable copal burner. To the garlanded cross they bowed deeply, and to the dolls in their baskets more deeply still. The step was little more than a rhythmic shifting from foot to foot. As they passed the little knot of men crouching in the corner of the arbour they gave them the flowery fans to kiss. When at last they stopped they brought offerings of food to the dolls, little plates each with two pieces of bread, one

271

straight and one in the shape of a double ring. Some they placed in the niches, others in a little 'garden of Adonis' beneath them, planted with *cempoalxochitl* and with maize cobs of bark paper.

Presently the dancing started up again. The clouds, which till now had obscured the waning moon, parted, and the moonlight flooded down upon the strange scene. The monotonous rhythms of the music, the still more monotonous steps of the dance hammered an unforgettable picture into my mind. At three o'clock we tore ourselves away to snatch a few hours' sleep before starting on the long, hard ride to Huehuetla. There would have been little more to see. The dancing would be kept up till the first glimmer of light in the east. Then the food offerings would all be eaten in a communal feast, the procession would form up anew, and by the time the sun rose the vegetation gods would all be back in the darkness of their coffer.

Santa Rosa had been right not to commit herself about the weather. Francisco was less cautious. In the small hours of that Saturday morning he prophesied with an appraising look at the moon that it would not rain till Sunday or even Monday. Yet when we woke at seven o'clock San Cristobal was wrapped in cloud and a fine drizzle was falling. We scarcely saw the sun during our week's ride to Huehuetla through Tenango de Doria and San Bartolo and back to Pahuatlan by way of Tlacuilotepec. The clouds never left the mountain tops. When we were not actually in them we were only just below them, and we gained little idea of the magnificent country through which we were passing. The mountains are all but razor-edged, and the valleys narrow to a river-bed twenty or thirty yards wide. In addition to its grandeur, the scenery has a delicate bloom rare in arid Mexico, and even under grey skies the fields of sugar-cane gleam like sunshine travelling across the hillside. I was reminded of the anecdote, possibly apocryphal, about Cortes and Charles V. The monarch asked the returned conquistador to describe New Spain. For all answer Cortes took from his pocket a crumpled handkerchief and tossed it on the table, thus portraying the Mexican landscape.

The joke goes that it is better to visit this *sierra* in the wet season than in the dry, for in the former it rains every afternoon while in the latter it rains all and every day. There is truth in the seeming paradox, but it leaves out of account the swollen rivers and washed out trails which make travel perilous from June to October. The trails are bad enough at the best of times, rocky ladders climbing the precipitous mountain sides. When we travelled them on Antonio's trusty mules they were deep in mud, which in one place came up to the girths. In summer all this mud is washed away by cloudbursts in the mountains, and only the slippery, still more treacherous rock remains.

During the six hours' ride from San Bartolo to Huehuetla we forded the river twenty-one times, the bed irregular with boulders, the water often coming up to the girths. There are no bridges, only wire hawsers stretched from bank to bank, well above the flood level, across which the Indians pull themselves hand over hand or with the aid of an ingenious contraption consisting of a rope with a wooden 'fastener' which closes on the wire.

As we followed the torrent towards the sea the vegetation grew more tropical. Huehuetla is only 1,000 feet above sea level and is rich in nameless trees, flowers and ferns. Unlike most Indian *pueblos*, the village eschews the hills and lines the right bank of the stream. Here we found our friends Robert and Simone Gessain making an anthropological study of the little-known Tepehua tribe who live only in this and three neighbouring villages. The Gessains were the second as we were the third party of foreigners to visit Huehuetla this century. The first, four years before, were the indomitable Mrs. Larsen and her sister.

When they first arrived, all the Tepehuas fled from them and shut themselves into their huts. When at last they recovered confidence, it transpired that they had taken the Danish ladies for witches. Why? Because, in their ignorance of local traditions, they had 'taken the witches' path to the river'. We, too, unwittingly took the witches' path to the river, but with less sensational consequences.

The Gessains had had a fantastic stroke of luck in the discovery of such an informant as they might have sought in vain in every Indian village in Mexico. Pancho was the son of a sorcerer and had obviously gone far in his studies of witchcraft. Then, disgusted with the way in which the sorcerers exploited the ignorance of the Indians, he had turned away from them and had become the Sacristan of the church and the director of the religious dances. Here, therefore, was a man who knew the pagan ritual from A to Z and yet was not averse from expounding its closely guarded secrets. For hours on end we sat in the Gessains' little room, while the rain poured down outside, listening with fascination to Pancho's description of Tepehua life and manners, hearing him play the tiny *teponaztlis* of Hue-huetla and sing the ritual chants of his people. While Robert Gessain took the words and I transcribed the music, he sang us the ten chants for healing, four for a man and six for a woman; the songs of the maize ceremony, the tune of which changes every quarter of an hour through the night; and those of the *costumbre general*, the initia-tion rite of a new sorcerer, with its special songs for waking the idols, for killing the turkey and even for craving the idols' pardon if any of those present profane the proceed-ings with quarrels or loud words.

Pancho remains in my mind as one of the most remark-able men that I met in Mexico, a perfect specimen of the pure Indian with fine, thin features, a soft, musical voice, gestures graceful yet precise, and a sensibility as delicate as his intelligence was keen. His hands followed his lips, underlining his words and making us not only understand but visualize the things which he described.

After leaving Huehuetla, we had further opportunities of investigating Indian sorcery which is not confined to the Otomis and Tepehuas but is no less rife among the Aztecs and Totonacs of the *sierra*. In essence it is rather a continuation of ancient, pagan cults than the nefarious practice of the black arts, and thus affords a striking paral-lel to Europe where mediaeval witchcraft is now recog-nized to have been neither more nor less than the under-ground survival in a debased form of the old pagan reli-gions, the open profession of which was suppressed by the Christian churches.

Earth Magic

Near Pahuatlan we explored, unknown to the Indians, two caverns which are centres of the cult. The *Cueva del Aguila* proved to be a small cave near a bend in the river, running far into the hillside, and narrowing so that one has first to stoop and then to proceed on all fours. A few yards in, by the light of a torch, we discovered a variety of offerings including candles, copal and *maxochils*, wands formed by winding sticks round with corn husks and tipping them with *cempoalxochitl* blossoms. There was also a tiny human figure of wax used probably for laying a spell or for exorcising it. Crawling further in, I came to a place where a strange rumbling noise suddenly became audible, probably caused by some subterranean torrent. Here the rotting carcase of a sacrificed hen lay a foot or two away from the thick red pool formed by the drained-off blood.

All these things indicate the nature of the cult, a worship of the Earth conceived as a female deity, to whom offerings are made and invocations addressed with dance and song. Although we had missed hearing the chants during the San Cristobal ceremony, I was later able to take down their music with rough translations of the words. The following are hymns to Shimhoi, the Holy Earth:

(1) SONG FOR GIVING THE EARTH TO DRINK

Now that we have come here
I bring wax to thy place, Little Mother,
Paper I bring and flowers,
Deign to receive them . . .
Seven times I bow the knee before thee,
I bring thee combs, good combs,
I bring soap for thee, good soap I bring,
I bring thee good silken thread,

276

Earth Magic

Craving thy pardon I bring thee all
That thou mayst lack nothing,
Flowers and all I bring thee,
Great is my respect for thee,
Violin and guitar I bring thee,
I bring thee a turkey to kill,
That its blood may be a delicacy for thee,
Little Mother, craving thy pardon,
That thou mayst bless all that I bring.

(2) HYMN TO THE EARTH

It is well, it is well, it is well.
I will sing a good song,
One that is called a good song.
Countless flowers I bring thee,
And these flowers I offer to thee,
I will sing a good song,
To know what thou hast disposed.
I would attain the sky to know the world,
I would know of each of the poor,
Now I will offer thee the pleasant things which I
    have prepared,
And I will pass over the whole face of the earth,
That I may know what has happened to all its offspring,
I bring thee that which makes green the whole face of the
    earth
In colours of green and white and yellow . . .

In these terms is Shimhoi invoked by those who crave good crops, health, freedom from spells or the bewitching of an enemy. Besides the Holy Earth, however, there are lesser earth spirits, both male and female, such as San Cristobal's *Dueño del Cerro*, Lord of the Hill. On the hill-

top the *fiesta grande* is still held by the whole village once
every five or six years or in times of pestilence or drought.
Then, and then only, are the sacred drums brought out
and used to accompany the chants. Herr Weitlaner had
divined the existence of a *teponaztli* from the way in which
the sorcerer who sang to him appeared to play an invisible
drum with the fingers of both hands. But before ours none
save Otomi eyes had seen it. By its guardian we were taken
to the place where, with a companion *huehuetl*, it lies hidden. Half way up the hill we left the narrow footpath and,
hacking through the thick undergrowth with machetes,
worked our way along an almost vertical hillside until
we came to a crevice in the rock where the drums are
kept, sheltered by an overhanging cliff-face. When, at
long intervals, they are taken out their pardon is craved
for disturbing them.

It was not only in San Cristobal that I saw these sacred
drums or discovered their existence. The sorcerer of
Xolotla has one, for instance, which is dressed in a little
cotton garment and is given the personal name of Tlaltic-
pactli, meaning the earth. It seems almost to be regarded
as an earth god and to play the same rôle as the stone idol
which each of Huehuetla's several sorcerers possesses.
Sometimes, unbeknownst to the priest on his rare visits to
Xolotla, it is taken into the church and laid behind the
altar. When asked questions it is said to answer them.

At Xico some six hours' ride away I was able to see another *teponaztli* which is kept with great secrecy and
reverence in a hut by two old men who, there is little
doubt, are *brujos*. Of ebony, it is carved in the shape of a
monkey[1] with ear-plugs and eyes which, once of gold, have

[1]The monkey was regarded by the Aztecs as companion, and
sometimes as symbol, of the god Xochipilli.

been replaced by bits of china since the Conquest. It makes its annual public appearance at Midsummer for an obsolescent pagan festival held at a place called the Tower of Xochipilli, where the ruins of an early colonial chapel crown a grass-grown knoll which was probably once a pyramid. On this occasion an Aztec hymn is chanted in honour of the god of dance and song, of which, incomplete and incorrupt as they are, I was able to transcribe the words:

> *Xochipile, Xochipile,*
> *Nochan, nochan,*
> *Otihualla capitan.*
> *Chimalli xochitl ticuicas*
> *Ac xon tenamas*
> *Chimeco, chimeco.*

The first four lines appear to mean:

> *Xochipilli, Xochipilli,*
> *To my house, to my house,*
> *Thou art come, O captain.*
> *Of shields and flowers thou wilt sing . . .*

The last two lines defeat Aztec scholars, but according to the guardian of the drum they bear some reference to fighting with the Indians of Tlaxcala. According to a tradition in the village there were once two drums, of which one took wings and flew away to Tlaxcala.

To the sorcerers, hereditary priests of the cult, the Indians pay large sums, especially in cases of sickness. A nocturnal ceremony such as we saw may easily cost 150 pesos, and the sorcerers are often summoned from great distances. Their curing ceremonies vary greatly. If, as in one case which came to my ears, their diagnosis is that the

279

idols have been offended by the patient, a ceremony of homage to the earth may be enough to put things right. Montezuma, they believe at San Cristobal, is the Lord of Sickness and must be threatened and exorcised in song. This is all the more strange in that the Otomis of Cuaxtla, only a day's ride away, conceive Montezuma as bestowing crops, health and well-being on his people. He will come again, they think, and meanwhile they hold an annual feast with sacrifices of which they believe he partakes with them.

Sometimes the sorcerers use bark paper dolls for curing, first transferring the disease to one made from the dark paper, then burning or otherwise destroying it and substituting one made from the light paper.

The following detailed account of a 'cure' shows another method. In the early autumn of 1937 B—— A—— of Pahuatlan, was ill with pains in the neck, the small of the back and the heel. Accordingly, he summoned a sorcerer from San Cristobal who set to work at midnight. The sorcerer first sucked the three places and produced in turn a stone, a small piece of glass and a metal bottle-top which he claimed to have removed from them. Then in a corner of the room he covered a packing-case with a cloth and held a dialogue with a voice issuing from behind it, which he said was that of the *Dueño del Cerro*. The Lord of the Hill announced that a live chicken must be brought, and the brother was sent off to fetch one. As soon as it crossed the threshold, the chicken was seen to stagger as though it was drunk. If it died before the treatment was completed, the sorcerer announced, the patient too would die. Drawing blood from its neck, he proceeded to anoint the affected parts. Next he rubbed the patient's whole body with the chicken and, hastily wrapping it up in bark paper, he gave it still alive to an assistant who went out into the night to throw it away in some remote spot. This treatment cost B—— no less than 25 pesos. Since, however, he claims to have been completely cured, he does not grudge the money.

In a long shallow cave behind Atla which we visited secretly, we found not only fresh offerings of flowers and chicken and turkey feathers, but also two wooden tables with *petate* mats stretched round the top forming a small chamber. In such shelters, an informant from Xolotla told me, the sorcerers hold dialogues with the Sun, the Moon and the Wind who, they say, see and know all things. Recalling Santa Rosa and the Lord of the Hill, this suggests that ventriloquism may play a part in the sorcerers' ritual and would argue some measure of charlatanry. Although I am persuaded that the sorcerers delude themselves almost as much as they delude the faithful, their occupation is a profitable one, and there may well be quite a few tricks in their trade.

It is curious that, while the Church naturally frowns upon sorcery, this antagonism is not reciprocated. Not only the devotees of the cult but its very priests go to church upon occasion, although, on the whole, they keep church and sorcery distinct. They wish no doubt to make the best of both worlds, and are by no means averse from borrowing some of the church's magic and its more powerful symbols. The sorcerer of Xolotla actually bought a complete set of ecclesiastical vestments, including a biretta, in which to perform his unhallowed rites. In Santa Catarina, the Saints are kept in the *oratorio* all the year round and only taken to the church on the annual *fiesta* day, being 'fed' with *mole* and *tamales* the previous night to strengthen them for the ordeal. In particular, the sorcerers profess great devotion to the cross. Here, however, it must be remembered that the cross was the emblem of the four points of the compass before Christianity reached Mexico, and the veneration in which it is held may be related to the worship of the rain gods. In many of Mexico's *sierras* chapels dedicated to the *Santa Cruz* are found on mountain tops. A good example is Santa Cruz Ayotusco in the Sierra de las Cruces, its church a white chalk mark against the green hillside beside an ancient grass-grown pyramid surmounted by a tiny chapel, where according to a local Otomi tradition Montezuma lies buried. In such places, the rain-clouds gather before discharging their burden on the thirsty earth, and pagan rain-making ceremonies were once, and may be still, performed.

Envoi

Soon, too soon, came the time when we must leave Mexico. Paradoxical as it may appear, we had far more to see when we left than when we came. Then, there had been but a handful of places which we knew we must visit: Taxco, Oaxaca, Patzcuaro, Acapulco and one or two more. All these we had seen, but each one had opened up at least half a dozen more possibilities, and our agenda, instead of diminishing, had steadily grown. Here we had discovered the name of a reliable muleteer, there we had conquered the confidence of a witch-doctor. Elsewhere we had found out the dates of festivals, Christian or pagan, never before chronicled. With more time we could have found out for certain whether there is a Dance of Eagles and Tigers at Malinalco in Easter Week, we could have been present at the Tepehua corn festival at Huehuetla in September, and accompanied the people of San Cristobal in February on their pilgrimage to the cave with the stone idol, two days' journey away. My plans for visiting the Maya ruins of Yucatan, the dancing matriarchs of Tehuantepec Isthmus, the pagan Huicholes of Nayarit had been brought to nought. Yet even if these plans had not miscarried, there would always have remained as much or more to see and to do, for Mexico is inexhaustible.

We left, as we had come, by way of Vera Cruz. I did not know the date of my departure until two or three weeks previously, and the intervening days were taken up with illness and innumerable occupations, so that there was no time to 'look our last on all things lovely' or even to feel that most poignant of all nostalgias, the sense of being still in a place yet no longer of it.

Now, before we could fully realize it, Mexico lay behind us. We travelled by night, and there was nothing but memory and a shouting of names in the darkness to conjure up that world which was still so near and yet now so remote. Apam, Esperanza, Orizaba, Córdoba, Paso del Macho. . . . With the names came memories, polished and rounded like gem-stones of many hues; blue of cloudless skies, of jacaranda trees, of rebozo shawls across brown shoulders; green of velvet hills in the rains; pink of silk shirts and rococo walls; scarlet of *Moro* dancers in the bright fiesta sunlight; white of billowing clouds, of virgin snow-fields on volcano flanks, of distant figures stooping in brown *milpas* fresh turned by the plough; gold of the *cempoalxochitl* flower, emblem of all that has endured of ancient ways of life and thought. With these were inextricably mingled sounds and scents. Gobbling of turkeys, hidden clapping of tortillas, the blare of a mariachi band, the subdued chatter of an Indian market. Even the stale odour of pulque and the sour-sweet smell of herbs in Indian cooking, had become lovable for their associations.

I treasured a string of sensory memories, the beads of a rosary, the little fragments of coloured glass of which a mosaic is made. They were all that was left to me as the train rumbled down from the high plateau and out into

Envoi

the lowlands of Vera Cruz. It would be idle to suggest that the mosaic which they formed would display the whole pattern of Mexico. Too much was left out for which I could find no place: archaeology, history, politics, economics, all those aspects of the country which belong to public affairs. Yet Mexico has not one pattern but many patterns, and it was my hope that in the pages of a book my fragments of coloured glass would fuse to form a Mexican Mosaic.

Glossary of Spanish, Mexican and Indian Words

acocote: gourd for sucking sap from the maguey.
agua miel: the sweet, unfermented sap of the maguey.
aficionados: 'fans' (principally in bull-fighting).
ahuehuete: the American cypress.
ajolote: a fresh-water fish.
atlatl: the Aztec spear-thrower.
atrio: churchyard.
aventón: a 'lift' (slang).
ayate: a carrying-cloth often used as a shawl.

barranca: gorge.
barrio: a parish or district of a town or village.
brujo: a sorcerer or witch-doctor.

cacique: originally an Indian ruler, nowadays a political boss.
calpulli: section of an Aztec town.
cempoalxochitl: a yellow flower, sacred to the Aztecs, belonging to the marigold and arnica family, used in many pagan and Christian ceremonies, especially connected with All Souls.
charro: a Mexican horseman.
china poblana: a female national type and the costume which she wears.

286

Glossary

chinampas: floating gardens.
chincuete: a woman's skirt of pre-Cortesian type.
chirimia: a musical pipe.
coa: planting stick.
comali: griddle for tortillas.
comparsa: a group, generally of dancers.
corrido: a popular ballad.
cotones: the white cotton pyjamas worn by Indians.
criollo: of European origin but born in Latin America.
cue: a Caribbean word applied at the time of the Conquest
    to pagan temples.

ejido: the communal smallholding peculiar to the Indian
    system of land tenure.

frijoles: haricot beans.

gachupín: a slang term, of doubtful origin, applied to
    Spaniards.
gallina: hen.
gallo: cock.
grito: shout.

hacienda: a ranch or rural property.
huarache: sandal of pre-Cortesian type.
huehuenche: type of Carnival dancer or mummer.
huehuetl: vertical pre-Cortesian drum.
huipil: pre-Cortesian type of female garment.

ixtle: fibre obtained from the maguey aloe.

jaripeo: a Mexican rodeo.

lienzo: the enclosed ring where jaripeos are held.

Glossary

machete: cutlass.

machincuepa: somersault.

maguey: the American aloe.

mayordomo: name given to the head of a religious brotherhood or the organizer of a fiesta or group of
dancers.

mecapal: the tump-line by which the forehead takes the
weight of an Indian's load.

mescal: a raw spirit distilled from the root of the maguey.

meseta: tableland.

mesón: a caravanserai.

mestizo: half-caste of mixed European and Indian blood.

metate: stone on which Indian corn is ground.

metlalpilli: stone roller for grinding corn on the metate.

milpa: cornfield.

mole: a meat stew with a rich sauce plentifully seasoned
with chile pepper.

muñeco: a paper 'doll' for witchcraft purposes.

nixtamal: maize dough.

ochtli: the Aztec name for pulque.

oratorio: a small shrine or chapel, Christian or pagan.

petate: a mat of woven reed or palmetto.

poncho: a South American term denoting a sarape with a
hole in the middle, through which the head is placed.

promesa: a religious vow.

pueblo: any village large enough to have a church.

pulque: a name of South American origin given to a drink
made from the fermented sap of the maguey aloe.

quexquemitl: a pre-Cortesian type of female garment.

Glossary

ranchería: a hamlet too small to have a church.

reata: a lariat.

real: an obsolete coin of twelve and a half centavos still used as a unit of calculation.

rebozo: a woven shawl of European origin.

refino: sugar-cane brandy.

sarape: a woven woollen rug.

sierra: a mountain range or mountainous district.

taco: cooked food wrapped in a tortilla.

tamal: cooked food with corn paste wrapped in maize leaves.

teocalli: an Aztec temple.

teocentli: the original wild maize.

teponaztli: horizontal pre-Cortesian drum giving two tones.

tezontli: a reddish stone much used in building.

tianguis: market.

tierra caliente: hot country from sea-level to 3,000 ft.

tierra fria: cold country above 6,000 ft.

tierra templada: temperate country between 3,000 and 6,000 ft.

tilma: ancient Aztec mantle.

tlachco, tlachtli: the ancient Indian ball-game.

tolvanera: whirlwind duststorm or dust-spout.

tortilla: flat griddle-cake of unleavened maize-flour.

zopilote: turkey buzzard.

Index

Index

292

Index

293

Index

Index

295

Index

Index

Index

Yautepec 96, 131, 157, 164, 166–9
Yecapixtla 76
Yucatan 19, 45, 146, 223, 283

Zaachila 218, 221–4
Zacan 255
Zacatecas 43, 198
Zacualpan 130

Zapotec Indians, 43, 53, 117, 207, 217–32, 238
Zempoala, Pico de 83
Zimapan (Hidalgo) 118
Zimapan (Oaxaca) 218
Zirahuen, Lake 249
Zócalo 23, 28, 31, 187
Zopoco 253–4
Zumarraga, Fr. Juan de 93
Zumpango 211